T'AU EMPIRE

ENLIGHTENMENT AND UNITY

CONTENTS

PRODUCED BY GAMES WORKSHOP IN NOTTINGHAM

With thanks to the Mournival for their additional playtesting services

Games Workshop Ltd, Willow Rd, Lenton, Nottingham, NG7 2WS
games-workshop.com

INTRODUCTION

On the galaxy's Eastern Fringe, a new empire is rapidly rising. Ambitious and united in purpose, the T'au seek to spread their enlightened ways across the galaxy, believing that now is their time to rule. Those who do not willingly bow down to the Greater Good of the T'au Empire must be taught the error of their ways.

The T'au are a relatively young species seeking to carve their own realm out of the havoc-filled galaxy of the 41st Millennium. They mean to bring enlightenment and harmony to a barbaric and unordered universe, and many races, whether through persuasion, coercion or subjugation, have already joined their cause. Their core philosophy requires all individuals to set aside their own desires and cooperate for the benefit of their growing empire. The T'au believe that this tenet, combined with their superior technology and scientific knowledge, can overcome all obstacles, and the stars themselves will be moved if the Greater Good demands it.

None can match the sophisticated equipment of the T'au Empire on the battlefield, but to assure victory a commander must truly embrace the philosophy of the Greater Good by combining each diverse asset into a powerful army. An infantry gun-line supported by anti-grav tanks, drones and alien auxiliaries will hold the foe at bay. All the while, battlesuits bristling with devastating weaponry that represent the apex of T'au technology airdrop from on high to strike the killing blow that the enemy never even saw coming.

Whether you decide to collect a force belonging to a single powerful sept world, or one drawn from across the empire and its mercenary allies, the T'au's clean yet imposing aesthetic provides hobbyists with the chance to create a distinctive collection that will truly stand out amidst the grim darkness of the war-torn future.

This codex contains everything you need to assemble a T'au Empire army and bring it to life on the tabletop.

A NEW EMPIRE DAWNS: In this section you will learn of the origins of the T'au race, their caste system, the rise of the T'au Empire and their continued campaigns of expansion in an increasingly hostile and perilous galaxy.

ARMIES OF EXPANSION: Here you will find a showcase of expertly painted T'au Empire miniatures, replete with examples of markings and colour schemes employed by the many T'au Septs.

FORCES OF THE T'AU EMPIRE: This section contains datasheets for every T'au Empire unit for you to use in your games of Warhammer 40,000, as well as wargear lists and weapon rules.

SUPREMACY THROUGH UNITY: The final section of this book provides additional rules for your T'au Empire army, including Warlord Traits, Signature Systems, Stratagems and matched play points.

> *To play games with your army, you will need a copy of the Warhammer 40,000 rules. To find out more about Warhammer 40,000 or download the free core rules, visit warhammer40000.com.*

The advent of the Great Rift has drawn the T'au into an escalating conflict with the twisted powers of Chaos. As they begin to understand the true horror of this relentless foe, they are filled with appalled revulsion. Nevertheless, the warriors of the Fire caste remain steadfast in the belief that there is nothing that can stand in the face of their empire's righteous destiny.

A NEW EMPIRE DAWNS

The T'au Empire is spreading, its boundless ambitions yet to be checked. Although world after world has been subsumed under their control, the T'au believe it is only the start of their new unified order, the first steps of a long journey that will end in a better existence for all. In their hearts they know it is their destiny to bring the light of truth to a galaxy drowning in darkness, and none have the right to deny their progress across the stars.

Like a newborn sun shining its light into the darkness, the T'au Empire radiates outwards, its power ever growing. The T'au's dynamism, unity of purpose and superb grasp of technology have enabled them to make rapid advances. Where once the T'au looked up to see the distant pinpricks of unexplored stars, now they see the shimmering lights of their own interstellar empire.

In their expansions, the T'au have planted thriving colonies where before there was only desolation. In their wisdom, they have transformed lifeless and poisonous orbs into fecund worlds capable of supporting burgeoning populations. Artificial planets, orbital docks and strings of relay stations now light interstellar pathways all across what was once the empty blackness of space. Although considered upstarts and fledglings by the elder powers of the galaxy, the T'au have supreme confidence in themselves and see only the unfolding of the natural order of things. New stars are born out of swirling nebulae, replacing those suns that collapse or blaze out in supernovas. So too do empires rise and fall.

MANIFEST DESTINY

The T'au believe that their destiny is to rule and that the time to do so is now. They fully accept the superiority of their culture and technology, and have recognised that they are the only hope of bringing an enlightened philosophy to a bleak and backwards galaxy. There is no feat beyond the range of their engineering, no quandary that their scientists cannot solve and no foe that their warriors cannot overcome. In time, all other races will come to accept these truths, and the very stars will be reshaped and realigned in the name of the only cause that ever mattered.

A strong ideological concept drives the T'au – *T'au'va* – which translates as 'the Greater Good', a phrase that means the good of the many (society) is greater than the good of the few (the individual). That one must set aside personal desires to work for the Greater Good is of prime concern to the T'au, and it is impossible to underplay the importance of this ideal – all working together to achieve the advancement of the whole society.

RELENTLESS DRIVE

The T'au Empire continues to grow, stretching outwards in ever-increasing bands. This unending expansion ensures that the T'au regularly encroach into already occupied territory, where they encounter much ignorance and hostility. However, this has not dissuaded them from their mission. If anything, each conflict only strengthens the T'au's collective will and lends further clarity to their purpose.

Although the T'au seek to annex all territory and assimilate any alien races they discover, they attempt to do so through enticement rather than hostility. The T'au have become masters of diplomacy, offering great rewards for those who acquiesce. In these matters the T'au are patient, content for the incorporation process to take years, or even decades, until an alien world is fully subsumed. Oftentimes, T'au rule is so subtly insinuated that the natives even assume it was their idea. However, if resistance is encountered, negotiations quickly grow more aggressive in nature. If these do not proceed in a satisfactory manner for the T'au, the talks are swiftly replaced with a purely military solution.

To see the T'au go to war is to witness a finely tuned instrument of death. Their warrior caste is prepared for battle from birth. Each soldier is equipped with high-tech weaponry and is unquestionably committed to the cause of the Greater Good. Their elite troops wear advanced battlesuits bearing truly fearsome arrays of weapons. A combined arms force, their mechanised infantry and gravity-defying gunships work in deadly cohesion while their air fleet dominates the skies above. T'au Commanders are master tacticians, well versed in the arts of war, and few foes are prepared to deal with their strategic brilliance and swift, incisive assaults.

'It is not solely our technology that will enable us to prevail in this hostile galaxy. It is our shared sense of honour and commonality of cause that unites us, and will give us the power to defeat our enemies.'

- Shas'el Sa'cea Or'es, Fire caste Commander

THE CASTE SYSTEM

So completely have the T'au absorbed the concept of the Greater Good that it has come to shape not just their purpose, but also their race's physical appearance. Since the time of their prehistory (known as the *Mont'au* or 'death age'), the T'au have been divided into rigid castes, with each segment responsible for specific functions within society – each caste contributing its expertise to the almighty whole.

All T'au are humanoid in shape, with two large hoof-like feet and blue-grey leathery skin, although the exact tone can vary, growing more blue based on a colony's proximity to the sun. Over time, each of the T'au castes has further evolved to better meet the requirements associated with their roles, effectively developing into a subspecies within the larger T'au race. T'au are born into their caste and interbreeding across these distinct classes is outlawed by the Ethereals, the mysterious fifth caste that are the leaders of the T'au Empire. The castes are as follows:

 Fire Caste: The Fire caste provides the warriors of the T'au. It is the duty of these soldiers to protect the other castes and to eliminate any foes foolish enough to oppose the will of the T'au Empire. Long ago the Fire caste originated from the hunter tribes of the plains, and even then they were already the strongest and most aggressive of all the T'au. Through the years, the Fire caste's desirable traits of strength and physical size have continued to increase, and any weak strains are quickly weeded out. They are guided by an enduring creed known as the Code of Fire, which stresses martial arts, loyalty, and merciless war tempered by wisdom. The Fire Warriors spend their entire lives either in battle or preparing for it, constantly honing their tactics and relentlessly working to improve their combat skills.

 Earth Caste: The Earth caste contains the artisans, builders and workers of the T'au, and is by far the most numerous of the castes. It is they who construct the machines, erect dwellings and provide food for the rest of the T'au Empire. Without the Earth caste, the farms would not produce and factories would sit idle. The menial levels of the Earth caste are sturdy labourers who toil ceaselessly. The foremost minds of the caste become engineers and scientists, inventors beyond compare. It is they who build the sophisticated machinery and create the many technological innovations that are so prevalent throughout all levels of society in the T'au Empire.

 Water Caste: Water is the element that can be found in all living things, flowing continuously to allow life to function. So it is that Water caste members are bureaucrats, politicians, negotiators and administrators – in essence, they are the civil servants that make T'au society run smoothly. The Water caste make up the merchants, traders and diplomats, moving fluidly among the other castes and any aliens incorporated into the T'au Empire. They assuage fears and ensure all negotiations are handled with great efficiency. This subset of the T'au has always displayed a gift for linguistics, a talent that has grown even more refined over time. The Water caste are able to learn alien languages with ease, and show a remarkable ability to pick up and emulate even the subtlest of communication nuances.

 Air Caste: In ancient times, the T'au of the Air caste were messengers, but they now fill the role of pilots and spaceship crews, transporting goods and warriors to where they are needed. The Air caste are the unseen force (sometimes called the invisible caste) for they rarely, if ever, set foot upon planets – most Air caste members spend the majority of their lives in space transit or docked upon space stations. Their bodies have evolved to their new circumstances, no longer bearing wings as they once did, but instead exhibiting longer and lighter frames in response to their low-gravity existence. Hollow bones allow the pilots of the Air caste to withstand great acceleration, although they are conversely weak and ungainly when on worlds with even moderate gravity. In battle, the Air caste can rain death from the skies while crewing either attack fighters or bomber craft in support of the planet-bound Fire Warriors.

 Ethereal Caste: Ethereals are the unquestioned leaders of the united castes that make up the T'au Empire. Their unique role is a combination of spiritual and political command, and their declarations shape and steer every facet of the T'au Empire in an indisputably complete way – and they have absolute authority. Were an Ethereal to order a T'au to kill himself, he would be met with instant obedience.

'The T'au'va frees us from the anarchy of disunity and the tyranny of the self. It frees us from corruption, jealousy and petty ambition. What more wondrous gift can there be than to understand from birth one's place in the universe? Than to know, with utmost surety, that you live and die in the name of enlightenment and reason. We will bring this precious freedom to the galaxy's suffering masses, even if we must do so at the barrel of a pulse rifle.'

- Ethereal Aun'Lan

THE RISE OF THE T'AU

The T'au say 'from out of darkness bursts the light', a phrase in their language that is laden with meaning – referring at once to the sudden and dramatic sunrise typical of the planet T'au, of the legends told of the coming of the Ethereals, and of the vigorous surge of expansionism that even now is spreading further out into the blackness of the galaxy.

Near the Eastern Fringe of the galaxy lies the small planet of T'au. It is an arid world with a few lush areas and shallow oceans. The planet is dominated by a massive continent, whose lands are composed of game-rich savannahs and sweeping plains, broken by patches of rocky desert. Long before the T'au took to the stars, they began as hunters on these plains; as their tribes grew they spread across the lands following migrating game, avoiding natural disasters and seeking to escape growing rivalries. As the centuries passed, each branch of the dispersed T'au began to adapt to its unique environment.

Some soared above isolated mountain peaks on thin membranous wings; these found plentiful employment amongst the other T'au as messengers and scouts. Those whose migrations carried them to the river valleys began establishing farming communities, developing their metallurgical, tool-making and mining skills to create the first settlements. Others realised that different communities could produce what they could not, and negotiated trade agreements between the disparate tribes. The T'au who remained on the plains grew stronger, becoming skilful and aggressive hunters.

ADVANCED EVOLUTION

The story of evolution from stone tools to a more advanced society is a common enough tale throughout the galaxy. What makes the T'au story notable is the speed at which their culture leapt from stage to stage. It was not many generations after they established their first settlements that the T'au began building fortresses, and using combustion firearms to defend them from marauding tribes of plains dwellers allied with the T'au of the air. Trade routes were cut and the T'au who negotiated between the various tribes were attacked to prevent alliances from being formed. Soon, vast inter-tribal wars ravaged the main continent, with T'au tribes turning on each other in savage battles utilising primitive firearms. The fighting dragged on for many years, with no end in sight. Squalid conditions caused by

the endless fighting allowed plagues to spread, until more T'au were dying of disease than were being killed in battle. It seemed as though the T'au race would surely destroy itself.

THE COMING OF THE ETHEREALS

The T'au had entered their darkest age, in which the entire race was being ravaged by war and sickness. At this time, strange lights were seen in the sky and many believed these were signs that they were living in the last days – that extinction was nigh. From these times come many different myths of how the race was pulled back from the brink of annihilation, of which 'The Ethereals of Fio'taun' is the foremost.

The legend tells that on a mountain plateau called Fio'taun, an alliance of plains dwellers and airborne T'au laid siege to the mightiest walled city of the builder T'au. In vain, the traders attempted to negotiate with the fierce plains warriors, but their blood was afire and they would brook no treaty. For five seasons the cannons of Fio'taun held the attackers at bay, but supplies dwindled and disease became rife within the city. The leaders within Fio'taun fell to despair, little knowing that succour was on the way.

Emerging from the darkness, a T'au of unusual appearance walked into the besiegers' camp, asking to see the army's commander. He was softly spoken, yet bore an undeniable authority, and the sentries to whom he had announced himself found themselves compelled to grant his request. At the same time, within the walls of Fio'taun, a similar individual presented himself to the guards, requesting audience with the castellan of the fortress. Again, his request could not be denied. Within the hour the fortress gates were opened, the stranger guiding the citadel's leaders towards the torchlit camp of their attackers.

As the enemies met, the newcomers, who called themselves Ethereals, bade all to sit. Beneath a maiden moon of purest white, they began to speak. The mysterious strangers explained that the skills of each tribe were unique and should be harnessed, and they spoke of a Greater Good that could be achieved if only they would put aside their feuding ways and instead work together. The two strangers talked through the night, their words heavy with great power. As the sun crested the horizon, a truce was agreed between the warring factions. Fio'taun was just the beginning. Soon, more Ethereals appeared and their message of the Greater Good spread to every corner of the planet. The new philosophy took hold quickly, and the T'au flourished as never before. Well-constructed towns and cities sprang up across the main continent, commerce routes were re-established and, everywhere, the winged T'au provided speedy communications.

As the most aggressive of all T'au, the warriors that dwelt on the open plains had the hardest time accepting the new ways. Yet as they saw the larger and more impressive settlements being established by the other tribes, they could not help but admire the great progress, and finally submitted to the Ethereals' entreaties. From that time forth, the Ethereals and a council of the eldest from each tribe decreed that the T'au would be formalised into castes, each known by the element that most befitted its role in the Greater Good. The builders and artisans would be the Earth caste, the scouts and messengers became the Air caste, the traders and civil administrators formed the Water caste and the warriors of the plains would be known as the Fire caste. Having saved the T'au from extinction, the Ethereals were revered with the utmost devotion. Although always the least numerous of the castes, the Ethereals became the guiding force for all T'au, as it was they who saw the vision of what the future could hold for their race.

DYNAMIC EXPANSION

The T'au entered into an unprecedented period of rapid change, heralded by new inventions and great leaps of advancement in many fields. Each caste became relentlessly driven in its pursuit of the next achievement for the Greater Good. The successes that followed were plentiful, with vast step changes discovered in metallurgy, engineering, energy production and weapons manufacturing. With breakthroughs occurring almost daily and hardship and disease greatly reduced, the planet of T'au was soon showing signs of overcrowding. The Ethereals pointed towards the stars. At their bidding, the Earth caste began building and testing rockets, while the Air caste began training for their new roles as pilots.

During this time of progress, only the Fire caste did not seem to advance. Although they used their new weapons and technology to hunt the larger predators of T'au to extinction, there was little call for a standing army. The Ethereals anticipated this growing frustration, focusing the Fire caste instead on the development of a new and tightly disciplined regimen. For guidance, they used the teachings of the Code of Fire, the ancient way of honour passed down the generations since the hunter tribes roamed the plains. With this 'way of the warrior' at its core, the Fire caste began the formalised traditions that are still carried on today.

The notion that the T'au's future lay in the stars was keenly grasped by all castes. After the first few rockets successfully escaped the planetary atmosphere, the T'au rapidly moved to establish orbital communities, followed by a base on Lu'val, the nearest moon. Scouting ships and far-ranging probes were sent deeper into space. Scans identified many neighbouring worlds capable of sustaining life. The construction of a massive orbital dock allowed larger space-faring craft to be built, and soon colonising efforts were underway – the nearby planet of T'au'n became the first of these bold new enterprises.

ART OF WAR

Although their technology has evolved, the T'au are proud to preserve many ancient customs. Much of the military tradition of the Fire caste can be traced back to the early hunter tribes that stalked the plains of T'au, including unit organisation, tactics and the warrior's Code of Fire. It is with great honour that the Fire caste continues such ancient traditions today.

The Fire caste are professional soldiers. In some ways, their training regimen begins moments after their birth, for the great communes are fully given over to raising the best soldiers and nothing else. Discipline, fitness, hard work and following orders are drilled into the growing warriors. It is customary for teams to be raised and trained together, allowing the troops to form strong connections – a comradeship-in-arms that will serve them well no matter where in the T'au Empire they are sent off to fight.

To be named a *shas'la* – a full-fledged warrior of the Fire caste – is to have completed the rigorous training and passed the final rite of passage signifying that one has proven successful at this crucial stage; those not healthy or bright enough to pass these tests are never heard from again. The Fire caste never stops readying for war, and their academies are purpose built to refine training and educate their students in the ways of battle. To the Fire caste, war is an art form – a discipline to be studied and applied.

TACTICAL PHILOSOPHIES

By far the two most common forms of Hunter Cadre tactics used by the T'au are the *Mont'ka* and *Kauyon*. Each method is taught in depth by the great Fire caste academies, and each has its own adherents amongst the masters. Both styles are based on ancient hunting techniques, each representing one of the two broad

approaches to slaying your quarry: one involves luring the prey to the hunter (Kauyon), the other involves the hunter running the prey to ground (Mont'ka). Although some Commanders or septs favour the use of certain teams or weaponry for certain styles, ultimately it is the tactics being used that make the difference. This is a concept the masters of the academy, all preeminent warriors in their day, stress to their pupils.

MONT'KA

Roughly translated, Mont'ka is 'the killing blow'. The most aggressive style of T'au warfare, its tenet is all about the art of identifying a target of opportunity and attacking it swiftly with a Hunter Cadre. There are many famous variants of the Mont'ka, with most revolving around rapid strikes with a mobile force and taking the fight directly to the foe. The theory behind it is that landing a swift and decisive blow to the vitals of the enemy will eventually win the fight. Common to all methods of T'au warfare, Mont'ka places a strong emphasis on target prioritisation and concentration of fire – attacking the right foe at the right time with an overwhelming application of force. Attacking too soon will cause the assault to lose impetus, while attacking too late will hand the foe the initiative.

A cadre pursuing the Mont'ka may stand in readiness for several days awaiting the command to strike. During this time they will review the plan: choreographing the moves they will perform when the call to strike comes, charting out all the nuances of targets, terrain and timing. Often, the attack will be delivered in varied stages, with elements of the assault arriving in different manners and quite often from separate directions. The coordination of such events is pre-planned, although, naturally, there are a range of contingencies and adjustments that can modify the plan in response to the variables of the battle.

The final decision to launch a Mont'ka comes from one who has a good view of the foe – often a Pathfinder Team that has worked its way forwards into enemy territory. There is a great bond of trust between the cadre that conducts the Mont'ka and the Commander who orders it, and a well-honed attack will bring great honour to both. The attack will be called off immediately if the prey remains resilient or proves especially troublesome or evasive. Escalation or grinding battles are not the way of the Mont'ka, and rather than enter into a fight of attrition, the T'au find it far more preferable to pull back out of range and begin planning for another strike. Moreover, these swift disengagements often tempt unwise enemies into pursuing the retreating T'au, believing them to be on the verge of a rout. Such aggression leaves the foe exposed to a second wave of precision strikes.

COMMANDER PURETIDE

Commander Puretide embodied the Code of Fire and complete dedication to the Greater Good. Grievously wounded towards the end of his life, Puretide became a hermit, spending his last years committing his accumulated wisdom and experience to posterity. He wished to pass on his unique, balanced style of war so that, after his death, others could build upon his successes. All Fire caste academies teach Puretide's work and, to this day, the most promising students, perhaps only one every generation, can still apprentice directly under the tutelage of Puretide himself. These elite disciples spend time with the old master thanks to the Earth caste's holographic programming technology. However, this is no mere recording of old images, but an interactive AI-assisted projection that thinks, responds and contemplates. The Ethereals tightly control access, but those few who meet the requirements join Puretide at his retreat atop the peak of Mount Kan'ji, on Dal'yth Prime, where the brilliant commander instructs, questions and teaches. Despite all his efforts – both when he lived and in his current form – few, if any, of Puretide's students have grasped the full scope of his balanced enlightenment. Even now, there are rival philosophies of the execution of warfare, with opposing sides each championing a single aspect of his teachings to the exclusion of the others.

KAUYON

The Kauyon art of war is the oldest of the T'au techniques, and the words for hunter and patience are both derived from this same root. This style of combat relies on the interaction of the hunter and the lure. The lure can be almost anything – most likely a friendly unit deployed in an intervening position upon the battlefield, or perhaps an objective known to be vital to the foe. Using wisdom and foresight, the patient hunter will anticipate the enemy's path and deploy in the most advantageous manner to attack them. For example, a cadre practising Kauyon might set up an attack along a known enemy advancement, placing a team far forward to inflict some initial damage before falling back. As the friendly troops withdraw, they are sure to be followed by the vengeful foe. How best to attack that advancement is where the art of Kauyon comes into play.

True masters of the ambush attack have so many layers of plans within plans that only at the end do their opponents come close to realising that all of their actions have been anticipated, even orchestrated, to achieve the attacker's end result. Many a foe has been drawn in by the spider-web plans of a Kauyon, lured by intentional weak spots left in the T'au battle line, or induced into a killing zone by teams feigning retreat. There are many subtleties to the T'au ambush strategy, with canny Commanders using multiple distractions to split a foe's forces, or actively moving their lures in order to spread the enemy out, leaving them vulnerable to impending attacks.

MOBILE WARFARE

The Fire caste is entirely committed to mobile and rapid-strike warfare. Movement is key, whether launching the aggressive attacks of Mont'ka, racing to get into the key positions demanded by Kauyon, or attempting any of the lesser known hunting styles such as the encirclements of Rinyon or the thousand daggers approach of Rip'yka. On these grounds, the Fire caste is built and equipped for fluid battle-tactics. The T'au regard close combat as primitive, and always plan their attacks around the application of ranged firepower. After a plan has run its course, whether in victory or defeat, Hunter Cadres are extricated from the battlefield using one of many planned exit strategies.

As a general principle, T'au forces do not hold positions by choice. While they recognise the tactical advantage of terrain, and always attempt to use it to their benefit, they do not see the wisdom of fighting over ground and regard territorial gain as irrelevant compared to the destruction of enemy forces. Skilled Commanders always look for the best opportunities to destroy the foe, and the ground is only valuable as a position from which to make the kill; once the enemy is gone, the territory is for the taking. With planning, advanced scanners and scouts, the T'au identify, track and kill targets in an efficient manner, preferring to keep as much distance between themselves and their prey as possible.

A T'au army will gladly retreat from a strong enemy attack to preserve their people's lives, while waiting for an opportunity or opening to strike back decisively. Unlike many races, T'au attribute no dishonour to prudent retreat and perceive last stands as incompetent defeats or the final refuge of an unimaginative Commander. When seeking to wear out or reduce a numerically superior foe, the T'au prefer a disconnected series of rapid strikes and ambushes, each planned to deliver maximum damage for the least cost in lives and resources.

While sacrifice for the Greater Good is considered heroic, unnecessary losses are disdained. Even after leading a cadre to a remarkable victory, a Commander whose army has sustained a large amount of casualties that might have been prevented does not rejoice, but is instead greatly shamed. Duty requires that he ask to step down and rejoin the ranks to atone for his failure. If the breach of conduct is more severe, the Ethereals themselves might step in and demand the *Malk'la* ritual, an event that scars all who witness it.

THE CHANGING FACE OF BATTLE

As the T'au Empire expands, the need to fight larger scale engagements has grown and caused the purist Fire caste approach to be questioned. At the suggestion of the Ethereals, large numbers of auxiliaries (largely made up from warriors of allied races) have been incorporated into the military to swell the ranks. Meanwhile, the new armaments and advanced equipment invented and produced by the Earth caste continues to provide new technological options. Yet the aged masters of the Fire caste academies continue to stress the old maxim: 'Our technology advances with the years; our tactics do not'.

A DESTINY TO RULE THE STARS

The T'au continued to push their realm outwards at an explosive rate, although losses were high amongst these early explorers. Not only did space travel and new and unusual environments take their toll, but as they ventured further from their home world, the T'au also began to encounter alien beasts, many of which proved a grave threat to the process of colonisation.

With the fledgling empire getting its first taste of a hostile galaxy, at last came the time when the rigorous training of the Fire Warriors could prove its worth. The colossal reptilians of D'yanoi consumed many colonists, before the quick deployments and disciplined volleys of the Fire caste drove the monstrous creatures back. On Sa'cea, the desert planet was so overrun with fierce flesh-eating predators that the Fire caste had to hunt down and destroy them all before settlers would even dare to land.

During these early expansions the T'au also encountered alien races – whole civilisations of other sentient creatures. While the Fire caste sought to destroy any who opposed them, hunting them in the same manner in which they eradicated savage creatures, the Ethereals saw an opportunity to bring enlightenment instead of war. Just as the Ethereals had stopped the fighting on T'au and bound the tribes to work towards a common purpose, so too should the aliens be embraced and given a chance to contribute to the Greater Good. The Ethereals guided the other castes to accept these alien races, no matter how strange. It did not matter whether these newcomers were mired in barbarism, enslaved to crude superstitions or simply unaware of the magnitude of the great destiny unfolding before them; the Ethereals said all should be welcomed into the emergent T'au Empire.

Henceforth, whenever a new alien culture was encountered, the Ethereals employed a master strategy in which each T'au caste performed a designated role. Planets were first scanned by the Air caste, and those classified as desirable were investigated further. If civilisations were discovered, the ambassadors of the Water caste, long trained in the subtle art of negotiations, were sent to make contact.

Honourable greetings and invitations were extended to the multi-armed Thraxians, the invertebrate Greet, the Nicassar and many others. All were called upon to join the T'au Empire, to ally themselves through the appeal of mutual security, trade and technology. The more primitive and docile aliens quickly bowed before the fair-speaking Water caste emissaries, while others acquiesced only gradually. Ultimately the results were the same, and within a short span of years the T'au's cultural hegemony was dominant, with each race doing their part to aid the Greater Good.

Not all alien peoples proved so accommodating. Those who refused cooperation outright were given harsh ultimatums. The full might of the Fire caste was unleashed upon any aliens that did not comply. Upon command, T'au Fire Warriors descended out of orbit onto a designated planet and delivered a series of rapid strikes to their foe before pulling back to avoid major retaliation. After such attacks, all but the most unrepentant were given another chance to reconsider. With key industries crippled and long-ranged communications jammed, many aliens found themselves fractionalised and unsure if others of their kind had already accepted the T'au's terms. Such divide and conquer tactics dragged most foes back to the negotiating table, although in some cases wars of annihilation were inevitable.

Although the population of the empire was increasing exponentially, its expansions were on such a vast scale that Fire caste warriors were already in short supply. They often found themselves outnumbered, although their astutely tactical Commanders quickly learned that even the largest enemy army could be brought to its knees by well-planned and rapidly executed strikes, as well as the judicious use of overwhelming firepower. Given the choice of bloody genocidal war and extinction, or assimilation and survival within the borders of the growing T'au Empire, all but the most stubborn of races bowed to the inevitable. One species, however, has proven a notable exception.

THE ORK THREAT

Orks are a prolific, green-skinned and brutal race that solves even the most trivial problems through violence. The T'au first discovered Orks on the planets surrounding their first major colony, T'au'n. Signals soon arrived reporting disparate Ork tribes scattered across every star system they investigated. The sophisticated T'au quickly learned to pinpoint the telltale Ork signature on their scanning equipment, and it appeared with alarming regularity on planets, moons, asteroid belts and virtually anywhere that could support life.

Initial attempts by the diplomats of the Water caste to broker a treaty with the Orks ended in bloodshed and tragedy. Several brave negotiators were killed on the spot, butchered for the amusement of the savage beasts. Retributive attacks by the warriors of the Fire caste seemed only to excite the scattered greenskin tribes, who soon united in vast hordes and set about raiding and pillaging T'au space. It took many battles before the T'au at last abandoned their futile attempts to absorb the Orks in the manner that had proven so successful with a dozen other alien civilisations; there was simply no bargaining with such creatures. The Ethereals themselves eventually conceded that these aliens were a lost cause, and amended the protocols to forego any attempt to integrate the Orks, declaring, at last, that the Greater Good would be better off without them.

Now, when the troublesome aliens are discovered, the standard procedure is to approach the Orks in one of two ways: either by destroying them as quickly as possible in all-out war, or by marking the territory with warning beacons in order to establish a safe perimeter around the savages. While these tactics are sound in theory, the T'au have learned from bitter experience that neither method is foolproof and that the greenskins are utterly unpredictable. The Orks actually enjoy prolonged wars and have proven nearly impossible to fully eradicate, reappearing on worlds long since deemed clear of their menace. Entire Ork invasion fleets also have a disturbing tendency to bypass all sensor readings and emerge unexpectedly to wreak havoc in some distant corner of the T'au Empire. Over time, constant vigilance and a rapid overwhelming response seem to be the only effective countermeasures against the seemingly endless green tide.

THE SPHERES OF EXPANSION

The rise of the T'au can be seen to develop through distinct phases of exploration, conquest and settlement, periods of intense growth known to the T'au as 'spheres of expansion'. Each of these waves of colonisation is marked by a long building up of resources, after which continual waves of exploratory missions are launched, followed, where needed, by military campaigns to solidify territorial gains. Once a colony transforms itself into a stable settlement, it then serves as a jumping-off point for the next expansion. In this way the T'au ensure that they do not risk overextension, and that every new territory is properly ordered and consolidated before they embark upon any new campaign.

By the end of the millennia-long First Sphere Expansion – as it later came to be called – the T'au Empire had unfurled across the heavens and consisted of eight fully settled systems known as septs. Named after its prime or 'sept world', a sept can include any number of additionally colonised planets or moons, as well as other holdings such as listening posts, sensor fields, shield satellites, orbital cities and mining operations. Everything is connected, both by a series of space stations and a massive net of communications and sensor relays strung between major locations. Although it might take many generations to establish itself, each sept is unique, with its own cultural nuances and varying proportions of the different castes and alien populations.

Several factors combined to end the T'au's initial great period of rapid growth. Firstly, despite the terrific population explosion their race had been experiencing, their numbers were being stretched too thin, with the need for more of every caste being felt. Fire caste warriors were in particularly high demand; the wars fought to conquer new planets had proven costly, and ongoing conflicts still raged in outlying areas. Initial encounters with the Orks had taken a horrific toll, and forced the T'au to divert vast resources and several entire expeditionary forces towards suppressing and eliminating the belligerent marauders.

The second reason the First Sphere Expansion came to a halt was simply due to the vast distances between systems. After colonising the many dense clusters near T'au, the expanses between worlds became greater. At that time, it was already impossible to travel the span of the empire in a single lifetime, and crossing the black gulfs that surrounded their star systems would take many, many generations. The T'au clearly needed to innovate new methods of space travel if they were to bring word of the Greater Good to the wider galaxy.

SEPTS OF THE FIRST SPHERE

T'AU

T'au is the birthplace of the T'au race, and it is here that the High Council, led by the Ethereal Supreme Aun'Va, convenes, its decrees shaping the entire empire. The planet remains the centre of T'au culture and bureaucracy, and produces many Fire caste warriors. None can rival T'au Sept for prestige, and only Vior'la can match its power.

T'AU'N

The first new sept established, T'au'n, has a chain of enormous orbital docks and controls the largest of the Air caste space stations; every sept hosts ships of the T'au fleet (kor'vattra), but none can boast of more than T'au'n.

D'YANOI

Named after the twin moons of its sept world, D'yanoi has survived long isolation due to a space storm of fierce and unnatural qualities. It has also seen many infamous Ork invasions.

BORK'AN

The sept world of Bork'an is a centre of learning and academia, and its system has many rich mining planets. Bork'an has a high percentage of Earth caste, and Fire Warriors from here are not infrequently outfitted with prototype weapons and equipment.

DAL'YTH

Dal'yth Sept was ravaged during the Damocles Crusade; many of its outer colonies and several cities on its sept world were destroyed. It has recovered quickly, thanks to its busy trade ports. Large numbers of aliens can be seen here alongside its famously efficient Water caste merchants and diplomats.

FAL'SHIA

Fal'shia houses a vast quantity of munitions factories. The sept produces weapons renowned for their reliability and the quality of their craftsmanship.

VIOR'LA

The planet Vior'la orbits a binary star and its name translates as 'hot-blooded'. It is known to produce especially aggressive and skilled warriors. Many Ork invasions have been broken by the sept, and the most respected Fire caste academies reside upon Vior'la.

SA'CEA

The world of Sa'cea is the hottest and most densely populated of all T'au worlds, producing more colonisation fleets during the Second Sphere Expansion than any other. Warriors of Sa'cea are regarded as particularly honourable.

STRENGTH IN UNITY

Unlike many of the galaxy's warring races, the T'au Empire does not see all alien life as an abomination to be destroyed. The T'au'va offers a better existence for all, and wherever possible the Ethereals will seek to draw cultures into the empire peacefully. Each vassal race so absorbed brings its own unique skills, knowledge and capabilities – not to mention fresh warriors to fight in the T'au's endless wars of expansion.

The Kroot are perhaps the most ubiquitous of the T'au's many vassal races, but there are countless others who play a vital role, whether militarily or otherwise. Humans are a common sight within the empire, commonly populating the T'au's colony worlds. Most accepted the Greater Good in a desperate attempt to escape the uncaring brutality of daily life in the Imperium of Mankind, but many are almost as devoted to the concept of the Greater Good as their T'au neighbours. The Nicassar, a race of psychically attuned ursine creatures, are nomadic explorers who provide the T'au navy with swift scouting and reconnaissance vessels in exchange for the latest and most accurate star charts, and the opportunity to guide the empire's colonisation fleets into uncharted territory. The Demiurg are squat and powerful humanoids who are greatly valued for their skill at asteroid mining and mineral extraction – well attuned to existing in deep space, the Demiurg live aboard their bulky cargo-haulers and bustling spaceports. Many of the T'au's most trusted allies are former foes. The Nagi, for example, are a species of hyper-intelligent worms posessing formidable mind-control powers that were once feared and hated by the T'au after a series of violent encounters. Fortunately, efforts by the Water caste led to a lasting peace, and now the Nagi are willing servants of the Greater Good. Some even serve as advisers to high-ranking Ethereals.

Aliens who exemplify the philosophy of the Tau'va are greatly respected, and ocassionally raised to positions of relative importance within the empire – though they are always closely supervised by Water caste bureaucrats.

A FORTUITOUS UNION

At the close of the first period of expansion, an exploration fleet out of Dal'yth picked up long-ranged scans of Ork ships firing on Kroot Warspheres. The previously unencountered Kroot were defending their enclave on the planet of Krath, although they were hopelessly outnumbered. Intending only to observe, the T'au were drawn into the battle as both the Air caste Admiral and Fire caste Commander could not bear to watch the honourless Orks bludgeon their way to victory. Quickly deploying their superior fleet, the T'au destroyed the ramshackle greenskin ships. Too late, however, they realised that this was merely the vanguard of a mighty invasion force that was closing on them in an encircling pattern.

Thus began an extended war, both in space and over several planets, later named the War in the Place of Union, for it marked the first time the T'au and Kroot fought side by side. So effective was the sudden alliance that they withstood the Orks long enough for reinforcements from Sa'cea to arrive, and ultimately triumphed over the greenskins. The T'au were so impressed with the Kroot's fighting prowess that they agreed to extend the alliance in order to liberate the remainder of the Kroot enclaves, which were also under Ork attack. For the next ten years, the T'au helped drive all sign of Orks from the Kroot worlds, eventually coming to their home world of Pech at the behest of the greatest of Kroot leaders, the legendary Anghkor Prok. There, at the sacred Oathstone, Prok swore allegiance to the T'au Empire and pledged his warriors to fight for the Greater Good – and regular payment. That pledge, and the cooperation between the two races, is still honoured today. The Kroot are, by far, the most common alien auxiliary force to serve in T'au armies, often ranging ahead of the Fire caste battle line, scouting enemy movements and launching devastating ambushes upon vulnerable enemy positions. The T'au greatly value their military service, although they continue to hope that exposure to their own superior culture will eventually cure the Kroot of their cannibalistic tendencies.

PROGRESS UNBOUND

Although their realm was larger than it had ever been, the planet T'au remained the spiritual heart of the T'au Empire. Of those born on distant septs, only the most privileged were ever able to travel to see their ancestral home, although all paid great deference to the eldest of T'au septs. There, the highest-ranking officials of each caste assembled at councils within the shining domes that dominate the skyline, receiving the wisdom of the most ancient of the Ethereal caste. From that High Council, the orders of expansion have ever been issued and passed along the relay stations to the ends of the empire.

The Ethereals pushed the council relentlessly, driving all of the castes to further accomplishments. The T'au dedicated the next half century to rebuilding their thinly stretched armies, solidifying their infrastructure and readying themselves for the next expansion. Auto-response probes were launched to explore the gulf of empty space past the empire's borders, marking the T'au's first uses of a new technology: artificial intelligence.

The Water caste sought to supplement the shortage of the T'au population by redoubling their efforts to integrate their alien vassal worlds further into the empire. This was accomplished in myriad ways; for example, the sturdy, if dim-witted, Anthrazods proved very well suited for the arduous toils of asteroid mining, while the tiny, dextrous-limbed crustacean race native to Brachyura were unmatched at the delicate assembly of the minuscule plasma generators needed to fuel the latest Earth caste inventions. It was the alliance with the Kroot, however, that made the largest difference, as in a short period of time, the Fire caste armies were swollen by billions of additional warriors to aid the fight for the Greater Good, albeit in a more mercenary fashion than was considered ideal.

Only the Earth caste had failed to reach their prescribed goal. With engineering centres in every sept working diligently, the Earth caste provided innumerable innovations, but the invention demanded by the Ethereals – faster propulsion technology to drive spacecraft – eluded them. At last, the quantum leap came from Fal'shia Sept, where they finalised development of the ZFR Horizon accelerator engine. An ingenious design, this powerful new mechanism allowed ships to attain near-light speed. It was this device that would usher in the next phase of progress.

THE SECOND SPHERE EXPANSION

With a faster fleet and armies buoyed by an influx of Kroot kindreds, the T'au Ethereal Supreme, Aun'Wei, declared the massive build-up to be complete. With a single command that was heard throughout the empire, the T'au launched the Second Sphere Expansion. Branching outwards from each of the hub centres of the First Sphere colonies, great fleets speared into the dark, spreading the Greater Good to worlds that from distant T'au were mere specks of flickering light.

The Second Sphere Expansion was to prove even more dynamic than the first, pushing further into space and establishing over a dozen new septs. During this time, a legend arose from the Fire caste, the greatest military thinker and strategist of his age, and perhaps of any other – Commander Puretide. He led his warriors to swift victories, and star systems fell before his campaigns of conquest. Many of the Second Sphere septs, such as Elsy'eir and Tash'var, owe their existence to Puretide's brilliant strategies, and it was his masterful counter-attacks that warded off the Ork invasions that threatened to overrun Au'taal Sept. It was said that

even the Orks grew to fear facing an army led by Puretide, for while the greenskins loved to fight, the master tactician stole much of the joy from their battles with his evasive yet hard-hitting tactics. Puretide's application of strategy and military theory were thoroughly recorded, and are still taught at every Fire caste academy today. The Commander remains an icon and a hero to all T'au, and it is common to see statues and murals depicting his greatest victories in the plazas and forums of sept worlds – a rare thing indeed for a culture that typically venerates the collective over the individual.

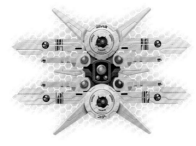

The last breakthrough of the Second Sphere Expansion was the successful crossing of the Damocles Gulf, a mysterious region to the galactic east that had long thwarted

all attempts by the T'au to pass through. Once on the other side of that roiling and unnavigable space phenomenon, the T'au swiftly established many colonies and outposts, soon making their first contact with the single largest power in the galaxy – the Imperium of Mankind. After a long and subtle campaign, the T'au Empire had peaceably encroached upon many planets within the area of space known to the humans as the Timbra Sub-sector of Segmentum Ultima. The T'au did not yet know it, but they had encountered perhaps their most stubborn and implacable nemesis yet, a tyrannical and fanatical opponent that possessed seemingly limitless reserves of manpower, munitions and engines of war.

To the xenophobic leaders of Humanity, there could be no peaceful coexistence with the T'au, and any attempt to spread word of the Greater Good was met with furious aggression. The two powers were set upon an inevitable path to conflict. The bitter and destructive wars that were soon unleashed across the Damocles Gulf were unlike anything the T'au had ever experienced, and that bloody fighting marked the beginning of the end of the Second Sphere Expansion.

SEPTS OF THE SECOND SPHERE

AU'TAAL
Au'taal Prime is a verdant and beautiful sept world, where only honoured heroes can retire.

N'DRAS
Long thought abandoned, N'Dras was in fact the site of a top-secret XV95 Ghostkeel testing facility.

KE'LSHAN
Situated near the Perdus Rift, this sept has suffered many invasions and is less trusting of aliens than other T'au. The Ke'lshan fleet and Fire caste forces are only recently back to full strength after their clashes with Hive Fleet Gorgon.

ELSY'EIR
Elsy'eir is a densely populated sept with many moons, most of which are mined for the valuable ores used in the construction of battlesuits.

TASH'VAR
A frontier sept, those of Tash'var have been subjected to frequent Ork invasions and pirate raids. As a result, its people have become tenacious and hardy.

VASH'YA
Known as the 'world between spheres', Vash'ya was settled near the end of the Second Sphere Expansion, as it took a long period for the Earth caste machines to make the air breathable. Major Air caste fleets and defence platforms are docked around the sept world.

T'OLKU
T'olku is known for its many large Ethereal temples, as well as the alien institutes, where numerous ambassadors from a multitude of different races and civilisations are brought to be instructed in the ways of T'au culture and society before being assimilated back into their respective home worlds.

CONTACT WITH THE IMPERIUM

Since first entering space, the T'au had experienced success after success. Guided by their Ethereals, each caste had overcome every obstacle yet encountered, and none could doubt T'au ascendancy. On the far side of the Damocles Gulf, however, the T'au faced an enemy unlike any other, and the epic clashes that followed heralded the beginning of a new age of war.

The T'au Empire's first introduction to Humanity came not with the ruling Imperium, but with dissident elements that were operating on the fringe of that mighty dominion. The Imperium of Man is the largest realm in the galaxy, although much within its sprawling borders has never been explored or has been forgotten over its history. The region of space around the Damocles Gulf is just such an area, a wilderness where the T'au Empire had found room to take root.

The T'au first encountered free captains, pirates and lost human colonies that had regressed so that they had long forgotten their origins and any connection to their distant birth world. Those initial contacts ranged from friendly trade negotiations to instant hostility. It was some time before the Water caste came to grasp the fact that the humans they encountered were merely the lost remnants or willing outcasts of an incomprehensibly large galactic empire. Worlds claimed by dissident humans were soon annexed into the T'au Empire, but there was much debate about how to approach those planets still bound to the Imperium. In typical fashion, the high ranking caste leaders debated the situation before the Ethereals.

To some of the High Council, the Imperium seemed so powerful that overt aggression might lead to a war that they could not win. The leaders of the Fire caste called for war, but it was Aun'Va, an Ethereal second in authority only to Ethereal Supreme Aun'Wei, who determined the plan. The Water caste were to integrate themselves into human worlds loyal to the Imperium, working their way into the courts of planetary governors. Eventually, a score of worlds within the Imperium were trading with the T'au, even in preference to each other. Alien goods, and especially coveted Earth caste technology, flowed through these markets in blatant contravention of Imperial law. The time soon came to initiate the second phase of Aun'Va's instructions.

Upon those worlds that were deemed ripe, Water caste envoys whispered well-rehearsed words into willing ears. The seeds of rebellion that had been long cultivated now bore fruit as, one by one, the planetary governors declared themselves and their worlds free of the shackles of the Imperium's totalitarian rule. It had taken decades to achieve, but the T'au spread more rapidly and with fewer losses than even the most brilliant military campaign could have achieved.

The Imperium's response to such sedition was slow in coming, but when it finally arrived, was characteristically brutal. The T'au were designated as a highly dangerous xenos species, and the Damocles Crusade was launched to expel them from the region. The Imperial forces were vast, based around a dozen capital ships, and included nineteen regiments of Astra Militarum and five provisional companies of Space Marines made up from a dozen Chapters. The initial battles were stunning victories for the Imperium, as the power of their fleet and the suddenness of their attacks smashed isolated outposts and eliminated outlying colonies. In a short period of intense conflicts, the T'au were pushed back across the Damocles Gulf, although in the later stages of this drive, the Imperium's victories were not so easily won.

The planets from which the T'au were driven were subjected to harsh recriminations; the Inquisition descended upon the remaining human populations and meted out cruel punishments to those who had rejected the Emperor's tenets. Meanwhile, the crusade followed the retreating T'au across the Damocles Gulf, entering the T'au Empire itself.

DAL'YTH DEFIANT

The first sign of the invasion came from the scanners of Pra'yen, the outermost planet of Dal'yth Sept. After picking up unusual readings, the T'au switched to long-ranged optics and were shocked to see great rents opening in space, with the massive Imperial battleships and their supporting craft emerging out of nowhere. Although the T'au fleet and Pra'yen's well-armed orbital station took a toll upon the Imperial Navy, the way was soon cleared for the crusade to advance towards Dal'yth Prime.

In the largest conflict of the war, Imperial forces landed upon Dal'yth Prime. In this case, they were not taking on a recently converted Imperial world or newly founded colony, but instead were treading upon a heavily populated T'au sept world. The Imperial drop was contested by swarms of atmospheric fighters, but was eventually successful in establishing a beachhead. Soon, the Imperium's ground forces, with Titans and armoured formations as a spearhead, ploughed relentlessly towards the conurbation of Gel'bryn.

The Imperial advance was stalled by storms of missiles raining down from beyond the hills. When units were detached to drive back the T'au spotters, they were instead engaged by jump troops protected by cloaking fields. Each time Imperial forces attempted to regain momentum, they were met by the timely counter-attacks of the Fire caste. These thrusts were orchestrated with precise and deadly effect by Commanders Farsight and Shadowsun, two heroes of the T'au Empire who would solidify their burgeoning reputations by masterminding the defence of Dal'yth Prime. Night was the worst for the invading forces, as under the cover of darkness, T'au in advanced battlesuits made swift, hard-hitting strikes. With the T'au's superior optics technology, major losses were inflicted upon the Imperial armour, while little damage was suffered in return. Mankind's elite Space Marines attempted to land behind T'au lines and regain the initiative, but they were defeated by teams of heavy battlesuits whose formidable firepower quickly downed their transports.

With more T'au reinforcements arriving at the front and the Imperial fleet's ability to hold orbit becoming tenuous, the Imperium's momentum was spent; they were finally forced to withdraw, leaving much of their equipment behind. It is conceivable that the T'au could have encircled the crusaders, but at the Ethereals' insistence, the Water caste opened a dialogue and agreed a truce, allowing the invaders an unimpeded retreat.

PREPARING FOR THE STORM

After the great battle on Dal'yth, an uneasy peace descended upon both sides of the war-torn Damocles Gulf. Even as many in the Imperium readied themselves for another offensive, more pressing concerns called for a hasty redeployment of Mankind's gathered armies.

The Imperium had demonstrated but a fraction of its power, and that had proven enough to hurl the T'au Empire backwards. Yet the T'au had also learned from the engagements, the Fire caste gaining invaluable insight into Mankind's methods. They had fought a foe that, like the Orks, was willing to absorb huge losses, but unlike the greenskins, the Imperial forces used a wide range of tactics and employed an expansive and impressive arsenal.

In the aftermath, the Ethereals demanded a full study of captives and recovered equipment. The Earth caste declared much of the technology to be inferior, and some was simply too unstable to contemplate using, such as Imperial plasma devices. There were some eye-opening discoveries, however, and the Earth caste was in absolute wonder over a warp engine they obtained. With no knowledge or understanding of the realm known as the warp, they found the strange apparatus utterly unfathomable. To their further frustration, the captured humans that had operated it seemed to possess no actual understanding of its mechanisms either, running the equipment solely through the application of superstitious rituals and chanting.

THE IMPERIUM'S VIEW

Most within the Imperium saw the T'au as just another disgusting xenos form to be obliterated, but a few of the deeper thinkers were unpleasantly surprised by this new race. Although no match in close quarters, the aliens had proved tactically savvy – bold masters of ambush and counter-attack warfare. Their technology was clearly advanced and some weapons, such as the railgun, were rightly feared. Next to a hive world, the T'au cities seemed like paradises of efficiency. Many, particularly the Space Marine Captains, found the T'au to be honourable adversaries that were worthy of respect.

Inquisitor Gallius was more alarmed by the T'au than any of his brethren. What struck him most about them was that their naivety, technological prowess and unwavering belief in progress reminded him of what he had read of Mankind in its glory days, a time known as the Age of Technology. Although much of that period is unknown, some believe that Mankind's intellectual hubris and unworthy reliance on machines and artificial intelligences brought about the dreaded Age of Strife, a nightmare time of horror and violence. If the T'au were indeed upon that same path, then they represented a larger threat to the Imperium of Man and indeed, the whole galaxy, than any would easily believe.

THE ADVANCE CONTINUES

In the wake of their war with the Imperium, Aun'Va stood up in the High Council and voiced his concerns. He implored the Ethereal Supreme, Aun'Wei, then in the twilight of his days, for the rights to reclaim T'au losses. The T'au harbour an unquenchable confidence in their own destiny and are determined that their methods are the best. However, after their long retreat across the Damocles Gulf, and their first-hand experience with the formidable forces of the Imperium, many of the T'au were filled with self-doubt. This was not a race that had tasted defeat before, in any of their prolonged endeavours. Aun'Va argued that without action, cracks would form in the foundation of their carefully orchestrated beliefs – and this must not come to pass. Sensing the truth of this, the ancient Ethereal nodded, leaving the details for Aun'Va to organise.

Aun'Va knew that those worlds disenfranchised by the Imperium could be manipulated, and from communications intercepts, he knew that the sectors around the Damocles Gulf could expect no further reinforcements. Therefore, Aun'Va ordered that an expeditionary force be assembled to cross that shifting barrier in space once more, the burgeoning T'au Empire stretching again into Mankind's realm in order to reclaim their recently lost colonies.

Although he had some reservations about his choice, Aun'Va selected Commander O'Shovah to head the military aspects of the reclamation effort. A protégé of the legendary Commander Puretide, O'Shovah was a dynamic and strong-willed leader who had risen to fame during recent campaigns against the Orks. The young Commander's tactical brilliance had already earned him the name of Commander 'Farsight' – for he was able to anticipate and exploit an enemy's course of action as if he already knew the foe's full battle-plan.

Initially, Aun'Va's choice proved judicious – every planet marked for reconquest was quickly taken. With much of their armed forces called away to war on other fronts, the Imperium's remaining defenders stood no chance against the devastating close-range strikes and bold thrusts that were Commander Farsight's signature tactics. The whole T'au Empire cheered with news of each of his victories.

A PARTING OF THE WAYS

With but a single world left to recolonise, Commander Farsight was drawn off-mission by his age-old enemies, the Orks. What started as swift raids to repel those greenskins that they found probing the edges of the newly recaptured space, soon turned into a prolonged war against a sizable conglomerate of Ork clans who travelled aboard crude asteroid bases. In time, O'Shovah's forces cut deeply into the Ork invasion, chasing the ruling Warboss to a nearby artefact world, a forlorn place long abandoned by the Imperium. Its name was Arthas Moloch, and there, Farsight's forces were engaged by a savage yet unidentified enemy, while the Orks escaped in the confusion.

Little was reported from the battle, save that all the Ethereals that had been accompanying the expedition as part of its coalition assembly were slain during the combat, and that their mysterious attackers had disappeared, leaving Arthas Moloch desolate once more. Undaunted by his losses, and despite direct orders to return, Commander Farsight refused to rejoin the other forces of the T'au Empire. Instead, he led the remnants of his army back onto the Orks' trail. Their pursuit soon took them beyond communication range, eventually passing further from home than any of their race had before.

The T'au Empire sent many desperate messages via the chain of communications beacons, accelerator relays on the ends of the system broadcasting their messages deep into the unknown space that Commander Farsight's expeditionary force had disappeared into, but no response came back.

It was possible that the vastness of space or some strange interference prevented the messages from reaching their recipient, but after many years with no reply, it was eventually deemed that the expedition was lost. The T'au Empire mourned the loss of one of their most illustrious Commanders. Years later, however, probes penetrated deep into the region where Commander Farsight's forces had last been seen and beamed back ominous reports: O'Shovah yet lived, and had established his own colonies on the far side of the Damocles Gulf. This mysterious, unprecedented and unthinkable betrayal of the Greater Good still haunts the T'au Empire to this day.

ATTACK FROM BEYOND

During the period of consolidation in the wake of the Second Sphere Expansion, outposts alerted the T'au to an encroaching menace. It was Hive Fleet Gorgon that penetrated their realm, and although only a minor splinter compared with some of the larger incursions that had entered the galaxy, the T'au had never faced a threat like that of the Tyranids – an intergalactic alien race whose voracious invasions stripped and devoured planets of all living matter.

The Tyranids showed a remarkable ability to physically adapt, evolving between battles to better counter the defenders. Against their onslaught, the T'au were forced to constantly alter their battle plans as new strains of Tyranid creatures morphed to overcome each advantage of tactics, terrain or technology that the Fire caste employed. The Tyranids annihilated many holdings before grinding to a halt against the T'au's major defensive actions on the forested planet of Sha'draig.

Although the planet was ultimately consumed, the aliens had been stalled long enough for the T'au to better prepare their defences at Ke'lshan Prime.

In a strange twist of fate, the sept world of Ke'lshan was first attacked by the forces of the Imperium; a fleet sent to aid in the Damocles Crusade over a hundred and fifty years earlier had only just emerged from the warp. Faced with a common enemy, the T'au and Imperial leaders agreed an uneasy truce. The Tyranids could not adapt to the two forces acting in concert, and were eventually massacred, with only a small remnant of Hive Fleet Gorgon fleeing into deep space. The opportunity to pursue this escaping splinter and destroy it utterly was lost as, with the immediate danger thwarted, tensions between the T'au and their Imperial allies swiftly escalated. The Earth caste of Ke'lshan immediately began to rebuild their battered sept, the Ethereals telling them to prepare for the eventual return of one, if not both, of their previous invaders.

A NEW AGE OF ASCENDANCY

Throughout the T'au Empire, recently built colony fleets were filling up orbital docks in anticipation of the call to launch a new sphere of expansion. Even as preparations were underway, warning signals flashed across the T'au Empire's relay lines. An age-old foe had returned in numbers beyond imagination; the Orks were back.

UNITE TO LIVE

They came from beyond the shroud of the Western Veil Nebula, the ragtag Ork armada emerging from the swirling gas clouds as suddenly as if they had materialised out of nowhere. As the first scans were picked up, the Earth caste technicians believed their sensors were malfunctioning, for the size of the greenskin fleet was staggering. The Ork invasion was composed of some dozen separate Waaaghs!, each with a Warboss vying for overall supremacy. Only the decrepit state of the Orks' spacecraft and their incessant infighting allowed the T'au Empire time to react.

Whilst many of the T'au panicked over the immensity of the looming threat, there was one who saw that, as always, if the empire worked together, they could defeat even an invasion of this magnitude. Aun'Va – now Ethereal Supreme – remained as calm as still water. He gathered the leaders of every sept in order to form a comprehensive plan of action. Those septs closest to the Ork menace – Vior'la, Sa'cea, and T'au'n – would combine forces in a delaying attack. Behind them, all other septs would rush troops and spacecraft towards the front to serve as the next wave of counter-attacks.

Across the empire, the Air caste scrambled their fleets, converting trade ships and colony transports into troop carriers to accommodate the armies needed to stem the green tide. As the united T'au advanced to confront the oncoming Orks, initial engagements took place along the outermost regions of the empire. The T'au navy launched hit-and-run attacks to lure pursuing Ork ships within range of orbital defence stations. The combined firepower of the fleet and orbital bases caused heavy Ork losses, although several stations were destroyed when sabotage ships crashed into the vast structures, allowing numerous greenskins to disembark and wreak havoc. Fire Warrior defenders were soon deployed aboard the remaining orbital stations and many desperate battles in the depths of space ensued, some lasting for months. Tu'val Base, one of the largest kor'vattra shipyards, was not scoured of Orks for over a year. During this time, almost constant skirmishes and close-range firefights took place across its enormous skeletal frame.

As the individual clans of the greenskins separated to follow their own pursuits, the fighting spread across space and over more than a dozen surface locations. Wherever Orks made planetfall, additional T'au ground forces were landed to reinforce the area, even on barren moons, for the aliens had to be denied any chance to scavenge supplies or set permanent roots within the territory of the T'au Empire. No sooner had one cluster of the primitive creatures been wiped out than reports would emerge of another roving band wreaking carnage.

With the possibility of being overrun forestalled, Aun'Va deemed the time was right for the next step of his master plan. Centuries before, when the Ethereal High Council knew that Commander Puretide was rapidly degenerating and would soon die, contingency plans were put into motion. The Earth caste had long been preserving Puretide's memories in an attempt to build an AI holograph that would look, act and most importantly, think like him. At the time, however, there was no assurance that this would successfully replace the indispensable instructor. So, as a safeguard, it was ordained that several of Puretide's top students would be placed in stasis – a time-proofing process that was then newly devised by the Earth caste. Now, with the largest Ork invasion ever seen already within their borders, Aun'Va determined that a leader of great destiny, one who had truly mastered the art of warfare, was needed.

A NEW HERO OF THE PEOPLE

One of those cryogenically frozen was a recently promoted Commander by the name of O'Shaserra. Of her generation of Fire Warriors, there was only a single rival who could match O'Shaserra's boldness and tactical abilities. That other warrior, O'Shovah, was not frozen, but rather chosen for glory, leading a T'au expeditionary force to reclaim the empire's colonies after the war with the Imperium.

By the time O'Shaserra had completed her reindoctrination, the fighting had been going on for half a dozen years; the massive Ork invasion was now spread across the borders of many septs. With their superior weaponry and the cohesion of their forces, the numerically inferior forces of the T'au Empire had been able to check the disorderly Ork hordes. It was a stalemate, as the disparate greenskins could not gain the momentum or unity to drive towards a sept world, and the T'au could not eradicate the monstrous aliens from their realm.

Taking leadership over a Hunter Cadre, Commander O'Shaserra joined the fray. After a daring string of victories, she earned control of a contingent – a formation of many cadres. By the time Sa'cea Prime's largest moon, Vay'harra, was proclaimed clear of Orks, Commander O'Shaserra's name was already becoming well known. From there, she led major victories on the dawn worlds of Kormusan, and finally on the K'resh Expansions. With each triumph, more T'au forces were freed to apply additional pressure to the fractionalised greenskins. After the total massacres of the K'resh Expansions, the power of the Orks was broken. Knowing full well how resilient these aliens could be, O'Shaserra dispatched her cadres upon hunt-and-kill missions, tracking and eliminating the most potentially troublesome pockets of greenskin resistance before they could reunite and become a greater threat. This diligence and ruthless precision doubtless saved thousands, if not millions of lives over the decades that followed.

The Great War of Confederation, as it came to be known, lasted a dozen years and firmly established a new hero in the hearts and minds of the T'au. O'Shaserra, now called Commander Shadowsun, had proven herself to a new generation – her tactical manoeuvres at every level of command were executed flawlessly and she was not without personal heroics. Her penchant for infiltrating battlefields and launching deadly ambushes was already legendary. A bright new future for the T'au Empire lay ahead.

THE THIRD SPHERE EXPANSION

With the Ork invasion defeated and a new hero risen to lead the Fire caste, Aun'Va knew the time was ripe to declare the Third Sphere Expansion. With more established septs to draw resources from, this drive to expand the size of their realm was undertaken on a scale never before attempted by the T'au Empire.

As bold and dynamic as the previous spheres of expansion had been, they had been confined to the dense star clusters that surrounded the planet T'au. The scope of such expansions was limited – the T'au did not have the population needed to spread further, and they had not yet fully learned to harness the power of alien auxiliaries to aid their cause. Technical constraints proved a barrier as well, for the Earth caste have constantly been seeking ways to develop spacecraft with faster engines to allow them to bridge the vast gulf of empty space between star systems.

Aun'Va knew that now was the time for his people to seize their destiny. The Great War of Confederation had served to put the T'au on a total war setting as the Ethereals pressed each caste for greater production and higher efficiency. The Ork invasion had proven a harsh training ground for the Fire caste, but they had now replaced the casualties of the drawn-out campaign. Furthermore, many Fire Warriors and their Commanders had gained invaluable experience from their encounters with the greenskins. They were now better trained than ever to coordinate their efforts with other septs and with the T'au navy. The number of alien auxiliaries at hand for deployment to the Fire caste was also greatly increased, and in terms of numbers they had never been stronger.

In order to reach those more distant systems earmarked as desirable by advanced scouts, the vast armadas of T'au spacecraft had been outfitted with the latest Earth caste modifications. The ships' propulsion systems were upgraded so that when magnified by impulse reactors, the engines could obtain faster speeds, propelling ships forwards at hitherto unthinkable velocities. To further lessen the burden on those space-faring craft with the longest journeys, the Earth caste had outfitted transport vessels with large stasis chambers, allowing Hunter Cadres or whole commands to shift to far distant battle zones months or years away without actually aging a day in the process.

BOW BEFORE THE GREATER GOOD

Every sept in the empire sent fleets to aid in the great expansion, resulting in an armada several times larger than any the T'au had previously assembled. The expedition's military forces were to be led personally by the newly appointed Commander Shadowsun, the highest ranking Fire caste officer. Its course was to cross the Damocles Gulf, travelling past the Gri-lok asteroid fields. Target destinations had been meticulously planned out, with all planets and moons desired for colonisation well marked on the fleet's holo-maps. Those worlds that had indigenous populations had already had many pre-emptive visits by Water caste traders and ambassadors in order to explore possibilities for a peaceful annexation.

Some of the planets branded for absorption into the T'au Empire were worlds that belonged to the Imperium of Mankind. In these cases, Aun'Va's timing of the Third

Sphere Expansion could not have been better. Water caste agents and *gue'vesa* – human helpers who had sworn loyalty to the T'au – confirmed what the Earth caste had already reported via intercepted transmissions: due to wars elsewhere, the number of Imperial defenders at the borders of their territory was much reduced.

The northernmost sector past the Damocles Gulf was soon wholly in T'au hands, while to the galactic west, the sectors adjoining the Red Sun Systems were cleared of Hrud, Orks and rebel humans. Fleets of Water caste Indigenous Inhabitants Liaison conclaves were deployed to begin their long integration process for those aliens that wished to seize upon the enlightenment that was being offered. Many human worlds actively sought out annexation, their people desperate to escape the tyrannical grasp of the Imperium. The Earth caste, eager to exploit these new domains, was already dropping producer domes upon recently seized planets rich with resources. In order to keep the drive going outwards, the T'au needed to establish fuel sources closer to the front lines of expansion. Linked back to the T'au Empire by long chains of relay comms, the expansion efforts had already claimed dozens of new worlds – yet this was only the start.

SEPTS OF THE THIRD SPHERE

The Third Sphere Expansion established several new septs, with more expeditionary forces launched in this period in search of new colonies than throughout the whole of T'au history.

KSI'M'YEN
The first of a handful of new septs, Ksi'm'yen is one of the many worlds previously claimed by the Imperium. Those human inhabitants who swore fealty to the Greater Good have been removed deeper into the T'au Empire to assure their safety and proper assimilation.

FI'RIOS
The T'au occupying the prime world of this sept wrested it from the grip of an Ork Warlord, and cleansing the star system has proven quite costly.

MU'GULATH BAY
The gateway to the Dovar System, Mu'gulath Bay was almost entirely destroyed during the Damocles Crusade. The sept's survivors bear a fierce hatred for the armies of Humanity.

When the warriors of the Fire caste met the armies of Mankind in battle, they swiftly realised this foe was like none they had faced before. The Space Marines, the Imperium's superhuman champions, brought the horror of total war to the T'au's nascent colonies.

SHADOWSUN TRIUMPHANT

Buoyed by her initial successes, Shadowsun led her armies deeper into Imperial territory. She seemed to be everywhere at once, driving her forces relentlessly onwards. At the forefront of the offensive, the Fire caste spearheads were already en route to their next targets before the consolidation forces that followed hard on their heels had fully landed on the newly conquered planet.

As Shadowsun pressed further into the Imperium of Mankind she encountered ever greater resistance, and she saw that to overextend her forces would risk disaster. Instead she split her fleets, scattering them to a dozen headings. Each began a devastating series of hit-and-run attacks against which the Imperium could mount no effective counter. At length, the humans settled into a static defence of a few key worlds. This allowed Shadowsun to marshal her forces and launch a mass assault on the target of her choosing. She decided upon the hive world of Agrellan, whose orbit safeguarded a rich cluster of Imperial worlds.

Transports of fresh Fire caste warriors and many of the newest weapon prototypes were rushed to this battlefront for what would surely be a pivotal conflict. Aun'Va himself came to inspire the Fire caste, and upon seeing him, the T'au knew that victory was assured. At last, the latest class of battlesuit was unleashed, and under Shadowsun's inspired leadership, it proved a resounding success. Fittingly, it was this new XV104 Riptide battlesuit that delivered the killing blow during the final engagement, laying waste to the massive heavy tanks that had so long protected the world's capital hive. Although the Imperial defenders fought with fatalistic grit, it was not long before they were cut down, and only isolated pockets of resistance remained. The planet, renamed Mu'gulath Bay, belonged to the T'au. Soon the whole system would follow.

THE IMPERIUM'S REVENGE

So thick and fast came the victories for the T'au that many Fire caste strategists believed the war to be won, and the Imperium of Mankind to be in full retreat. These naive hopes were dashed with the emergence of an enormous Imperial battle fleet in orbit above Mu'gulath Bay. Humanity had come to either reclaim their lost world or see it burnt to ashes.

The battle that followed was a brutal meat grinder the likes of which the T'au had never experienced before. There seemed no limit to the manpower and armoured assets of the Imperium. Fire caste defenders fought until their last breath in the name of the Greater Good, yet even Commander Shadowsun's flawless Kauyon could not hold back the Imperium's ferocity. It was then, when all hope seemed lost, that red-armoured figures dropped from the skies into the heart of the Imperial formations, blasting the enemy into atoms with close-range barrages of searing energy. The pariah Commander Farsight had come to aid his people.

The rebel Farsight's noble intervention prevented the complete obliteration of the T'au forces on Mu'gulath Bay, but the Imperium of Mankind would not simply accept defeat at the hands of an upstart xenos empire. The humans deployed nightmarish assassins to hunt down the T'au high command, hoping to cut the head from their foes. In a further act of retaliation, agents of the Adeptus Mechanicus utilised bizarre archeotech to set light to Mu'gulath Bay, an unnatural fire that would spread across the entire Damocles Gulf. The dream of the nascent sept world ended in flames. With this atrocity, the Third Sphere Expansion came to a halt. Shadowsun and the remnants of her coalition force retreated from Mu'gulath Bay, and began the long hard work of consolidating their significant gains elsewhere.

FATE OF THE FOURTH SPHERE

The Third Sphere Expansion had brought many worlds into the fold of the Greater Good, but it had ended in fire and destruction, isolating the T'au from the wider galaxy. The empire required new technologies to push beyond the Eastern Fringe, but in their pursuit of rapid expansion at any cost, the T'au would court disaster...

TO CROSS THE STARS

As the T'au Empire recovered from the brutality of the war for Mu'gulath Bay, the expansionist power was faced with a dilemma. Utilising archeotech and eldritch science, the Tech-Priests of the Adeptus Mechanicus had engulfed a vast swathe of space in flames, cutting the T'au off from their destined coreward path. To the east of the empire lay an expanse of dead space, barren worlds left in the wake of Hive Fleet Gorgon's ravenous invasion, and to the west the Sautekh Dynasty of the Necrons arrayed their fleets for war. The T'au found their space lanes cut off on all sides, with no obvious route towards new conquests.

At this time of great tension, a further cataclysm unfolded across the empire and beyond. The galaxy-scarring phenomenon of the Great Rift – known as the *Mont'yhe'va*, or 'Devourer of Hope' – marked the skies of the T'au Empire, and heralded a succession of vicious stellar storms that tore across several vital colony worlds. Millions of lives were lost. Many high-ranking T'au strategists feared that if these ructions were to continue, even the shining Sept worlds themselves would be at risk.

Upon the world of T'au, at the heart of the empire, the Ethereal High Council debated the issue behind closed doors. A small faction suggested negotiating passage through territory belonging to the Imperium of Mankind, but the humans were judged too mercurial and hostile for such a diplomatic approach. Others proposed the construction of vast cryo-ships, which would be hurled out into the void to colonise new worlds, even if this took hundreds of years. Yet such slow and unreliable proliferation was not the way of the T'au. The process of bringing enlightenment to the lesser races could not be delayed any longer, for with every passing day, more of the galaxy was lost to their thoughtless squabbling.

So it was that the Ethereal caste chose a far more dangerous path, but one that might solve their problems entirely. Ever since the T'au's first brutal encounters with Mankind, Earth caste science divisions

had been assigned to study the primitive technology of the Imperium, assessing the means by which the humans made their far-reaching jumps through the vast expanse of space. After decades of examination and alteration – during which Imperial technology was combined with the wreckage of Kroot Warspheres recovered in secret from the battle sites of earlier expansions – a breakthrough had been made. The AL-38 Slipstream module was a prototype device that could be fitted to the propulsion system of any deep-space craft, forming a powerful bubble of anti-matter around the vessel and propelling it at such speed that it could pierce the fabric of reality itself. In this manner, huge tracts of realspace could be circumvented and journey times significantly reduced. Initial tests of the module were incredibly successful. T'au ships fitted with the Slipstream prototype were able to cross the entire expanse of the empire in only a few days, a journey that would have taken many months with previous propulsion designs. The raging star-fire that consumed the Damocles Gulf could theoretically be entirely bypassed.

TRAGEDY AT NUMENAR POINT

The empire accelerated production of vessels equipped with the sub-realm module, and selected veteran Fire caste cadres from every sept world to join the next wave of colonisation. Overall military authority was granted to Commander Surestrike, a calm and considered veteran whose performance in the wars of the Third Sphere Expansion had garnered much prestige and respect. He had fought beside Shadowsun herself at the Battle of Mu'gulath Bay, and O'Shaserra spoke of his abilities in the highest regard.

With great fanfare, a broadcast from the most glorious Aun'Va announced the commencement of the Fourth Sphere

Expansion. The Ethereal Supreme declared that it would pierce the fires of the Damocles Gulf like a shining spear of truth, spreading word of the Greater Good further across the galaxy than ever before.

Surestrike's armada gathered at Numenar Point, in the northern outskirts of the T'au Empire. Earth caste scientist Fio'vre Ka'buto, the genius behind the AL-38 Slipstream prototype, expressed great concern at the sheer size of the venture. The AL-38 had previously only been utilised for single-vessel faster-than-light travel, he argued, and there had been little research into the potential ramifications of multiple breaches in the fabric of space-time occurring simultaneously and in such great concentration. The Ethereal High Council dismissed his fears calmly, pointing to the near-total success rate of the prototype's trials. The Fourth Sphere Expansion would proceed as planned.

Facing towards the fires of the Damocles Gulf, the fleets of the Fourth Sphere Expansion made ready to jump, preparing to usher in a new age of exploration and expansion. At Commander Surestrike's mark, each vessel routed power to its Slipstream module. It was at this moment that the galaxy tore open.

The combined disruption of hundreds of anti-matter fields activating at once acted like a trans-dimensional pulse bomb, blasting apart the veil between realities. A ragged wound in realspace yawned open before the fleet of the Fourth Sphere Expansion, vomiting forth unnatural colours and roiling half-formed shapes. The horrified T'au looked on helplessly as the breach, growing wider with every moment, raced towards their vessels. Reverse-thruster fusion-jets kicked in as Air caste commanders attempted to escape the onrushing doom, but they were as helpless as shimmerhawks in a hurricane. The storm of unreality swept over the Fourth Sphere Expansion and devoured it whole, leaving nothing but a vortex of sickening colours behind. These images were broadcast across every sept world, from far-flung D'yanoi to T'au itself. Gasps of horror echoed around great plazas and view-platforms, as signals fizzled out or were desperately disconnected. The Ethereal caste moved quickly to contain all knowledge of the disaster, creating elaborately doctored holo-reels that showed the Fourth Sphere Expansion successfully completing their sub-realm jumps into the great unknown. Meanwhile, long-range Recon Drones blinked and whirred in the blackness of space, searching for any hint of a distress signal or emergency holo-beam. Not a sign was found.

A LIGHT IN THE DARKNESS

Years passed. The T'au, far from embarking upon a new age of discovery, found themselves on a defensive footing. The ceaseless cosmic disturbances that ravaged the Empire similar showed no sign of abating. Enemies arose on all fronts. It seemed as if the birth of the Mont'yhe'va had whipped up the unenlightened races into a primal frenzy. The Orks were gathering in great numbers once more, and the shadow of Hive Fleet Gorgon, once thought effectively destroyed, had returned to haunt the Perdus Rift. Many alien populations across the sept worlds, particularly those closest to the Mont'yhe'va, were struck by outbreaks of violent insanity. This was particularly common amongst the human gue'vesa colonies. Several armed uprisings were put down with uncompromising efficiency, though fortunately the malady did not spread amongst the T'au. The Fire caste kept the borders of the empire safe through their bravery and bloody sacrifice. The fighting was fierce, and many glorious victories were won. Yet in their heart, each Fire Warrior longed to end these grinding wars of consolidation and return to the T'au's great task: to travel the length and breadth of the galaxy, bringing word of the Greater Good to all.

Though the T'au continued to strive together in the name of progress and enlightenment, it could not be denied that a malaise had settled over the citizenry of the empire. The AL-38 Slipstream project was scrapped, all traces of the prototype disassembled and returned to storage in the laboratories of the Earth caste. With it disappeared the dream of faster-than-light travel. The Ethereals would not risk another Numenar Point. It seemed as though the loss of the Fourth Sphere had signalled the dawn of a dark era for the T'au'va, where uncertainty and constant danger had replaced the ideal of peace amidst the stars.

And then, after years of silence, came a signal. A deep-space holo-relay captured a solitary drone drifting through the Zone of Silence, pinging an encrypted data-flow upon a decades-old frequency. Recon ships moved to intercept the drone, but upon reaching its location they were shocked to discover a previously unrecorded cosmic phenomenon – a spiralling wormhole that had appeared as if from nowhere in the midst of this lifeless stretch of space. The drone orbiting this anomaly contained high-level identity codes and micro-phase security keys dating back to the launch of the Fourth Sphere Expansion. Further, embedded within its mainframe was a series of coordinates far to the north of the T'au Empire, amidst a swathe of territory known to Humanity as the Chalnath Expanse. With this discovery came a miraculous realisation: the Fourth Sphere Expansion had endured, and even now it called to its distant kin from the far side of the wormhole.

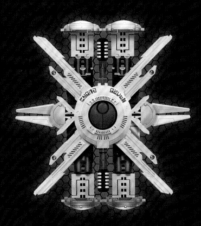

The Ethereal High Council ordered that work begin immediately on the construction of defensive positions around the wormhole, which the T'au named the Startide Nexus. A hexagonal ring of immense stellar fortresses and interwoven ionic minefields would safeguard the anomaly, and several kor'vattra defence fleets were assigned to permanent sentry patrols around its shimmering depths. The raw material required for these fortifications was staggering, the equivalent of hundreds of battle fleets. To ensure that the resources required were gathered in sufficient time, the T'au initiated a series of resettlement programmes and so-called Labour Freedom Decrees, moving entire populations, both alien and T'au, from their home worlds and organising them into work divisions. The manpower and resources dedicated to the defence of the nexus soon rivalled even those surrounding the T'au home world.

Meanwhile, a division of elite Earth caste scientists, assembled from across the empire and led by the team behind the creation of the AL-38 Slipstream module, studied and probed the wormhole in search of answers.

'The tragic loss of the Fourth Sphere fleet was the most terrible event I shall ever witness. It will haunt my dreams until my dying days. Yet even in disaster there is opportunity. Even in the darkest moment, there is the flickering light of hope. Progress cannot be halted by tragedy, and innovation must not be stymied by hesitation. Our work continues. With clear minds and steady hands we build upon the harsh lessons of the past.'

- Fio'vre Ka'buto, inventor of the AL-38 Slipstream module

NEW HORIZONS, NEW DANGERS

Miraculously, the T'au discovered the location of the Fourth Sphere Expansion's survivors. With fresh hope in their hearts, the warriors and colonists of the Fifth Sphere Expansion prepared to reunite with their lost kin. They could little imagine the awful truth behind the Fourth Sphere's disappearance…

REUNIFICATION

Fortification of the Startide Nexus was achieved in an astonishingly short time frame, far ahead of the estimations provided by the Earth caste scientists in charge of its construction. Without concrete proof of the Fourth Sphere's survival, however, the Ethereal High Council would not sanction any expedition through the spatial rift. A recon probe was sent through the portal with a series of code queries and genetic markers. It took more than a T'au solar cycle for the probe to return. Analysis of the blood sample and data-reels it contained confirmed the identity of the recipient as Commander Surestrike himself. This explicit evidence would finally herald the launch of a new sphere expansion.

Following the miracle of the Fourth Sphere message, a new sense of optimism had invigorated the empire, and waves of colonists sought to take part in the grand expedition of the Fifth Sphere Expansion. Commander Shadowsun herself was revived from stasis to lead the journey to reunite with Surestrike's expedition. At her demand the assembled armada was divided into eight great fleets, each led by a Fire caste Commander of her own choosing, every one a veteran who had fought alongside her in the wars of the Damocles Gulf. Earth caste builders and Water caste politicians were present in their thousands, for there would surely be many challenges, both logistical and political, that would need to be overcome.

Soon, the assembled armada of the Fifth Sphere Expansion was arrayed in tight formation ahead of the moon-sized dimensional portal, which rippled ominously before them, its flickering corona washing across their vessels in a pale blue light. Engines were primed and anti-matter fields activated. With a single word, Commander Shadowsun gave the signal to jump. The Fifth Sphere Expansion fleet streaked forwards and leapt into the void.

Shutters and view ports slammed closed across the fleet as the vessels bucked and rattled. Skeleton crews and AI pathfinders guided the fleet along a strict trajectory, while the rest of the colonists slumbered in deep stasis. How long the journey took, none could say. It felt like decades, but also somehow only a few cycles. Eventually, with a gut-wrenching jolt, the ships of the Fifth Sphere expansion fleet were spat back into realspace. Shutters whirred open and stasis pods wound down with a hum of idling power cells. The view-ports slowly opened to reveal a scattering of battered vessels, deep-space arcologies and drifting habitat pods. Several ships had been disassembled and arranged in a hexagonal structure around the stellar anomaly from which the Fifth Sphere armada emerged, their heavy pulse cannons and mass driver arrays facing off into space. A hail came from this ragged collective, welcoming all newcomers to the Nem'yar Atoll.

Commander Shadowsun emerged from her ship's docking pod into the largest of the space-borne arcologies, accompanied by several high-ranking Ethereals. Commander Surestrike himself greeted her. He looked to have aged several decades since the two had last met. Even in the presence of the Ethereals, the veteran Fire caste warrior seemed to find no spiritual contentment, and his eyes were flecks of cold steel. The Ethereal delegates debriefed the Commander over the course of several weeks. The content of these conversations was severely restricted, and vessels from the Edification Corps were a common sight around the Fourth Sphere Gate, as the T'au's political officers cross-examined the survivors of the ill-fated expedition. Nevertheless, disturbing rumours swiftly began to circulate. Something had assailed the ships of the Fourth Sphere Expansion as they drifted, lost in the sub-realm's roiling tides. Nearly three quarters of the expedition's ships were cracked and torn apart, their occupants dragged into the screaming maelstrom. Bizarre, unnatural forms manifested within the depths of merchant starships and Kir'Qath frigates, alien creatures that obeyed no known laws of physics or nature. Many vessels were gutted from the inside out, their crew and occupants slaughtered and devoured. One by one, the ravenous creatures of the sub-realm were picking off their prey. It seemed almost as if they were prolonging the game, feeding upon the T'au's rapidly increasing sense of terror and agony.

No survivor of the Fourth Sphere Expansion could say how long they endured this torment. Nor would they speak of what had saved them from oblivion, beyond the revelation that something possessing a hideous sentience had dragged them free of that nightmare realm, tearing a great furrow through the fabric of unreality in the process – the very wormhole through which the Fifth Sphere Expansion had travelled. The primal horror in the eyes of those who spoke of their salvation chilled the hearts of all who saw it. Whatever it was that they had witnessed had irrevocably changed these unfortunate souls. They spoke little, and could hardly meet the eyes of those who had not shared their experiences. Yet it was in the presence of non-T'au species that they seemed most discomforted. It was only with firm insistence from the Ethereal caste that Surestrike allowed alien auxiliaries and support staff to board the gate. Even then, his warriors had pulse rifles trained upon any non-T'au that entered their territory. What had become of the Fourth Sphere's own auxiliaries was a mystery, though dark whispers spoke of forced exiles and even mass liquidation. Some theorised that the Fourth Sphere T'au had witnessed something pure being corrupted beyond countenance during their traumatic odyssey, and now placed the blame at the door of those alien races inducted into the T'au'va.

COLONISATION

Despite this less than auspicious reunion, the momentum of the Fifth Sphere Expansion did not slow. The T'au could not afford to halt for a moment. This new frontier was a deadly place, and the ongoing trauma of the Great Rift rendered space travel an unpredictable hazard. Worse still, old enemies of the T'au were on the move. Thousands of Ork fleets roared across the Ful'na Nebulae to the east, massacring anything unfortunate enough to fall in their path. Scattered remnants of Tyranid hive fleets drifted south along the galactic plane, the survivors of some apocalyptic battle. Of the Imperium of Mankind – the T'au Empire's star-spanning nemesis – little was seen, aside from several lost fleets that strayed into the empire's newly claimed territory and were quickly captured or destroyed. Captives from these isolated fleets knew little of value. Humanity's archaic methods of communication and interstellar travel had clearly been devastated by the galactic turmoil, and the T'au took advantage of their enemy's weakness to sway several nearby Imperial worlds to the Greater Good, excoriating any rogue elements that challenged this forced emancipation.

The warriors of the Fourth Sphere Expansion partook in these purges with unrestrained eagerness, to the astonished disapproval of their kin. They displayed a ruthlessness quite unheard of amongst adherents of the Code of Fire, slaughtering prisoners with fusillades of pulse fire, and disregarding – even intentionally maximizing – any loss of non-T'au life. Such dark events as the Massacre of the Dul'un Lakes and the Eight Days of Infamy caused great consternation to Commander Shadowsun and the Ethereal High Council. Several T'au Commanders of the Fourth Sphere were subjected to the ritual punishment known as Malk'la for their callous actions and unnecessary brutality, before being returned to the ranks or sent back to the empire for re-assimilation. After a spree of killings and a bloody Kroot uprising upon the colony of Ky'san, all alien auxiliaries were removed from contingents of Fourth Sphere T'au.

Despite these unsavoury incidents, the T'au's expansion efforts continued at a formidable pace. In a matter of several months, several planets had been occupied and transformed into thriving colonies, and new sept worlds flourished under the savvy statesmanship of Water caste officials. Orbital defence stations and patrol fleets lined the borders of the Nem'yar Atoll, for after the bloodshed of Damocles, the T'au fully expected the Imperium of Mankind to attempt to reconquer their lost domain with a great crusade of blood and fire. Yet it was not only the zealous warriors of Humanity whose gazes were drawn towards the Startide Nexus, an open pathway to the heartlands of the T'au Empire…

SEPTS OF THE FIFTH SPHERE

FE'SAAN SEPT

The first sept world established by the fleets of the Fifth Sphere Expansion, Fe'saan is a starkly beautiful planet dominated by soaring mountain ranges. The Water caste has established a colonial headquarters here, from which it governs the processing and integration of conquered foes and newly encountered races into the T'au'va. Fe'saan's three tide-locked moons are now home to vast kor'vattra shipyards; the sept's position at the heart of the Nem'yar Atoll makes it a key strategic location, from which colonisation and patrol fleets are continuously dispatched across the nascent Fifth Sphere colonies.

KOR'TAL SEPT

The sept of Kor'tal orbits not a sun, but a black hole. Only thermo-inductive shields and artificial satellite flares render this harsh planet of permanent darkness liveable. Nevertheless, it is one of the most vital Fifth Sphere septs, for the Earth caste have established dozens of AI-automated droneports that harvest pure dark matter from the event horizon of the system's black hole. This priceless resource is most notably used to power the nova reactors of XV104 Riptide battlesuits, but it has many other potential applications, both military and industrial.

YO'VAI SEPT

Yo'vai was founded upon a planetary disc – a flat, circular expanse of solid matter orbiting a dwarf star. The origin of this anomaly continues to be the subject of intense debate amongst the astrophysicists of the Earth caste. The most popular theory posits that the entire disc was shaped by some ancient terraforming technology – this would explain the oddly geometric shape of its major landmasses, and the lack of a planetary core. The soaring valleys and great plains of the planetary disc have been claimed as Fire caste training grounds, and have proven especially popular amongst gunship pilots, who engage in endless mock battles across its rolling grasslands.

THE NEM'YAR ATOLL

KOR'TAL

YO'VAI

Startide Nexus

FE'SAAN

ON THE RISE

The map below provides a view of the T'au Empire's territories at the time of the Fifth Sphere Expansion, and identifies several points of interest.

FI'RIOS

KSI'MYEN

DAL'YTH

MU'GULATH BAY

Gri-lok Asteroid Field

Farsight Enclaves

Arthas Moloch

Pech

VIOR'LA

SA'CEA

DAMOCLES GULF

Sha'galudd

KE'LSHAN

WESTERN VEIL NEBULA

T'AU'N

Gas Clouds

T'AU

AU'TAAL

Startide Nexus

N'DRAS

VASH'YA

THE ZONE OF SILENCE

Q-15

Ironrok

Gurgit's Mekworld

Red Sun Systems

T'OLKU

ELSY'EIR

Landfall

TASH'VAR

D'YANOI

BORK'AN

FAL'SHIA

Vespid

Isla'su

KEY
Communications Routes

- ○ Relay Beacons
- ◯ 1st Phase Septs
- ◯ 2nd Phase Septs
- ◯ 3rd Phase Septs
- ◯ 5th Phase Septs
- ▯ Kroot World
- ◎ Other Worlds
- ◈ Farsight Enclaves
- Fortress Stations
- Orbital Cities
- Sunburst
- Mining Fleet

A BURGEONING EMPIRE

Since the T'au first left the atmosphere of their birth world, their empire has grown, spreading across the stars in distinct spheres of expansion. In addition to the settled systems, or septs, the T'au realm is rife with all manner of space phenomena, T'au-made structures and important alien home worlds.

FORTRESS STATIONS (TA'SHIRO)

Positioned in the deep space between septs are ta'shiro bases – fortress stations capable of enough thrust to resist drift and maintain permanent interstellar positions. Several patterns of development have been followed in the construction of these enormous floating fortresses, with the largest comparable in population to a continent-sized city.

KROOT WORLDS

The Kroot are the most common of the alien auxiliaries in the T'au Empire, and dozens of Kroot enclaves can be found among the septs. Although they are a far-flung and migratory race, all Kroot eventually feel the pangs that lead them to return to their birth world of Pech, bringing with them a wealth of evolutionary traits to be absorbed by the race at large.

SHA'GALUDD

Sha'galudd is the home world of the Nagi, a small species of highly intelligent worms known for their mind-control abilities. When first discovered, the Nagi were hated creatures known as mind-worms, but since the early violent conflicts, they have agreed a peace accord and joined the T'au Empire. Many Nagi now serve as advisors to the Ethereal caste.

VESPID

Benighted gas giant and home world of the Vespid race, this planet is also known for its rich crystal mines.

SUNBURSTS

In attempts to drain stars of energy, many suns have been accidentally sent into supernova. Thus far, the Earth caste has failed to collect this resource, and travel into these regions is not advised. Since failing at fuel-collection, the Earth caste are experimenting with weaponising the intense power of this cosmic phenomenon, with varying degrees of success.

THE ZONE OF SILENCE

Devastated region where Hive Fleet Gorgon left behind many barren planets, scoured of all life forms. Has recently been heavily fortified as a result of the discovery of the Startide Nexus.

RELAY COMMUNICATIONS BEACONS (TAL'HYEN)

T'au communications can only travel so far before their signals fade, so relay stations are positioned to form chains capable of crossing the gulf of space. This is an effective solution, but each holo-vid can take months to cross interstellar distances and the quality can vary based on the number of relays and the amount of interference, such as dust clouds and solar winds.

NEM'YAR ATOLL

The region of space colonised and fortified by the survivors of the Fourth Sphere Expansion after their escape from the sub-realm dimension, and later expanded with the arrival of the Fifth Sphere Expansion fleets. This cluster of sept worlds, stellar fortresses and habitation spheres surrounds the swirling portal of the Startide Nexus. The Nem'yar Atoll is stranded amidst a wild and dangerous frontier, and is under almost constant assault from raiders, hostile aliens and other, darker threats. As such, the military resources allocated to the defence of this key region are considerable.

FARSIGHT ENCLAVES

Although not a part of the T'au Empire, the breakaway faction led by Commander Farsight are known to have settled throughout this region. Up-to-date intelligence on the martial-led septs is difficult for the High Council to obtain, as armed fortress stations have proven effective at destroying probes.

FIRES OF DAMOCLES

The Damocles Gulf has been enveloped in a stellar firestorm, unleashed by a strange techno-arcane device of the Adeptus Mechanicus. Pockets of T'au forces remain within, isolated from the wider empire and desperately defending their shattered colony worlds from rampaging aliens and roving battlefleets of the Imperium.

RED SUN SYSTEMS

Probes have marked the dense cluster of planets around a string of six distinct red suns; however, the massive Ork population has deterred any further T'au colonisation. The systems are ringed with sensor buoys, in hopes of offering early warnings should the greenskins ever cease their internal fighting and seek to menace neighbouring systems.

STARTIDE NEXUS

This trans-dimensional channel was torn open when the surviving vessels of the Fourth Sphere Expansion were hurled back into reality, and connects the nascent colonies of the Nem'yar Atoll to the region known as the Zone of Silence. The exact nature of this cosmic phenomenon remains an utter mystery to the Earth caste, which has established a number of research stations at both ends of the wormhole in order to carry out further studies.

LANGUAGE AND CULTURE

The language of the T'au is a complex, highly evolved form of communication. In sound, it is deeply lyrical and soft, with many words and meanings varying greatly depending on a user's intonation, glottal emphasis and even posture. Its multiple arrangements of polysyllabic word groups make it difficult in the extreme for human speech organs to pronounce correctly. Without voice translation technology, only the most skilful linguist would have any hope of speaking even the most basic T'au words and phrases.

T'au names are multipart, with the prefix that names the caste they were born into considered by far to be the most important part. The castes are as follows: Fire (Shas), Earth (Fio), Air (Kor), and Water (Por). The name of the fifth caste translates most often as Ethereal (Aun).

With the caste established, the second portion of a T'au name refers to their rank within society. The T'au are unusual as a culture in that there is no stigma attached to rank or profession. Each individual has his or her place in society and commands equal respect no matter how menial a task they perform. Each role is recognised as being part of the greater whole and a furtherance of the common good. When non-T'au, such as alien races just beginning to enter contact with the T'au Empire, point out that some classes, such as Fire caste Commanders or any of the Ethereal caste, are clearly given respect bordering on reverence, the Water caste envoys simply speak one of over two dozen subtle variations in the T'au language that translates roughly as the phrase 'first amongst equals'.

There are five major levels of rank within society, each of which has a subtly different meaning dependent on the caste to which it is suffixed. In ascending order of seniority, these ranks are as follows, including the best translation of each rank based upon the Fire caste.

'La	- *Warrior*
'Ui	- *Veteran*
'Vre	- *Hero*
'El	- *Noble (or possibly knight)*
'O	- *Commander*

Next in a T'au's name comes his sept, which can translate as either his extended family or place of birth. This portion of the name has wide interpretations that are not easily picked up by aliens. For example, a T'au from one of oldest septs may be perceived as wiser or more sophisticated than one from a more recently established sept. Certain septs also contain meaning in themselves, as they embody a particular trait. For example, the name of Vior'la means 'hot-blooded' and those who hail from that sept are considered particularly aggressive, while those from Bork'an Sept are regarded as quick learning and contemplative.

Lastly comes a T'au's individual name, which is earned in recognition of some achievement, rather than given at birth. These are sometimes the most puzzling elements of the name and while some may be relatively easy to understand, such as 'Shovah' (far-sighted) or 'Kais' (skilful), others are more obscure. The meaning of an individual name may also change quite dramatically depending on the preceding and subsequent names. For instance, 'Kais' would read as something more akin to 'ingenious' to a T'au of Bork'an Sept, while a Vior'la native would likely associate the word with skill in battle. It is possible for remarkable individuals to accumulate

T'AU WORD	BEST TRANSLATION
Aun	Ethereal/celestial
Be'gel	Orks
Da'noh	Mystery not yet unravelled by the Earth caste
Fu'llasso	Political mess, to be unscrambled by the Water caste (literally 'cursed mind knot')
Gue'la	Humans
Gue'ron'sha	Space Marines (literally 'engineered human warriors')
Gue'vesa	Humans who have joined the T'au Empire (literally 'human helpers')
Kor'vesa	Drone ('faithful helper')
Ko'vash	To strive for (literally 'a worthy cause')
Lhas'rhen'na	Euphemism for worthy or noble sacrifice (literally 'shattered jade')
Mal'caor	Spider
Mal'kor	Vespid
Mont'au	The Terror, the T'au's worst nightmare
Mont'yr	Blooded
M'yen	Unforeseen
Or'es	Powerful
Por'sral	Propaganda campaign
Run'al	Small blind or bunker
Shas'ar'tol	Fire caste High Command
Shas'len'ra	Cautious warrior
Shi	Victory
Ta'lissera	Communion/Marriage/Bonded
T'au'va	The Greater Good
Ves'ron	Robotic being
Vral	Undercut, work to undermine
Y'eldi	Air caste name for a particularly gifted pilot (literally 'winged one')
Y'he	Tyranid ('ever-devouring')

more than one name over the course of their lifetimes, and some of the most notable T'au have literally dozens of names. In the interest of expediency and simplicity, it is common to truncate one's full list of names and be known by a simplified appellation.

As an example of how a full T'au title translates, the name Shas'o Vior'la Shovah Kais Mont'yr can be broken down as follows: the individual is a member of the Fire caste (Shas), holds the rank of Commander ('o), hails from the world of Vior'la and has the personal names that translate as far-sighted (Shovah), skilful (Kais) and blooded (Mont'yr). However, this T'au is more commonly known as O'Shovah or Commander Farsight.

FIVE CASTES, ONE PEOPLE

Although they are one race, the T'au castes are so evolutionary distinct at this stage in their development that the differences run more deeply than mere appearances. Each caste acts, speaks and even thinks in its own unique manner. With a glance it is easy to identify a T'au's caste; however, it takes closer scrutiny to reveal their rank in T'au society and possibly which sept they originate from.

A T'au's caste is the easiest to distinguish, as the physical traits of each are immediately recognisable: the larger framed and more muscular Fire caste, the tall, willowy Air caste, the stout and prosaic Earth caste, the facially expressive Water caste, and the gaunt yet graceful Ethereals. Most T'au appear stern and impassive, their flat faces registering little to no emotion, with the exception of the Fire caste, who can be roused to an intense anger, and the highly demonstrative Water caste, whose facial features are softer and more expressive than any other of T'au kind.

The colour of a T'au's skin offers hints as to their caste as well which sept they call home. In general it can be said that the Fire caste tend to have the darker pigmentation, while the Air caste have the palest. The darker the T'au's bluish-grey skin, the closer to the sun they live – therefore those hailing from Vior'la have much darker skin than those from Bork'an. Some strange quality in the green-tinged sun of the N'dras Sept can leave those from that region slightly mottled.

Although all T'au speak the same language, each caste has adopted a unique pattern of speech and each sept has a distinctive dialect. Ever pragmatic, the Earth caste speak in matter-of-fact tones, similar to, but more monotonous than, the clipped orders of the Fire caste. Both, however, are audibly different from the shrill tones of the Air caste or the calm yet unnaturally penetrating speech of the Ethereals. As the Water caste usually adopts the speech patterns, mannerisms and tones of those with whom they converse, it is more difficult to gauge what their dialect actually sounds like; however, when on their own or only amongst others of their caste, their speech patterns and voices are the most melodic of all T'au. Those T'au from the elder septs (those from the First Sphere Expansion) are generally considered more sophisticated and erudite than those from the newer, outlying worlds, and not surprisingly, the T'au accent is regarded as the most prestigious.

As a culture, the T'au have put aside individual gain in favour of the Greater Good. Thus, such things as personal possessions or sole ownership are rare, with communal ownership of everything being the norm. Each T'au is taught to be loyal to Ethereals, the empire, their sept and their caste, in that order. As they are raised by caste institutions, family allegiance is an alien concept, with perhaps the closest thing in T'au society being those who are bonded in a ta'lissera – a pact where groups of T'au pledge support to each another. This is the highest form of T'au affection for one another, as it symbolises the sacrifice of the individual to become part of a greater whole. In all castes, age and experience are venerated. It is common for T'au to bear a single scalp lock, sometimes adorned with ornamented ringlets indicative of rank. The more elaborate the decoration on the scalp lock, the higher the rank and position. Also, no matter which caste the T'au is from, the higher up his position, the more he will be surrounded by technological upgrades and gadgets, such as drones or larger communication vanes.

As different as each of the castes are, all are possessed of the same unwavering self-confidence in the righteousness of their empire's cause. Even the most overworked and overlooked of their number are assured that their culture, beliefs and technology are manifestly superior to those of other races, and all T'au are united by the ambition of conquering the galaxy for the Greater Good.

T'AU ALPHABET

Below is a diagram that translates the T'au alphabet into Low Gothic. The T'au's language is incredibly complex, so certain words or phrases may differ from this established paradigm.

Note also that the T'au alphabet does not have an equivalent for 'Q' or 'Z', and that both 'I' and 'Y' share the same symbol and pronunciation.

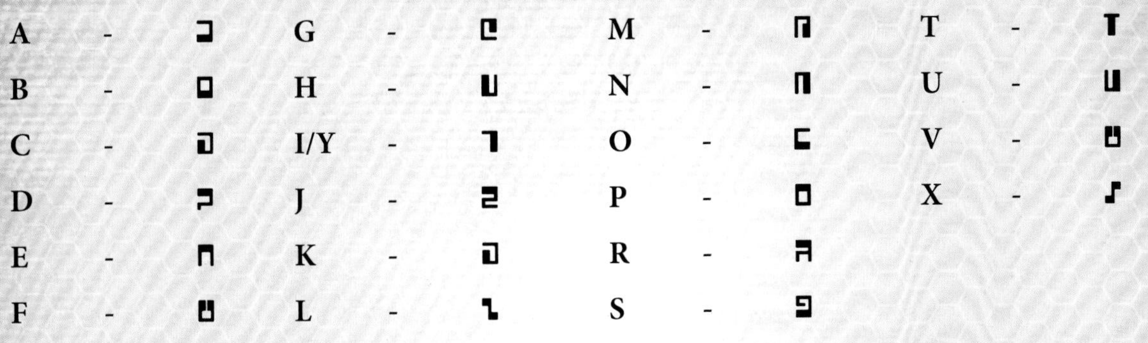

A	-	�	G	-		M	-		T	-	
B	-		H	-		N	-		U	-	
C	-		I/Y	-		O	-		V	-	
D	-		J	-		P	-		X	-	
E	-		K	-		R	-				
F	-		L	-		S	-				

T'AU NUMERALS

The Tau numerical system is rendered as shown to the right, and used to identify their fighting vehicles. Characters from zero to seven are used in varying combinations, marking out squadrons and applying ascending identifier numbers within them.

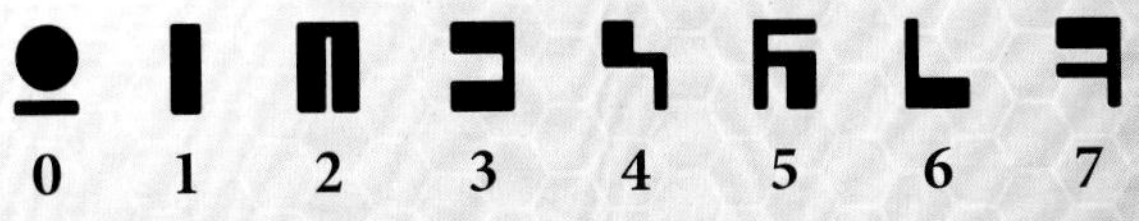

0	1	2	3	4	5	6	7

T'AU MILITARY ORGANISATION

The T'au Empire's military campaigns vary in scope and requirement, and may require the contribution of any of the castes. Thus, the T'au's strategic composition must be flexible and adaptable, with every unit and detachment able to operate in perfect conjunction in order to fulfil the dictates of the Greater Good.

COMMANDS (UASH'O) AND COALITIONS (SHAN'AL)

A command is the term used for all the forces of a single caste in a given location. For instance, all the Fire caste on the world of Nimbosa were part of Fire Caste Command Nimbosa, while all Air caste formations were part of the Air Caste Command Nimbosa.

The four commands are drawn together into a strategic organisation referred to as a coalition, and are presided over by a specially assigned Ethereal council. Thus, a coalition will consist of all T'au and auxiliary forces on a given world or within a particular system.

These coalitions are often assembled as expeditionary forces. In such instances, a Fire caste commune will form the military arm, an Earth caste command will be organised into a support workgroup, an Air caste command into a transport task force, and the Water caste command will function as a diplomatic corps.

COMMUNE (KAVAAL)

Sometimes translated as 'battle', a commune is a temporary grouping of contingents and the highest level of Fire caste organisation thus far committed in the field. Communes are often formed by contingents from different septs, and although rarely seen before the Damocles Gulf conflicts, they are now more regularly formed, most famously during the decade-long campaign against the Orks known as the Great War of Confederation. Only the combined forces of many septs could have hoped to stop the gargantuan Ork Waaagh! that threatened the empire.

CONTINGENTS (TIO'VE)

A contingent is a grouping of cadres, normally three to six in number. The most senior Commander is designated as Contingent Commander, and their own cadre is nominated as a headquarters guard. An Ethereal might be present in a force at cadre level, but there is always at least one when a contingent is formed. Ethereals often stay at the headquarters position, as it is a hub for incoming reports and their councils can be best received there. Should an Ethereal wish a closer observation of a situation, they will attach to or even assume leadership over a cadre.

Unlike a cadre, a contingent is not a permanent formation, though efforts are made to preserve contingents that have served efficiently together during prolonged campaigns. Once objectives are achieved – such as a breakthrough of enemy lines or the elimination of a foe – the contingent is dissolved or reformed into another arrangement.

CADRES (KAU'UI)

A cadre is a collection of teams joined under a single Commander. There are many types of cadre, but by far the most common one is the versatile Hunter Cadre. It is a combined arms group, fielding infantry, battlesuits and gunships together. A cadre is comparable in size and power, if not in composition, to what the Imperial Guard might call a company. Hunter Cadres are a standing formation, although their exact structure is variable, subject to change due to the tactical situation on the ground, the quarry they are hunting, the available reinforcements or a Commander's favoured mode of attack.

The core of most Hunter Cadres is its Fire Warriors, but these can be supported in a number of ways. Pathfinders scout ahead and mark prospective targets, elite battlesuits provide hard-hitting support, Sniper Drone Teams pick off the foe's greatest threats and Hammerhead Gunships use their deadly armaments to blast enemy armour or break up massed infantry attacks. The doctrine of T'au battle tactics is all about the efficient coordination of different groups – from the infantry to the battlesuits, the gunships to the aircraft, all must work as one to defeat the foe. A Hunter Cadre is fully integrated at the tactical level, so that all teams are considered to be part of the same fighting unit.

There are a number of different cadres in addition to the Hunter variety, although they tend to be smaller in size and more optimised for individual roles. There are Rapid Insertion Forces made exclusively of fast-striking battlesuit teams, Infiltration Cadres of Pathfinders and Stealth Battlesuits, and Auxiliary Reserve Cadres, battle groups made entirely of alien warriors. A particularly formidable group is the Armoured Interdiction Cadre, a force composed of Hammerhead and Sky Ray Gunships. Its heavy firepower is used to counter enemy tanks, and is capable of toppling even the mightiest targets. During the Hive Fleet Gorgon invasion, Armoured Interdiction Cadres blunted the Tyranid bio-titan spearhead – pitting shoals of Hammerheads against towering Hierophants flanked by the tank-sized Hierodules.

TEAMS (LA'RUA)

The smallest standard unit in the T'au military is known as a team. The most commonly deployed is the Fire Warrior team, the backbone of most T'au armies. Each team of Fire Warriors consists of between five and twelve soldiers. All members of a team come from the same sept, and most likely have gone through Fire caste academy together. All teams have a team leader, although he can only earn the higher rank of shas'ui after extensive battlefield experience.

Teams that serve together in the field often bond themselves through rituals, of which the most famous is the *ta'lissera*, which roughly translates to a type of communion or binding oath. Those who have sworn such an oath as part of a bonding knife ritual may address each other by their individual names and have vowed to support one another unto death. It is not uncommon for teams to progress together as well – veteran Fire Warrior teams may even earn promotion to shas'ui together. Each might serve for a time as a squad leader for a different Strike or Breacher Team before the survivors are reunited as a Crisis Team.

THE DY'AKETH EXPEDITIONARY FORCE

The Dy'aketh Expeditionary Force was tasked with the colonisation of the Imperial world of Drachenvol, to be renamed Dy'aketh and absorbed into the T'au Empire. Its mission was to quickly eliminate any hostile forces and ensure as peaceful an integration as possible.

COALITION: DYA'KETH EXPEDITIONARY FORCE

EARTH CASTE COMMAND
SUPPORT WORKGROUP

WATER CASTE COMMAND
DIPLOMATIC CORPS

AIR CASTE COMMAND
TRANSPORT TASK FORCE

FIRE CASTE COMMAND
COMMUNE / BATTLE

Commander O'Namo took overall command of the commune, organising initial survey and reconnaissance missions, and countering the enemy's aggressive response with careful deployment of strategic reserves.

INSERTION CONTINGENT
Cadres (4):
Pathfinder Recon
Stealth Team
Dropstrike
Firststrike Assault

BREAKTHROUGH CONTINGENT
Cadres (3):
Crisis Dropstrike
Piranha Firestream
Riptide Rapidstrike

ENCOUNTER CONTINGENT
Cadres (3):
Hunter
Armoured Interdiction
Forward Stealth

ADDIT
CONTI

CADRES

A wide range of troop configurations were used in the ground attack on Dy'aketh, including the following cadres:

Hunter	Auxiliary Reserve
Mobilised Hunter	Armoured Interdiction
Firebase Support	Ranged Support
Advanced Insertion	Retaliation
Rapid Insertion	Skysweep Defence Shield
Optimised Stealth	Counterstrike
Crisis Dropstrike	Kroot Hunting Pack

COMMANDER O'NAMO'S HUNTER CADRE

This aggressive and mobile force was led by Commander O'Namo during the initial battle for Kighhauld Forest. Kroot auxiliaries were seconded to the Hunter Cadre in order to aid in navigation and scouting of the planet's dense woodlands.

O'Namo and Command Team [O'Namo & Crisis Bodyguards]	2 Kroot Carnivore squads
	1 XV104 Riptide
6 Fire Warrior Teams with TY7 Devilfish	4 XV8 Crisis Teams
6 Fire Warrior Teams	4 TX7 Hammerhead Gunships
4 Pathfinder Teams with TY7 Devilfish	3 TX78 Sky Ray Gunships
	4 AX3 Razorshark Strike Fighters

MARKINGS OF THE FIRE CASTE

The cadres of the Fire caste are a truly dynamic spectacle. Their wargear and vehicles are sleek and deadly, and their iconography is picked out in crisp, precise characters across camouflage patterns and striking sept colours. These markings indicate each unit's function, individual leadership structure and Sept of origin.

T'AU UNIFORM

Some battle-colours worn by the warriors of the Fire caste are determined by the nature, character and history of their sept. The majority, however, are camouflage patterns based upon the environment and climate of the war zone in which the wearer is fighting. Ever a practical race, the T'au favour tactical advantage over lurid displays of allegiance. More rarely, battle-colours are prescribed by the Ethereals, or derived from the complex Fire caste warpaint of old – these are often worn for ceremonial purposes, but it is not unknown for such esteemed warriors to carry their unique iconography. In any case, the wearer's identity, role, rank, cadre and even sept can be quickly ascertained by any other T'au.

SEPT MARKINGS

It is not the colour of their armour that denotes from which sept Fire caste teams originate, but rather the stripes applied to their weapons and armour. White is the colour for the T'au Sept. These markings are the same for all members of a team, and different patterns are used to distinguish teams of the same type.

FIRE CASTE BADGE

The symbol of the Fire caste is prominently displayed on the armour of all Fire caste warriors and vehicles, regardless of sept or uniform style. This icon symbolises the warrior's adherence to the hallowed Code of Fire, and their commitment to fighting for the empire with wisdom, bravery and skill. It also signifies that no matter the bearer's sept of origin or martial background, they are bound together with their warrior kin by the emancipating truth of the Greater Good.

T'AU SEPT — ELSY'EIR SEPT

T'AU'N SEPT — TASH'VAR SEPT

D'YANOI SEPT — VASH'YA SEPT

BORK'AN SEPT — T'OLKU SEPT

DAL'YTH SEPT — KSI'M'YEN SEPT

FAL'SHIA SEPT — FI'RIOS SEPT

VIOR'LA SEPT — MU'GULATH BAY SEPT

SA'CEA SEPT — KOR'TAL SEPT

AU'TAAL SEPT — FE'SAAN SEPT

N'DRAS SEPT — YO'VAI SEPT

KE'LSHAN SEPT

Every team has a unique marking design. This designator is prominently displayed upon armour or weaponry; the exact location can vary from warrior to warrior, and consists of multiple stripes in a specific configuration.

In each cadre, every member of every team bears a cadre marking somewhere on their wargear. This pattern of dots is always applied in the same fashion across the entire cadre, symbolising unity and the deferral of self-interest.

Shas'ui status is denoted by the application of the sept colour upon the shoulder guard and helmet sensor vane.

BATTLESUIT MARKINGS

On battlesuits, the application of sept colours reflects a T'au's rank: coloured sensor vanes for a shas'ui, fully sept-coloured helmets for a shas'vre and inverted sept colours on helmets for a shas'o. On rare occasions, renowned heroes of the empire may be granted dispensation to wear their own unique markings, signifying particular achievements of note.

The helmet of a shas'ui bears a sensor vane in the sept colour.

Shas'vre rank is shown by both helmet and sensor vanes in the sept colour.

This helmet denotes shas'el rank, as it is in the sept colour except for the sensor vanes.

A shas'o helmet is in the sept colour, but its markings match the wearer's armour.

ARMIES OF THE EXPANDING EMPIRE

Each of the T'au septs has its own traditional colours, which form the basis of the armour patterns used by its armed forces. However, the exact markings and camouflage applied to an army of the empire can differ greatly depending on a variety of factors – these include its specific battlefield role and the environment in which it will be operating. Veteran warriors may also earn the right to apply unique honour markings.

Shas'ui Vor'en's battlesuit is painted with the traditional Sa'cea blue. Note the cadre markings upon his thigh and shoulder plates.

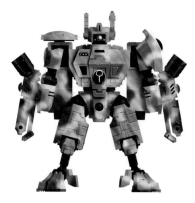

Shas'o Dur'am bears inverted colours on her thigh plate, an honour-marking occasionally granted for acts of particularly selfless bravery.

Shas'el Yaol wears the typical colours of Vior'la. The crimson sept markings reflect the hot-blooded and aggressive nature of these warlike T'au.

The inverted armour pattern of Shas'vre Or'tais marks him out as a member of Ethereal Aun'Hur's honoured battle retinue.

The camouflage on Shas'ui Bor's battlesuit was specifically designed to allow him to blend in amidst the nuclear tundras of Vanishpoint.

Shas'ui Lais wears the regulation T'au armour pattern. His red armour-blocking is shared amongst his ta'lissera bonded team.

Inverted sept markings can indicate a number of different honours or positions. Shas'el Ju'sa's denote her place in a pacification contingent.

Shas'vre Fain's Crisis suit has been painted with desert camouflage, in preparation for an invasion of the arid world of Catrangras.

As a warrior in Fal'shia Sept's advanced sciences contingent, Shas'el R'yos wields the latest refinements in Earth caste weapons technology.

Shas'vre Sut'an of Tash'var Sept earned his title during the defence of the Fen'tha River colonies against an Ork pirate fleet.

During the Battle of Kaspaneth, Shas'el Du'n of Vash'ya Sept destroyed no fewer than seven Imperial tanks with salvoes from her plasma rifle.

Shas'ui Nu'ma of D'yanoi Sept is a young warrior tipped for greatness after her heroic actions during the Karassin Pacification.

Shas'o Mas'mura earned retirement on the paradise world of Au'taal, but still fights as part of the sept's elite veteran contingents.

A survivor of the Fourth Sphere Expansion left disillusioned with the Ethereal caste, Shas'vre Kor'tav defected to the Farsight Enclaves.

Shas'el Hu'Jin fights for one of Ke'lshan Sept's elite ship-boarding contingents, clearing the way with his fusion blaster and flamer.

Shas'ui Fe'neth, survivor of Mu'gulath Bay, honours her destroyed home by displaying its sept colour across her battlesuit's thigh armour.

Shas'el Om'pui hails from T'au'n, famed for its massive orbital shipyards, and has trained to fight in zero-gravity conditions.

MARCH OF CONQUEST

The T'au have developed their own mode of timekeeping based on the annual cycle of their origin world, a unit called a T'au'cyr. Except on human planets that are still in the process of being subsumed, the T'au do not use the Imperium's dating system. However, for ease of translation, we have done so here.

M35-M36 BIRTH OF THE T'AU'VA

From the ashes of war rises a new empire of hope and reason. Guided by the Ethereals, this period is defined by the uniting of the T'au's divided castes in the name of the Greater Good.

Land's Vision

The Adeptus Mechanicus Explorator vessel *Land's Vision* makes the first discovery of primitive T'au.

End of the Mont'au

Strange lights are seen and the Ethereals arrive.

M37-M38 FIRST SPHERE EXPANSION

A time of great scientific and cultural evolution, during which the T'au advance into nearby space and colonise the first septs of their fledgling empire.

First Colony

The T'au colonise their largest moon, Lu'val; this is their first off-world holding.

T'au'n Established

Ethereals declare the colonies centred around the planet T'au'n will become their own sept – or realm, governed centrally from T'au'n, the sept world or prime planet.

Welcome Additions

The Poctroon become the first sentient race to join the T'au Empire, although within a few generations, disease destroys their indigenous population. The T'au, whose physiology is fortunately immune to the plague, inherit the Poctroon home world, turning it into the prime world of what will become Bork'an Sept. The Nicassar become the first race to join the T'au Empire and survive long enough to tell about it.

Campaign of Cleansing

In their first prolonged campaign against the Orks, the T'au suffer many defeats but are ultimately able to eradicate the greenskins, thanks in part to the Earth caste refinement of the first pulse rifle. During this period of bloody war, Dal'yth Sept is founded.

The Union of T'au and Kroot

In order to combat Orks, the fortunate alliance between T'au and Kroot is formed. Within a decade, the Water caste has established embassies upon Pech, the capital world of the Kroot realm.

M39-M41 SECOND SPHERE EXPANSION

The Ethereal Supreme, Aun'Wei of the Whispered Wisdom, gives the signal to begin the long-planned Second Sphere Expansion. Aun'Wei's famous speech is well remembered, ending with 'the nod that launched a million ships'. With new advances in propulsion technology and an already established space empire, the second expansion is marked by more contact with aliens and larger wars.

A New Ally

The planet Vespid is absorbed into D'yanoi Sept. They had long been courted by the Water caste, but little was established save for crystal trade agreements. Within days of Ethereal involvement, the Vespid Strain leaders submit wholeheartedly to the cause of the Greater Good.

N'dras Colonised

Despite reservations from those of the Earth caste who urge further study of N'dras' inexplicable sensor readings, the planet is chosen by the Ethereal High Council as the prime world of a new sept.

Steady Advancement

Improvements to anti-grav motors and new battlesuit technology (the T–series prototypes) help the Fire caste complete the annexation of Tash'var Sept.

Mistaken Identity

War is declared upon the cruel raiders victimising the new colonies of Ke'lshan. Believing they have tracked their foes down, the T'au instead destroy the Aeldari maiden world of Lilarsus. Future relationships continue to be strained.

Vior'la Triumphant!

A massive Ork fleet invades Vior'la Sept but is defeated by a masterful campaign. Vior'la annually passes through a gap between its two stars, a time called the Trial by Fire. It causes deadly plasma storms to ravage the planet, whose inhabitants survive by closing protective domes around their cities. Warlord Garskrak and his fleet are lured into this storm, where they are utterly destroyed by the raging plasma radiation.

Mass Migration

The greatest Water caste envoy, Por'o Dal'yth Kais Twi Lui'tan, better known as the Golden Ambassador, leads the effort to recruit alien worlds into the T'au Empire. During this period the Thraxians, Greet, and Formosians are welcomed into the fold. The Hrud and Arachen reject the proposals and are driven out of the region.

A Legend is Born

The T'au who will one day become Commander Puretide, the pride of Dal'yth Sept, is born. His brilliant campaigns later conquer half a dozen star systems. Under his authority, the T'au envelop those who can be embraced, seize what can be conquered and obliterate those who defy the Greater Good.

The Once and Future Master

The elderly Commander Puretide is urged to view the new colonies across the Damocles Gulf before retiring. While inspecting a colony, Puretide is wounded during a raid. Unable to walk again, the most revered of military leaders spends his remaining years atop Mount Kan'ji on Dal'yth, where he is kept alive for many more decades. Only those who attain perfect scores at the Fire caste academies are sent to sit at Puretide's hover-throne and learn his wisdom. Thanks to Earth caste holographic technology, this tradition is still maintained, although few students are deemed worthy of this high honour.

The Arkunasha War

A decade-long war in which a populous T'au colony is besieged by the resurgent Ork hordes begins. It is especially notable for the rise of the exemplary Puretide protégé named Commander Farsight, who swiftly follows in his master's footsteps to become a vaunted hero of the T'au Empire – and a key element of the High Council's campaigns of propaganda.

The Damocles Crusade

The T'au Empire comes under attack by an armada of the Imperium's warships on a crusade to reclaim their long-neglected territory. It is a bloody campaign, which is finally stymied at Dal'yth Prime. The retreat of Imperial forces marks the end of the Second Sphere Expansion.

The Stasis Chamber

Aun'Va makes the decision to place the favoured pupils of the rapidly declining Commander Puretide into stasis using prototype technology. This allows O'Shaserra and a few select others to be recalled at later need.

Rogue Commander

Following the Damocles Crusade, Commander Farsight recaptures much of the lost territory. However, the famed Commander defies orders to return, instead establishing a string of fortified planets known as the Farsight Enclaves.

Cano'var Destroyed

The T'au world of Cano'var is overwhelmed. Transmissions show robotic creatures using unidentified energy weapons.

Ally Unlooked For

An Ork invasion under Warlord Grog advances into the T'au Empire. The populated T'au world of Atari Vo bears the brunt of the attack before the Oks are finally defeated by the combined forces of Dal'yth Sept and, to the surprise of many, Commander Farsight and his separatists.

A New Menace

Tyranid Hive Fleet Gorgon smashes into the fringe of the T'au Empire and claws inwards. It is ultimately defeated upon the sept world of Ke'lshan, with the help of unlikely allies in the form of a fleet of ships from the Imperium of Mankind.

Great War of Confederation

Led by Vior'la, many septs combine to hold off the single largest Ork Waaagh! to have penetrated the T'au Empire. This campaign is also notable for the brilliant tactics and battle record of a shas'o recently awoken from stasis, who there earns the name Shadowsun.

Lagan System

Decades of Water caste work has converted many human worlds in the Lagan System. With the help of an expeditionary force, the star system is graded a class 1 colony, moving steadily towards becoming a fully fledged sept. However, all this preparation comes to naught as the sector becomes a war zone, targeted for xenos cleansing by the Ultramarines Space Marine Chapter. Many colonists are slain.

The Nimbosa Annexation

Commander Brightsword, a student of Farsight's way of war, leads an attack to claim the Imperial world of Nimbosa. By the time the Imperium brings reinforcements, the T'au are prepared to defend their new planet. The fighting culminates with the infamous Koloth Gorge Massacre, where the forces of the Astra Militarum are so brutally slaughtered that Brightsword is censured and summoned back to T'au due to the remorselessness of his acts. Since this attack, the planet has changed hands several more times and remains a war zone.

M41 THIRD SPHERE EXPANSION

After careful preparation, the new Ethereal Supreme, Aun'Va, launches the Third Sphere Expansion.

Ksi'm'yen Established

The first sept of the Third Sphere Expansion is declared and used as a staging ground for further advancement.

Defence of the Farsight Enclaves

With his spearhead of eighty XV8 Crisis Teams, Commander Farsight leads a counter-attack against a tendril of Hive Fleet Kraken that has entered his territory.

Shas'o Kais Victorious

It is unknown when Shas'o'Kais, another of Puretide's former protégés, emerged from stasis, but it is he that leads the victories that establish the Fi'rios Sept at this time.

Defeat at Zeist

An Imperial fleet enters the Zeist Sector. The Space Marines drive the T'au from many of their colonies there, and while the losses are regrettable, the gains elsewhere are on such a scale that, even to the casualty-conscious T'au, Shadowsun's diversion seems not just acceptable, but shrewd.

Mu'gulath Bay

In the largest battle of the Third Sphere Expansion, Commander Shadowsun leads the invasion of the Imperial world of Agrellan, beginning the rout of human forces now known as the Path of Blood. It is a bright day for the T'au, who saw a foe with vastly superior numbers crushed, and the process of integrating the newly designated sept world of Mu'gulath Bay into the empire is quickly begun. Of the numerous advanced weapon prototypes deployed in the campaign, all were successful save one: a fusion reactor whose meltdown destroyed Mu'gulath's moon.

Cataclysm

The Imperium of Mankind sends a colossal combined fleet to retake Mu'gulath Bay, spearheaded by the ships of Humanity's elite Space Marines. Battle is joined across the barren world, as T'au Fire Warriors exchange furious salvoes with the advancing regiments of the Astra Militarum, and thousands of tanks clash in a murderous maelstrom of explosions, churned earth and flying shrapnel.

The Pariah Returns

The vengeful ferocity of the Space Marines and the blunt force of the Astra Militarum's armoured regiments force the defenders of Mu'gulath Bay back at every turn. Commander Shadowsun delays the advance with a series of cunning strikes, but even her mastery of Kauyon is not enough to repel the invaders. Just as the T'au are on the verge of an open rout, crimson battlesuits fall from low orbit, smashing into the midst of Imperial formations and blasting the shocked enemy with hails of cluster-missiles and searing plasma. The legendary Commander Farsight, outcast of the T'au Empire, has joined the fight.

Uneasy Alliance

Commanders Farsight and Shadowsun forge a temporary alliance, with the reluctant assent of Ethereal Supreme Aun'Va. The elderly Ethereal refuses to abandon Mu'gulath Bay despite Shadowsun's pleas, and retreats to a hidden bunker, where he broadcasts messages of strength and unity to his loyal warriors.

Imperial Vengeance

The Officio Assassinorum unleashes the horror of an Execution Force upon the T'au commanders of Mu'gulath Bay. Ethereal Supreme Aun'Va is tracked down and murdered by a nightmarish Culexus Assassin.

Damocles Burns

The Adeptus Mechanicus deploys a warhead of astonishing power that sets Mu'gulath Bay ablaze. As the war-weary T'au survivors reluctantly abandon their devastated sept world, the unnatural fires continue to spread. Soon, a vast swathe of the Damocles Gulf burns, separating the T'au Empire and the Imperium.

Wrath of Ages

The Hrud ravage the T'au sept world of Vash'ya. Thousands of Fire Warriors are slain as the Hrud's bizarre chrono-entropic fields cause them to age several decades in a matter of hours. The surviving T'au retreat and regroup. Their Commander initiates combat protocol 'Avatar', unleashing waves of combat drones and remotely operated XV8 Crisis Battlesuits. Their super-alloys resistant to the Hrud's withering aura, these automated warriors scour the alien infestation from the surface of Vash'ya with flamers and fusion blasters, sending the hunched creatures fleeing into the depths of space.

Bright Dawn, Setting Sun

T'au forces under the nominal command of Ethereal Aun'Kir unite with the Aeldari of Craftworld Lugganath to assail a tendril of Hive Fleet Gorgon before it reaches the Perdus Rift. In a brutal naval battle the Tyranids are defeated, though many lives are lost. In the aftermath, Aun'Kir and his honour guard are granted audience aboard the Aeldari flagship. Soon after this meeting, the Ethereal High Council grants Aun'Kir control of his own pacification fleet, which heads beyond the Perdus Rift on a mission of utmost secrecy.

Tide of Fire

The oceans of Antrenex boil under relentless missile cascades from Stormsurge weapons platforms, as T'au of Vior'la Sept engage the colossal Ork navy of Rugg Rokktoof.

Unsought Liberation

An Insertion Contingent of T'au Pathfinders is deployed to Cadmon's Lock, a forge world dedicated to the construction of small arms and munitions. They escort several Water caste insurrection specialists, whose task is to incite rebellion amongst the hive-bound working classes. T'au spies report that the planet's underclasses have recently been stockpiling contraband weapons for an upcoming insurrection against their cruel masters. This information is in fact accurate, but it masks the true horror of the situation. A hostile cult known as the Disciples of the Bleeding Star has infiltrated the labour unions of Cadmon's Lock, spreading the worship of their strange gods. The T'au's entreaties are greeted with a hail of autogun fire, and several warriors and diplomats are snatched away into the darkness of the hive city's undertunnels by hulking razor-clawed figures. Surrounded on all sides by mutated demihumans, the contingent's survivors

are forced to battle their way to the surface of Cadmon's Lock for extraction. Before they depart, they activate a wide-band holo-signal that is picked up by the planet's Adeptus Mechanicus administration. Skitarii forces are dispatched to the underhives to investigate, and open warfare breaks out as they discover the extent of the cultist infestation. T'au high-orbit recon probes perform a thorough analysis during the ensuing carnage.

Kin Against Kin

A convoy of survivors from the fall of Mu'gulath Bay attempts to flee to the Farsight Enclaves. Commander Surestrike is dispatched to cut off the dissidents and return them for censure and reassignment. Surestrike's fleet reaches the convoy at the same time as a fleet from the rebel Enclaves. The rebels open communications and warn the Commander to retreat. A tense stand-off ensues, culminating in a vicious exchange of fire. Many of the fleeing ships are caught in the crossfire, though several dozen escape alongside the Enclaves' navy.

A Tempting Lure

Having tormented Dal'yth space for many seasons, a host of Drukhari raiders launches an assault upon the colony world of Shi'yen, a sparsely defended frontier outpost with a large population consisting almost entirely of various T'au client races. They sweep into the desert planet's great habitat-spheres, butchering with impunity. It is only when the raiders are fully occupied with their slaughter that the Dal'yth Fire caste springs its trap. Macro-camouflage arrays and wide-span refraction fields are deactivated, and scores of Breacher Teams emerge from concealed positions to deliver a brutal barrage of fire into the flanks of the startled Drukhari. Though losses amongst the T'au's vassal races are substantial, the devastating impact of the sudden ambush all but obliterates the foe.

Behemoth Slayer

A colossal Ork Gargant terrorises the cities of Hul'aan. Its black-iron armour seems impervious to even the most intense pulse-fire and missile bombardments, and its formidable array of solid-shot cannons and projectile launchers annihilate entire Fire caste cadres in mere minutes. The gruff, static-laden laughter of its Ork pilots booms out over the Gargant's enormous vox-arrays as it crushes entire buildings to rubble with each swing of its great metal arms. Swarms of greenskins follow in the wake of this behemoth, bellowing praises to their gods of war. Only the

Bork'an Earth caste scientist Tu'len and his experimental weapons division stand in the way of the monstrosity. Tu'len orders the deployment of six KV128 Stormsurge weapons platforms, each armed with multi-phase-locked pulse ARC cannons – a new refinement of these devastating devices. Even the enormous Stormsurge ballistic suits are dwarfed by the sheer size of the Ork Gargant, but when they fire their ARC cannons simultaneously the beams converge, melding into a ray of destructive energy as wide as a starscraper. This battering ram of pure annihilation burns through the Gargant's metal torso, setting off a chain reaction of detonations that tear the massive construct apart. Tu'len marks the first field test of his new technology as an impressive success, though the power of the channelled plasma energy has entirely immolated three of the six Stormsurge platforms.

M41 FOURTH AND FIFTH SPHERE EXPANSIONS

A new and darker age dawns for the T'au Empire, beginning with the greatest naval disaster in its history.

Tragedy at Numenar Point

Equipped with the latest sub-realm transition technology, an enormous armada gathers at Numenar Point, aiming to travel beyond the devastated Damocles Gulf. As the ships of this Fourth Sphere Expansion prepare to engage their jump drives, a breach in reality swallows the armada, dragging the entire assembled fleet into the roiling depths of the immaterium.

From the Master's Shadow

The Necrons of the Sautekh Dynasty launch a series of attacks along the western reaches of the T'au Empire. Crack Fire caste contingents from T'au and T'au'n are sent to repel the invaders. They are led by Commander O'Vash, a protégé of Commander Shadowsun who earned significant honours during the Third Sphere campaigns. O'Vash adopts the tactics of his tutor, splitting his forces into hunting packs and tearing at the flanks of the Necron invasion fleet, delaying its advance and buying precious time for the beleaguered empire to dispatch reinforcements.

Mutiny on Junica

The war against Chaos forces on Junica goes ill, and the Fire caste suffer horrific losses. The Ethereal Supreme Aun'Va is holding audience with Commander O'Ryn, responsible for prosecuting the offensive, when a tank shell strikes the war camp. Aun'Va's Ethereal retinue is slain, but the Ethereal Supreme – or rather, the solid-light hologram representing the deceased leader – is unharmed. Yet, when Aun'Va orders the Commander to send her remaining warriors to the front lines to buy time for reinforcements, O'Ryn feels no compunction to obey. Unthinkably, she refuses the order, judging it a waste of good warriors and claiming that Junica is lost. In doing so she becomes the first T'au since Farsight himself to disobey a command from an Ethereal. Several days later, an Edification Corps fleet descends upon Junica with the intention of detaining O'Ryn's entire command, only to find that the Commander and her loyal warriors have fled to the Farsight Enclaves. All witnesses to O'Ryn's act of treason are sequestered, and the remaining cadres on Junica broken up and dispersed across the empire.

Grim Sojourn

Commander Farsight travels back to Arthas Moloch alone, refusing to allow his loyal bodyguards to accompany him. For thirty days and nights, there is no word from the leader of the Farsight Enclaves. When he finally returns from his sojourn, Farsight immediately summons the Enclaves' chief strategists to a war council.

The Blooding

Elite city-fighting cadres from Sa'cea are sent to reclaim the colony of Ol'me from an Ork infestation. Advancing street by street, the Sa'cea Breacher Teams utilise airburst markerlight flares and overwhelming aerial support to identify and destroy the largest congregations of greenskins. So brutal is the close-quarters fighting that the sept's Fire caste refer to the Ol'me campaign as Mont'yren – the Blooding – and survivors of the war are held in the highest regard.

Hope Rekindled

After more than a decade, a deep-space probe is discovered drifting through the Zone of Silence, broadcasting signals on frequencies dating from the launch of the Fourth Sphere Expansion. When Air caste recon vessels locate this beacon, they discover a stunning phenomenon – a vast swirling vortex in space. This dimensional pathway, which the T'au come to name the Startide Nexus, is previously unrecorded on the empire's detailed star charts. The captured probe contains coordinates to a colony far to the north, in territory claimed by the Imperium of Mankind – now revealed to be home to the survivors of the Fourth Sphere Expansion.

Reunited

The Fifth Sphere Expansion travels through the Startide Nexus and arrives at the Nem'yar Atoll, a cluster of colonised worlds and star-borne arcologies that is home to the remnants of the Fourth Sphere Expansion. The survivors' experiences have transformed them into uncompromising hardliners, and they have developed an intense distrust of non-T'au, particularly the empire's gue'vesa auxiliaries.

New Worlds

Reunited with their lost kin, the T'au of the Fifth Sphere Expansion embark on an extensive campaign of colonisation and consolidation, establishing a cluster of new sept worlds around the Nem'yar Atoll.

Plague Wars

Commander O'Kais is sent to prepare the verdant world of Kellik for colonisation. Unfortunately, Plague Marines of the Death Guard have already made landfall, and are in the process of pouring the disease-ridden, liquefied remains of their sacrificial victims into Kellik's great lakes. T'au gunships and Piranhas knife into the Heretic Astartes, overwhelming dozens of Plague Marines with bursts of incinerating plasma fire. However, the Death Guard had already seeded their foul corruption deep into the bedrock of Kellik. Foetid creatures begin to crawl from the tainted waterways in their thousands, and clouds of fat-bodied flies block visor displays and clog helmet rebreathers. The Plague Marines rally and regroup, chortling wetly as they unleash brutal fusillades of bolter fire that burst open T'au bodies like ripe fruit. Commander O'Kais refuses to abandon his mission even in the face of this repulsive contagion, and the surface of Kellik becomes host to a deluge of blood and bile.

The Charpactin

Water caste diplomats from the Fifth Sphere sept of Fe'saan encounter the Charpactin, a race of sentient fungoid creatures who communicate entirely in bursts of ultraviolet colour. These strobing emanations prove surprisingly effective at subduing and transfixing living beings, rendering them docile and amenable. The T'au quickly negotiate a client-state treaty with the Charpactin, drafting many of these creatures into their growing Edification Corps.

The Voridium Sceptre

Amenex Soulrend, Exalted Sorcerer of Tzeentch, unleashes his Silvered Sons against the newly founded sept world of Dy'aketh. While his Rubric Marines march through recently constructed conurbations and laboratory-complexes, incinerating all in their path with salvoes of incendiary rounds, Soulrend and his personal retinue head deep underground. Far beneath the planet's crust lies an Earth caste research facility, which has spent several months studying a strange artefact – a sceptre crafted from voridium crystals that thrums with barely suppressed energy. Just as Soulrend nears the priceless relic, he is assailed by experimental battlesuits and Fire Warriors wielding super-charged pulse carbines. These weapons fire searing beams of green-white fire that burn through even the warp-blessed armour of Soulrend's warriors. Battle lines are drawn as sorcery meets cutting-edge technology, and the fires of war consume Dy'aketh.

Drowned in Fire

An Insertion Contingent of T'au Pathfinders from Vior'la Sept lures a blood-mad warband of Khornate Heretic Astartes onto the volcanic moon of Dxul, before activating a macro-pulse bomb that ruptures Dxul's tectonic plate and drowns the satellite in a tide of liquid magma. Many Pathfinder Teams willingly sacrifice their lives in order for the gambit to succeed, but the Skullsworn pack is almost entirely incinerated in the ensuing devastation.

Battle of the Startide Nexus

Mere months after the Fourth Sphere survivors rejoined their people, an enormous Death Guard armada tears its way from the warp and emerges in the heart of the Nem'yar Atoll, before the mouth of the Startide Nexus itself. The Chaos fleet launches attack ships and boarding claws filled with Heretic Astartes at the star fortresses guarding the spatial rift. The shocked T'au defence fleets react with remarkable speed, blasting many of these vessels to atoms, but many more slip through the barrage and spill packs of frenzied killers into tide-locked arcologies and stellar fortifications. A furious battle rages. The T'au know that if the Nexus falls, a route to the heart of the empire will be left open. The warriors of the Fire caste fight with desperate courage, selling their lives by the thousand to repel the invaders. Commander Shadowsun leads an immense counter-attack into the heart of the Chaos fleet, blasting daemonic enemies and hulking Plague Marines into a putrid mist with each cannonade from her twin fusion blasters. Yet even her desperate heroics surely cannot hold back Nurgle's chosen Legion for long…

The Fire Warriors of Vior'la eschew the staggered firing lines and long-range focus of conventional T'au warfare. Instead, these hot-blooded souls take the fight directly to the foe, charging forward while unleashing blistering, point-blank fusillades of pulse fire that punch through armour and melt flesh to atoms.

COMMANDER SHADOWSUN

HERO OF THE 3RD SPHERE EXPANSION, SPEARHEAD OF THE GREATER GOOD, THE TRUE DISCIPLE OF COMMANDER PURETIDE

O'Shaserra, better known as Commander Shadowsun, is a dynamic leader who rose to recent fame in the battles of the K'resh Expansions. There, she smashed the Ork menace, and her cadres suffered historically low casualties in return. All of Shadowsun's victories are marked by unrivalled efficiency, a trait not surprising from one of Commander Puretide's most promising pupils.

Over four hundred years ago, O'Shaserra was a brilliant young warrior; her successes and matchless performances at the Fire caste academies earned her recognition as one of the most able military minds in the T'au Empire. As such, she was granted the honour of studying personally under the ailing but legendary Commander Puretide. Despite being the youngest of all Puretide's protégés, O'Shaserra scored exceptionally well in all simulations, outstripping all others save one – the most highly favoured of all Puretide's students, Commander O'Shovah. From the start, theirs was a bitter rivalry, as the two most gifted Commanders strove to gain their wizened master's approval.

During the battle on the Dal'yth Sept world in which the Imperium's Damocles Crusade was finally halted, it was Commander Farsight's audacious counter-attacks that drew the most attention; however, they would never have been possible without O'Shaserra's patient ploy to draw out and overextend the Imperial battle lines. This ongoing competition between the two Commanders was abruptly halted by the death of the venerable Commander Puretide. The Ethereal High Council was not fully convinced the mind-capture devices and holograms of the Earth caste engineers would be able to recreate the teachings of their fabled teacher. So, to ensure Puretide's teachings were preserved for future generations, it was decided that several of his top students would be placed in stasis. Upon the orders of the council, a select few, including O'Shaserra, slept in frozen animation, untouched by the passing years, until a time came when they would be most needed; a time of great expansion and furious battle.

Although Aun'Va had planned to awaken Commander O'Shaserra at the dawn of the Third Sphere Expansion, the largest Ork invasion of the T'au Empire accelerated the Ethereal Supreme's meticulous calculations. Yet even this, the sagacious Aun'Va turned into an advantage. Appearing in a time of great need, O'Shaserra has once more proven herself a patient hunter, meticulous in her planning, yet swift in action. Her ability to draw foes into well-conceived killing zones lured numerous Ork armies to merciless deaths during the battles of what is now called the Great War of Confederation. Yet, as the situation dictated, O'Shaserra could be bold. In order to end the fierce fighting in the K'resh Expansions, she led a Stealth Cadre straight into the heart of the Ork encampment to deliver a killing stroke. Timing her strike to coincide with an artificial eclipse, the T'au forces used the jet packs of their XV25 battlesuits to deploy from low-swooping Orca dropships.

Under the cover of the unnatural darkness, the greenskins never knew what hit them. In an instant, their leaders were riddled by burst cannons before being finished off with searing shots from fusion blasters. It was O'Shaserra herself who personally sought

out and targeted the warlord, bringing down the hulking alien with precision fire. As the alien hordes milled in confusion, the rest of O'Shaserra's cadres joined the fray. Without their bosses to lead them, most of the Orks panicked and fled, only to run into well-placed ambushes. By the time the sunlight burnt through the obscuring veil, the battle was over and a new Fire caste legend was born.

Aun'Va was quick to promote the dedicated Commander, for he saw embodied in her all that was noble about the Fire caste's pursuit of the Greater Good. Here was a Commander who would not shirk from duty, who would not forget her vows to her people or her loyalty to Aun'Va himself. When he declared the Third Sphere Expansion, Aun'Va also announced the warrior who would spearhead the most important of attacks – Commander O'Shaserra, now called Shadowsun in honour of what was then her greatest triumph.

In her first speech as Supreme Commander, O'Shaserra made her address from the Mont'yr battle dome, the site where Farsight had famously trained. Arriving resplendent in her new prototype XV22 battlesuit, it was a sight to stir the martial hearts of all who viewed her. With the entire Fire caste watching, Shadowsun began by firing her weapons at the statue of Farsight, obliterating it in a burst of white-hot desecration. As the dust settled, she outlined the new campaigns they would soon embark on. She spoke of honour, the sacred Code of Fire and the all-important law of the T'au'va. After this address, every Fire Warrior shouted in one voice, ready to follow their new Commander to any end.

Within days, the Third Sphere Expansion had begun, and under Shadowsun's leadership, the T'au Empire was all but unstoppable. With Imperial attention elsewhere, and the Tyranid and Ork menace temporarily contained, Fire caste spearheads drove into the outlying systems of the Damocles Gulf. Leading from the front, Shadowsun seemed to be everywhere at once and her assault on Agrellan, a hive world of the Imperium, opened up the entire Dovar System.

The war for Agrellan – renamed Mu'gulath Bay by the T'au – would end in fire and destruction thanks to the dread technologies of the Adeptus Mechanicus. Even so, the gains of the Third Sphere Expansion were remarkable, forever enshrining O'Shaserra as an icon of the T'au'va. Where once statues and murals of Commander Farsight had bedecked the cities and plazas of the empire, now it was Shadowsun they depicted, the true heir to Commander Puretide's legacy.

Yet even these triumphs are not enough to appease O'Shaserra's restless soul. As long as there are new worlds to enlighten and hateful enemies that deny the truth of the Greater Good, her tactical brilliance and inspirational example is still sorely needed by the Fire caste. And as long as the Ethereals name her former comrade O'Shovah a traitor, she is compelled to treat him as one – Farsight's heroic intervention during the Mu'gulath Bay crisis has not erased his betrayal, nor swayed O'Shaserra from her tireless pursuit of the errant Commander.

COMMANDERS

A Commander, or in the language of the T'au, a 'shas'o', is the highest rank a Fire Warrior can obtain. It is a position of great honour, and can only be attained after years progressing through the ranks – there are no shortcuts or exceptions. The final test to advance from the shas'el level is to have repeated success on the battlefield. To be named shas'o is to be proven a master in the martial arts, a first rate tactician and a true disciple of the art of war. Depending on their situation, sept and renown, a T'au Commander can be called upon to lead anything from a cadre to a coalition. The number and size of previous commands is reflected in the rings confining their long scalp lock. The greatest military leaders, those whose names and victories are most honoured, can call countless millions to arms with but a single word.

There are vast differences in approach and philosophy between the varied T'au Fire caste leaders. Some T'au Commanders prefer to lead from the front, pushing their battlesuits to their fullest. These fearless warriors often opt for the rugged power of the XV85 Enforcer battlesuit, though many prefer to dominate the skies in the agile XV86 Coldstar variant. The Commanders of the Vior'la, Tash'var and Ke'lshan are particularly noted for their personal kills, and are often accompanied into the thick of battle by an XV8 Crisis Bodyguard Team. Conversely, T'au Commanders that hail from the Elsy'eir and T'olku Septs are typically considered more cerebral in nature, ordering their troops from behind the front lines and only entering the fray themselves upon great need.

There are times when hubris gets the better of these proud military masters, and in such situations, the Ethereal High Council reins them in. It is said that 'while there is no substitute for victory, its pursuit must be balanced by the Greater Good.' A triumph that sustains more losses than were necessary does not service the true needs of the T'au, and personal heroics, while lauded, are never an end unto themselves. Such wisdom is usually enough to correct the behaviour of an unruly Commander, but in rare instances, a malk'la must take place – a ritual discipline meted out by the Ethereals to those deemed to have erred in judgement in regards to the Greater Good. Those subjected to this punishment are rendered pariahs in the eyes of their comrades. Often, such souls actively seek to sell their lives in the name of the Greater Good, hoping that in death they can gain some measure of redemption.

Upon attaining the rank of shas'o, a member of the Fire caste will serve his sept until death or until he has earned honoured retirement, though the most successful Commanders are asked to join the military high command, or shas'ar'tol. Each of the spheres of expansion has its notable Commanders – great heroes whose teachings are still used at the Fire caste academies. There, the ways of the Wise Hunter, a great conqueror of the initial expansions, can be heard, as well as those of Commander Quickstrike, hero of Bork'an Sept. Many references are made to Commander Truestar, the military leader whose brilliant career was marred by a single tragic error, and to the Desert Beast, the wily Commander Dawnstrike, whose exploits of feigned retreat are often emulated but never bettered. Yet of all these great lords of the Fire caste, there are none whose battle record can come close to equalling that of Commander Puretide, the noble master behind the greatest victories of the Second Sphere Expansion.

ETHEREALS

The Ethereals make up the ruling caste within T'au society, and are born to steer their comrades towards the chosen path. They embody the roles of royalty and the priesthood, and the deference paid to them is the closest thing to mysticism in T'au society. For weighty decisions, a wise Ethereal will take counsel from the senior members of each caste, although ultimate sovereignty falls upon him and him alone. The Ethereals find themselves in a binding role – guiding the other castes to work together for the Greater Good. An Ethereal must be a consummate leader and motivator: pushing the Earth caste for more practical innovations, setting firm negotiation goals for the Water caste to strive for, giving perimeters to the great fleets of the Air caste and directing the sometimes overzealous aggressions of the Fire caste.

The absolute control which Ethereals exhibit over the other castes of the T'au Empire is a mystery. Many assume such manipulation is a form of innate psychic ability; others feel that the faultless loyalty the Ethereals inspire has been contrived by some unseen technology, or is even the result of some pheromone-based reaction.

The most primitive races T'au forces have encountered believe the Ethereals are deified beings, leaders of an advanced people chosen for greatness. Naturally, the Ethereals themselves help propagate and encourage this particular myth. As the T'au do their utmost to prevent any Ethereal from being slain or captured, there have been few opportunities to conduct tests, and those that have been performed offer no conclusions, and far more questions.

The presence of an Ethereal is motivational, but they are not mere figureheads; they are also reverential leaders for whom any T'au would willingly lay down their life. Battles uncounted have been turned in the empire's favour by the sudden arrival of an Ethereal on the field. By invoking the elemental truths, an Ethereal can inspire those around him to perform feats above and beyond what is normally considered possible – displaying bravery in the face of certain death, placing shots with increased accuracy, withstanding crippling pain, or pushing their bodies to their limits to quickly reach crucial locations on the battlefield. The T'au do not question the source of these powers, accepting the greatness of their leaders on faith alone.

'Remember the fires of Mu'gulath. Remember the horrors wrought by ignorance and hate. But do not be defined by vengeance, for that is a sickness which has no place in the T'au'va.'

- Ethereal Aun'Phor

AUN'VA

MASTER OF THE UNDYING SPIRIT, SPEAKER OF GREAT TRUTHS, FATHER OF HIS PEOPLE, THE GREAT LEADER, THE SHINING LIGHT

Aun'Va is the oldest and wisest of the venerated Ethereal caste, and his hand can be seen at work behind many of the greatest successes of T'au history. Ethereals have longer life spans than those of other castes, but the fact that their Great Leader continues to live many times beyond even the most venerable of Ethereals is never questioned – it is merely another facet of the legend of Aun'Va. As the highest-ranking member of the High Council, or Ethereal Supreme, Aun'Va's word is the ultimate law across not just the T'au Sept, but over the whole of the T'au Empire. All Ethereals are given the utmost respect, but Aun'Va is revered beyond others of his caste, and even the merest suggestion of a visit to a T'au colony by this esteemed figure is enough to double production in the Earth caste factories and spark planet-wide ceremonies.

Despite his advanced age and important symbolic status, Aun'Va regularly walks amongst his people, feeling he is most effective when he can lead from the front. History is replete with examples of Aun'Va in the midst of conquest, inspiring the Fire caste to great deeds or arriving in battle zones to bolster morale. It was his awe-inspiring presence that impelled the T'au to rid the Si'coa System of the hateful Reek, giving each cadre the will to see the bloody campaign completed. Upon the flanks of Mount Scion

it was Aun'Va who pronounced the fate of the Orks of Waaagh! Grognik – a sentence enacted by the assembled Fire Warriors with a righteous rage.

In perhaps his most famous pronouncement, Aun'Va declared the beginning of the Third Sphere Expansion. Flanked by a full ceremonial guard, the Ethereal Supreme gave a slow, deliberate speech culminating in a rousing call to arms, a demand to proliferate across the stars and make manifest the T'au Empire's glorious destiny. The guiding light of the Greater Good must reach those worlds trapped in the darkness of their barbaric ways. As his words echoed into silence, untold billions of T'au stood outside the council dome, or listened to the broadcast throughout the empire – all bowed low as one, humbled by the immensity of the moment.

During the long wars of the Third Sphere campaign, holo-footage of the Ethereal Supreme in the thick of the fighting was ever-present in the T'au Empire's propaganda transmissions: Aun'Va on his hover-throne entering a breach in a battered Imperial fortress wall, Aun'Va directing the devastating volleys of a Fire Warrior line, and Aun'Va standing next to the new technological marvel of the XV104 Riptide, with the still smoking wreckage of recently destroyed enemy tanks in the background. More than any previous Ethereal Supreme, Aun'Va desired to be seen at the forefront of the T'au Empire's military endeavours.

Since those heady days, the Ethereal Supreme's visits to the front lines have been less frequent, though still memorable and decisive. Although protected by his Honour Guard and a force shield that envelops him and his hover-throne, it is not Aun'Va's way to enter the conflict directly. Rather, through his wisdom and ability to inspire his followers to seemingly impossible feats, he guides the T'au soldiery around him. In his august presence, Fire Warriors have been known to unleash more accurate volleys, enabling them to cut down oncoming opposition, shrug off otherwise mortal wounds in order to continue the battle, or hold their position to the bitter end despite overwhelming enemy assaults.

Of course, this is all an illusion of unthinkable complexity and scale, for in truth the Ethereal Supreme is dead, slain at the hands of an Imperial assassin at the culmination of the war for Mu'gulath Bay. If this secret were to ever be unearthed, the ruptures throughout T'au society would be monumental – for Aun'Va is an icon of hope, stability and longevity, the calming and steady voice that guides the immortal dream of the T'au'va. Thus, the Ethereal Caste utilises the latest solid-light technology and AI personality matrix algorithms to give the Ethereal Supreme life, albeit in entirely hologrammatic form. Before his assassination, the aging Aun'Va was already in the process of uploading his memories and thoughts to an engrammatic shell, and it is this consciousness – expanded and altered by the Ethereal High Council – that now survives the Great Leader.

Aun'Va's stirring rhetoric continues to be broadcast across the T'au Empire, and the old leader – or rather, whatever simulacrum remains – still makes regular combat tours, inspiring all with his wise counsel and selfless bravery. His Honour Guard never leave his side for a moment, lest the grand deception be discovered.

AUN'SHI

MASTER OF THE BLADE, SAVIOUR OF THE FIRE CASTE, HERO OF FIO'VASH

Hailing from the proud martial sept of Vior'la, Aun'Shi is an indomitable Ethereal whose iron will has steeled the resolve of multitudes of T'au across many frontiers. A modest hero of numerous battles, Aun'Shi longs for peace but is bound by duty to his comrades, and he is wholly committed to furthering the cause of the Greater Good. Because of his exemplary service, and his habit of joining them for battle rituals and training, Aun'Shi is lionised by the Fire caste. Thanks to his long career and many exploits, Aun'Shi is also seen by the Fire caste as a sure sign of victory, and he is greeted everywhere he travels with many salutes and deep respectful bows. Even the renegades of the Farsight Enclaves, openly hostile to the Ethereal caste, bear a grudging respect for the grizzled old warrior.

At the time of the battle that catapulted Aun'Shi to the position of a full-scale hero of the empire, he was already nearing the age when an Ethereal can choose to retire to a life of contemplation within the temple-domes of their caste. Due to his many successes, Aun'Shi was entitled to spend his last years on the paradise world of the Au'taal – an honour accorded to only those who have excelled in their drive for the Greater Good. Aun'Shi's last assignment was to bolster a new colony named Kel'tyr.

Established on a planet that turned out to be infested with Orks, the colony's progress had been slow, but with the arrival of reinforcements and Aun'Shi's canny alien-fighting guidance, the Fire Warriors were soon able to clear the main continent. This allowed the Earth caste to construct great cities and better establish the exploitation of Kel'tyr's natural resources. On his final inspection tour, however, Aun'Shi became trapped in Fio'vash when a horde of Orks surrounded the compound. With their shas'vre beheaded by the Ork Warboss, the Fire Warriors began to panic. Leaping to action, Aun'Shi used his famed honour blade to cut the Ork leader in two, planting the weapon's haft between the shorn halves of the twitching corpse. Heartened, the Fire Warriors steadied their firing line.

Again and again the Orks were repelled from the ever-constricting perimeter. Despite the growing mounds of dead, the greenskins hurtled forwards and everywhere they reached the T'au lines, Aun'Shi was there to meet them. When his allies tired, the Ethereal's inspiring words and heroic actions granted them a second wind, and they rose once more to fire a fresh volley, hearts filled with hope and defiance. Tirelessly, Aun'Shi chopped the savages down, but always they returned. As the Orks finally closed for the kill, a relief force arrived. When they reached the only building that remained standing in Fio'vash, they were surprised to find Aun'Shi still standing guard over the few survivors, his blade dripping with Ork ichor.

News of Aun'Shi's deeds travelled fast. Aun'Va knew well that the T'au must have new heroes, and here was an Ethereal, a living legend amongst the Fire caste and the saviour of Fio'vash. Rather than allow such a valuable warrior to fade away, it was decreed that Aun'Shi should continue in his duties and lead fresh expeditions. Known as the 'aged wonder', Aun'Shi continues to bring great fortune to the Fire caste, leading them to victory after victory at the forefront of the T'au Empire's relentless campaigns.

COMMANDER FARSIGHT

**HERO OF VIOR'LA, PROTÉGÉ OF PURETIDE, THE BANE OF GREENSKINS,
RENOUNCED TRAITOR TO THE GREATER GOOD**

There is no figure in T'au history as divisive as Commander O'Shovah. The most famous warrior of Vior'la, Farsight's greatest victories were against the Orks on the oxide-deserts of Arkunasha. There, clad in his battlesuit, he led a masterful campaign that defeated armies numbering hundreds of times greater than his own loyal troops. Farsight's training, much of which was under the direction of Commander Puretide himself, had taught him the use of terrain and the importance of a bold, decisive stroke to cripple his enemies. Preferring to eschew long-ranged firepower, O'Shovah encouraged the aggressive spirit of the Fire caste in his warriors, and they won many bitter battles at close range. It was O'Shovah's tactical brilliance that earned him his famous title 'Farsight'.

Along with the forces of another of Puretide's pupils, Commander O'Shaserra, Farsight's Hunter Cadres were instrumental in holding off the advance of Imperial forces on the sept world of Dal'yth during the battles that raged back and forth across the Damocles Gulf. His attacking style left Imperial forces reeling, unsure where the next hammer blow would fall. Although victorious in eventually driving the forces of the Imperium from the face of Dal'yth, the T'au Empire was facing a time of great disconcertion. The T'au, always so assured of the superiority of their cause and of their abilities, had been swept away from dozens of newly colonised planets and even suffered an attack on one of their sept worlds. The Ethereals named this period the *Nont'ka* – the time of questioning. Realising that some were beginning to doubt their message of superiority, the Ethereals sought for a new hero to rekindle the spirit of expansion and to firmly re-establish the T'au's rightful destiny – the ultimate triumph of the Greater Good.

In the wake of their victory on Dal'yth, the Ethereal High Council ordered vast reclamation attacks to reconquer their recently lost colonies. Many successful Commanders were considered to lead the spearhead, but in the end, it was Farsight's flawless battle record and his flair for dramatic victories that earned him a formal ceremony of recognition from the empire's Ethereal rulers. The Water caste's top propaganda efforts were put behind Commander Farsight's Coalition – perhaps the largest fleet of warships, ground troops and colony ships yet assembled by the T'au Empire.

THE DAWN BLADE

The mysterious artefact that O'Shovah took up on Arthas Moloch is even older than the Imperium of Man. Fashioned aeons ago by the strange race that once inhabited that haunted world, the Dawn Blade has been forged from materials that even the finest of Earth caste minds cannot fathom. Its blade is sharp enough to cut through rock, and since taking it up on Arthas Moloch, and modifying it for use in battle, it has been O'Shovah's weapon of choice for close engagements.

Unbeknownst to Farsight, the ancient sword has a dark secret. Its blade is made from chronophagic alloys – whenever its wielder cuts a life short with it, the natural span that he stole from his victim is added to the wielder's own. This has allowed O'Shovah to live for almost three centuries. Though he has his suspicions that it is the Dawn Blade that has prolonged his lifespan to such a degree, if Farsight ever found out the horrible truth, he would likely end his own life in ritual suicide then and there.

However, there was no need for embellished accounts, for in the ensuing battles O'Shovah truly established his greatness. The bulk of Mankind's forces had been conscripted to fight a menace in another sector, and the T'au quickly re-established rule over planet after planet. With a skill bordering on prescience, Commander Farsight knew when to attack brashly and when to employ skilful manoeuvres and ambushes. Not since the peak of Commander Puretide's triumphs had the T'au Empire been so united by the deeds of a single warrior.

The Farsight Expedition, as it came to be known, ran into unexpected difficulties with Orks who had taken advantage of the T'au's war with the Imperium. With no opposing military power in the region to stop them, the greenskin forces were free to expand their territorial raids, subjecting many of the nearby planets to the brutal whims of their cruel overlords. O'Shovah abandoned his recolonisation efforts to confront the Orks, drawing his forces far from their assignments and eventually into a decade-long war across multiple star systems. The battles raged far beyond the borders of the empire, yet Farsight was wholly absorbed by this new campaign. Although claiming many victories, Commander Farsight grew increasingly embittered – feeling that his expeditionary force was not receiving the continued support it deserved. The loyal warriors beneath him, a dedicated troop of acolytes, strongly agreed.

Back on the distant planet T'au, the Ethereal High Council debated their next move, for many had grown wary of the strong-willed Commander, feeling a growing breach with their appointed leader that had nothing to do with the great distance between them. Even as Aun'Va came to the conclusion that the wayward Farsight must be relieved of command and recalled, a new disaster struck. It happened at the periphery of the Damocles Gulf during a battle on Arthas Moloch, a deserted world save for strange monuments and ruined shrines of some long-forgotten culture. All of the Ethereals in Farsight's expedition were slain by an unknown enemy.

Undaunted, Farsight weathered the savage attacks of the unrelenting foe, pulling back in the hope of learning more about the fiends that had attacked them before launching a retaliation. Soon, however, the mysterious beings disappeared with the same suddenness with which they had arrived. With the world apparently cleansed, Commander Farsight pushed ever onwards, pursuing the Orks lest they make good their escape. He did so in strict disobedience of protocol, for without the guidance of any Ethereals, it is a Fire caste Commander's duty to immediately report back to the High Council and await new orders.

Before long, Farsight was beyond the reach of even the most advanced communication relays and was no longer operating within the bounds of the T'au Empire. Years went by and no messages came back, until it was eventually assumed that their never-defeated Commander had, at long last, been vanquished – dying on a distant planet, far from the stars that lit the T'au Empire. All castes on every sept bowed their heads low when the loss of this revered hero was broadcast across the empire.

Yet Commander Farsight was not dead. Obstinately choosing to press on with his personal crusade rather than return to the bosom of his empire, Farsight instead established a string of heavily fortified strongholds across the frontier space on the far side of the Damocles Gulf, a region long forbidden to the T'au. Even now, sporadic signals from long-range probes are received

THE FORBIDDEN ZONE

The T'au Empire launches many probes towards the Forbidden Zone, the cluster of star systems beyond the far side of the Damocles Gulf – although few have ever returned. The strange eddies and unreadable energies that drift in that region doubtlessly damage or reroute a portion of those lost probes, but many more are destroyed by orbital defence stations that blockade all entry, save only for their own ships.

Beyond that formidable ring of floating fortresses are the Farsight Enclaves. Scans from those few probes to successfully beam back signals reveal a string of heavily built-up worlds with large populations, including nodal cities expanded from colony domes and entire moon-bases converted to manufacturing. When last seen trailing the Orks, Farsight's Coalition bore the symbols of their septs – predominantly Vior'la, but also Sa'cea, T'au'n and several others. When sighted generations later, these forces and fleets bore markings similar in design to those used by the T'au Empire, but in colours and patterns never sanctioned. Like any distant colony, much of the equipment and armour used by those within the Farsight Enclaves is slightly dated – the equipment most prevalent at the time of Farsight's disappearance. There has been, however, unsettling evidence of classified technology and recent prototypes present within the Enclaves. Time will tell whether this is the result of spycraft, theft or traitors to the Greater Good who have been aiding those within Farsight's domain.

Despite the T'au Empire's efforts to rewrite history – either avoiding mention of the fallen hero or painting him as a cowardly deserter – there is still support for Farsight amongst the existing septs, especially upon his home world of Vior'la. This secret admiration has only increased since Farsight's notable intervention during the battle for Mu'gulath Bay, during which warriors of the Enclaves fought alongside their former kin. Despite this temporary truce, the Ethereal High Council has not ceased its attempts to suppress support for O'Shovah, nor reneged on its classification of the Farsight Enclaves as enemies of the Tau'va. The Council has forbidden all travel and communications to that sector of the galactic west. Special councils, composed of Ethereals and auxiliary guards, are dispatched to question any who are rumoured to have contacts or sympathies with the Farsight Enclaves. Few who are questioned are seen again.

by the Ethereal High Council, which confirm the continued existence of the Farsight Enclaves. There has even been evidence – unique signature signals from his personalised early-model Crisis battlesuit and a few far-ranged visuals – that Farsight himself still lives. This is, itself, a great and confounding mystery, for it would mean that the Commander has lived for at least three centuries, considerably longer than the ordinary lifespan of any T'au, save only the unknowable Ethereals.

Rumours have spread within the empire that O'Shovah is extending his lifespan through some technological process or that a series of successors has taken up the mantle of Farsight. Regardless, the Ethereal High Council has labelled O'Shovah a renegade and traitor of the T'au'va, and has forbidden any communications with the rogue Commander and the rebels he leads.

DARKSTRIDER

THE SHADOW THAT STRIKES, THE ELUSIVE, HE THAT WALKS UNSEEN

Despite his many heroics, there is something unsettling about Sub-Commander El'Myamoto, the T'au more commonly called Darkstrider. Although all of the Fire caste regard him as a cunning tactician and a warrior to be reckoned with, his unconventional methods and disregard for proper protocol have stirred up much trouble and made many internal enemies.

It began when Myamoto, a shas'ui borne on T'au, passed his Trial by Fire. Scorning the honour of donning a battlesuit to join the Crisis Teams, he was next offered the opportunity to join the Stealth Teams – a formation noted for its unorthodox methods. This choice too, Myamoto derided, preferring to return to the Pathfinder Teams with which he had first served. Time and again, Myamoto led his team into the most deadly of situations, but always escaped, bringing glory to his cadre. It was he that shut down the strange mechanisms of the Necrons on the moons of Gal'yth, and he who hunted down the tri-headed beast that terrorised the mining colonies of Nep'tan. During the Great War of Confederation, when the grim leader earned the name Darkstrider, he infiltrated Ork camps and used markerlights to pick out components of Gargants under construction. It was his team that set the homing beacon on Warlord Gruzzguts' mechanical armour. Yet for all his heroics, Darkstrider always spurned offers to command, preferring instead to lead raiding missions and terror attacks behind enemy lines.

Myamoto regularly walks the fine line near insubordination – nearly unheard of in the Fire caste. Some Commanders refuse to work with Darkstrider, claiming that he refuses council. Yet others, most notably Shadowsun herself, value the sly tactics and obvious bravery of Darkstrider. Gifted with a prototype structural analyser that can identify the weaknesses in any target, Darkstrider is a proven asset on the battlefield, and his skill at baiting the enemy into attacking before coordinating the Fire Warriors around him in a fighting retreat has contributed to a string of victories that none can deny.

> 'We engaged and destroyed the enemy column in accordance with mission parameters. No, I received no such orders to disengage and fall back, shas'o. Perhaps there was some form of atmospheric interference.'
>
> *- Communication from Sub-Commander El'Myamoto to Commander O'Fai*

Tradition is everything to the Fire caste, and their adherence to the Code of Fire demands, above all things, respect for Ethereals, military rank and more experienced warriors. Through declined promotions and subtle inflections when speaking to his superiors,

CADRE FIREBLADES

Fireblades are the most grizzled and seasoned Fire Warriors of their cadre, whose mastery of the infantryman's art of battle leads them to eschew battlesuit technology. They are excellent field leaders, and their long experience has taught them exactly where to place shots to maximise damage. Whether breaking the impetus of an advancing horde of greenskins or seeking to bring down the heavily armoured Space Marines of the Imperium, no one knows a Fire Warrior's strength better than a Cadre Fireblade.

These officers were once Fire Warrior troopers like any other in the cadre, and as they gained experience, they rose to become shas'ui: veterans and squad leaders. Whereas most of these seasoned leaders eventually choose the great honour of donning a battlesuit, there are a few who instead prefer to remain with the Fire Warriors. For some, this is a practical realisation that the tactical versatility required by Crisis or Stealth Teams eludes them; for others, it is simply a preference to remain squarely situated within the heart of the T'au gun-line.

The military path that takes a soldier to become a Cadre Fireblade can never rise as high as the rank of shas'o – they are limited to a level just beneath that of shas'el. Nor does the title carry with it the élan associated with those who wear a battlesuit. Nonetheless, Cadre Fireblade, or shas'nel in the T'au language, is a highly respected role – not least because of their willingness to forgo prestige. T'au Commanders value their Fireblades as highly as any battlesuit-clad shas'o, for they provide an invaluable blend of experience and competence that makes them a priceless force multiplier. Moreover, the constant drilling and workman-like efficiency of a Cadre Fireblade is, to the T'au, a willing embrace of their most beloved concept – the T'au'va.

Other than the Greater Good, there is only one thing all Cadre Fireblades will extol: the efficacy of overwhelming infantry firepower. It is at close range that this discipline really comes into its own. Even as the enemy draw nearby, Fireblades radiate a steadying calm, driving and directing Fire Warriors as they pour volley after volley of merciless pulse fire onto the target, and instilling each trooper with the ruthless efficiency that is the hallmark of thousands of years of martial teachings.

PULSE WEAPONRY

Pulse technology is the foundation upon which the T'au's formidable ranged combat proficiency is built. Pulse weapons utilise refined induction fields to propel lethal bursts of plasma over great distances. This principle holds true for both the T'au's regulation small arms – including the iconic pulse rifles and carbines carried by Fire Warrior teams – and the devastating pulse driver cannons and blastcannons carried by advanced ballistic suits. A pulse rifle round can burn clean through Space Marine power armour, while the blast from a pulse driver cannon can reduce a battle tank to little more than a glowing pile of molten slag.

STRIKE TEAMS

To be born into the Fire caste is to be born for battle. Bred for generations to maximise size and strength, these warriors-to-be are enrolled in Fire caste academies as soon as they can walk, institutions whose sole purpose is to produce soldiers to serve the growing T'au Empire. There they are rigorously prepared, in mind and body, to become Fire Warriors – the professional infantry that forms the backbone of the Hunter Cadres of every sept. The greatest proportion of these warriors are then formed into Strike Teams, the familiar and devastatingly effective core of a typical sept army.

T'au Strike Teams are superbly equipped for battle, and a large part of their training is to grow proficient in the use of their high-tech gear. Each warrior wears multi-layered body armour that provides defence against high velocity or explosive rounds. Thanks to the T'au's mastery of metal fusions, the armour is lightweight, especially in comparison to conventional materials such as those used by Orks or the Imperium. The enlarged sinistral shoulder pad is particularly useful, as Fire Warriors are trained to use this as a shield, often positioning it towards incoming fire to increase their protection. Their helmets contain a number of digitised aids, including sensors, target-tracking readouts, air quality levels and communications uplinks.

The arsenal available to Strike Teams is formidable, with individuals carrying either a pulse rifle or a pulse carbine. With this advanced armament, Fire Warriors can lay down a withering fusillade upon their foes. Their range and hitting power outclasses the standard weapons of every race the T'au have yet encountered. Should their enemies advance too close, Strike Teams are equipped with disc-like photon grenades, defensive devices which explode with a dazzling blast of multispectral light to disorient foes. Although their potent pulse weapons can penetrate the armour of light vehicles, against heavier targets, Strike Teams often employ EMP grenades. These are technical marvels that send out an electromagnetic pulse on detonation which can overload electronic circuitry, causing anything from minor malfunctions to complete meltdowns.

Strike Teams consist of between five and twelve warriors. A team leader, or shas'ui, is a veteran warrior whose experience has prepared him to command. A shas'ui can draw upon additional equipment to aid both the team and the cadre, such as drones or a markerlight. Before the battle, the shas'ui will receive the orders for his team via relay comms, although due to the haphazard nature of war, these goals often change, and a shas'ui is expected to lead his team to fluidly react to every situation.

The Fire caste puts utmost importance on acting in a coordinated fashion upon the battlefield. Needless sacrifices or inadequately supporting nearby teams are considered great failures. Strike Teams drill endlessly in setting up overlapping fields of fire and positioning themselves so that they can efficiently protect other teams should they be attacked. Such rigorous training produces Fire Warriors to whom covering fire is second nature – able to send volleys of pulse fire at a foe closing upon their comrades with a single command flashed through the comm-system. While a Strike Team is formidable in its own right, an interlocking cadre of teams is even stronger than the sum of its parts. Such inter-unit dynamics have foiled many foes. During the T'au victories over the Orks during the Great War of Confederation, time and again the waves of greenskins almost closed with the T'au gun-lines, only to find their final charge defeated by the literal wall of pulse fire that the combined teams discharged. It is a lesson that resounds through the Fire caste academies: 'only by supporting our comrades can we defeat the superior numbers of our foes'.

DS8 TACTICAL SUPPORT TURRET
Carried in racks along the flanks of Orca Dropships, tactical support turrets are automated defence batteries that provide support for the Fire Warriors of the Strike and Breacher Teams. These armoured turrets plummet into battle and deploy in fixed positions to add their firepower to the fight. Each turret is programmed to self-destruct should its sensors register the possibility of capture or tampering, ensuring that the T'au's superior weaponry can never be turned upon them by their enemies.

BREACHER TEAMS

With their pulse blasters blazing, the courageous Fire Warriors of the Breacher Teams take the fight into the midst of the foe. Following newer tactical doctrines devised to dig stubborn foes from cover, it is the Breachers who seize key locations and tear the heart from defence lines with intense, point-blank pulse fire.

Blinding blue light flickers down corridors and illuminates the charnel confines of burning bunkers as the Breacher Teams press the attack. Before the high-impact fire of their pulse blasters, enemy warriors are blown apart in horrific gory sprays. Particle streams light up luckless targets, causing the panicked victim to glow vividly for a split second before screaming bolts of energy smash them apart. Meanwhile, the Fire Warriors advance with practised efficiency, overlapping their fire and covering one another perfectly. Sensor suites within the Breachers' helms read every inch of the local environment, providing relative personnel positioning, projected fields of fire and probable locations of enemy forces. Rigorously trained to absorb this wealth of information at speed, the warriors of a Breacher Team can stay one step ahead of their foes while laying down devastating fire with their powerful weapons.

The catalyst for the formation of Breacher Teams dates all the way back to the first T'au invasion of Imperial space. It was observed at that time that, while foes such as the Orks or the Barghesi preferred close assault and would often force the T'au onto the defensive, Mankind took a more static approach. The sprawling bunker complexes and strongpoints of the Imperium were on a scale never before seen by the T'au and, while crude compared to Earth caste workmanship, these fortifications were rugged enough to prove troublesome. Furthermore, an alarming number of Air caste spacecraft were lost to the aggressive boarding actions of the Space Marines, against which there seemed little defence. Increasingly, the Fire caste found themselves forced to commit their strength to one-sided close-quarters battles amid winding corridors and rooms in which there was no space for a battlesuit to deploy. Casualties were high during such costly actions, and so development was begun on the tools necessary to win point-blank fire fights with decisive firepower.

So were born the Breacher Teams. Drawn from the most aggressive Fire Warrior cadets, many of whom may have been deemed too belligerent for service in the past, these new teams were trained to take the fight to the foe. Protected by Drone-generated energy shields, the Breachers are able to blast a path into the most heavily defended strongpoint while weathering the blistering fusillades of the foe. Each warrior is trained to hold their fire until the perfect moment to maximise their kill potential, a trait that requires extreme self-control and bravery. Indeed, though their casualties are invariably high and their lives often short, the Breacher Teams have continued in the proud and selfless tradition of their founding ever since.

PATHFINDER TEAMS

Light reconnaissance units, Pathfinder Teams are the eyes and ears of their Commander in a way no drone can yet emulate. A Pathfinder's foremost role is not to engage the enemy, but instead to maximise the efficiency of the rest of their cadre. They operate ahead of their comrades, close to their foe, to accurately scout the enemy. In such a position, a Pathfinder's life is always under threat. For this reason and more, Pathfinders are held in high regard by every caste.

They are not protected by a battlesuit or stealth field generators, yet they are far from helpless. A Pathfinder's standard kit includes a pulse carbine – ideal for the close-ranged firefights they so frequently find themselves in. Pathfinders also bear markerlights to guide the firepower of the rest of the cadre to optimal targets. Holding a markerlight on a distant enemy while your own position is being overrun is a selfless act, but Pathfinders epitomise the Greater Good, and by their actions, many battles are won.

By infiltrating the battlefield, they can also activate homing beacons or positional relays, allowing reinforcements to enter the fray

with greater precision. Some teams also carry a few rail rifles – especially useful against power-armoured infantry. An even more recent addition to the Pathfinder's arsenal is the ion rifle. Able to fire in two distinct modes, the ion rifle can vaporise light vehicles and punch through ceramite, but is unstable when overcharged. Many Pathfinder shas'uis employ drones, and during the Third Sphere Expansion, new variants specially designed to assist Pathfinder Teams were developed.

Needlessly spending lives to gain ground is anathema to the T'au, and the Fire caste is trained to retreat and fight another day. While every sept has tales of Pathfinders escaping against impossible odds, even the best-laid extraction plans can fail. All T'au warriors are willing to lay down their lives for the Greater Good, but Pathfinders find self-sacrifice called for more often than all other cadre teams combined; during the early days of the Great War of Confederation, some septs reported Pathfinder casualty rates as high as ninety per cent. Despite this, or perhaps because of it, the Fire caste academies are inundated with volunteers wishing to be Pathfinders, eager to do their utmost for the T'au'va.

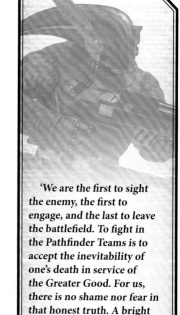

'We are the first to sight the enemy, the first to engage, and the last to leave the battlefield. To fight in the Pathfinder Teams is to accept the inevitability of one's death in service of the Greater Good. For us, there is no shame nor fear in that honest truth. A bright future can only be earned through sacrifice.'

- Pathfinder Shas'ui Mor'kami

TX4 PIRANHAS

The Piranha is a lightly armoured skimmer – a mobile weapons platform that is capable of great speed and manoeuvrability. Using its jet-thrusters and anti-gravitic engine, the Piranha glides over a planet's surface, its twin pilots well able to hug the terrain and make the best use of any cover. Along with a nose-mounted main armament, the Piranha carries two drones – either retained on the vehicle to add firepower, or detached into AI mode to perform some other mission.

On the battlefield, Piranhas often seem to be everywhere at once: hurtling over friendly troops to counter-attack approaching infantry, racing along the flanks to launch devastating enfilades at enemy armour, or streaking from behind cover to destroy vulnerable foes. After so many training drills that stress using co-ordinated attacks and mutual fire support, Fire Warriors are well accustomed to the thrum of a Piranha soaring just over their heads, and they no longer turn to follow the sudden swoosh of air as they streak past.

Piranhas are used in a wide array of capacities, and formations range in size from lone vehicles to a team of up to five working in conjunction. The larger schools of these deadly skimmers can use their burst cannons to annihilate enemy infantry units, while smaller formations are ideal for eradicating scouts or countering enemy teleporters. Lone Piranhas that are equipped with the deadly fusion blaster are proficient hunters of enemy tanks. Using its speed, the skimmer will attempt to manoeuvre so as to approach the target from an unexpected angle. During an attack run, Piranhas are a blur of motion, and the crew are more likely to trust their jinking ability over any amount of armour.

Piranhas have the ability to bring firepower quickly to wherever it is needed, but they are even more dangerous when working in conjunction with Pathfinder Teams. Using markerlights, the Pathfinders often set up Piranha runs, ensuring that the skimmers' volley of fire is as devastating as possible. In return, Pathfinders that find themselves in danger of being overrun request quick strikes by Piranha Teams to help wipe out approaching enemies or, at least, buy time for the Pathfinders to reposition. Unsurprisingly, the T'au's recon troops bear a great fondness for the daredevil pilots of these lightning-fast vessels.

TY7 DEVILFISH

The Devilfish armoured troop carrier is the workhorse of the T'au ground forces, granting the Fire caste infantry much-needed speed and tactical mobility. It can transport up to twelve fully armed and armoured warriors into battle in relative safety and then provide mobile fire support once they disembark. The highly mechanised Hunter Cadres rely on Devilfish to ensure that their Fire Warriors can travel to and deploy quickly wherever they are most required.

Powered by a complex dual anti-grav and jet-propulsion motive system, the Devilfish seems to glide over the ground. The advanced engines generate a 'cushion' for the Devilfish to float upon, and its armoured bulk is driven forwards by two powerful, multi-directional jet engines. By pivoting the propulsion units downwards, the Devilfish pilot can gain extra lift to clear obstacles, making the vehicle capable of boosting over impediments and terrain that mundane tracked vehicles could never hope to traverse.

Mobility is essential for any Commander, and the Devilfish allows an army's infantry to keep pace with its armoured gunships.

Whether manoeuvring troops to deliver the killer offensive of a Mont'ka, or rushing them into ideal firing positions to ensure a Kauyon ambush is properly set, the Devilfish is often key to victory. But the TY7 is not used merely to ferry troops to the battle lines. In addition to the fire of its burst cannon, the Devilfish is on hand to quickly extract troops should enemy formations penetrate too closely. Given the T'au's loathing of close combat, a common tactic is to redeploy their gun-lines when enemy units approach too closely, whisking their troops out of harm's way to set up new firing perimeters elsewhere on the battlefield. This re-embarking and relocating tactic allows Pathfinders to escape encirclement and helps Fire Warriors to keep their foe at arm's length, better enabling them to whittle down the enemy with repeated volleys of pulse fire.

A more aggressive ploy, employed by all septs but made famous by those from Vior'la, is a rapid delivery of Fire Warrior teams into close range of an enemy target. Although a risky proposition, this allows disembarking units to emerge from their Devilfish to shoot point blank into their foe. When it works effectively, they drive back or destroy the enemy; however, failure to do so leaves them vulnerable to assaults. These rapid counter-attacks are a hallmark of T'au tactics, and are often the final stroke in a well-planned Mont'ka. Such ploys are made even more effective by working in conjunction with other elements of the cadre, such as combining firepower with similar supporting assets, coordinating to arrive at the same moment as incoming battlesuits, or having Pathfinders light up the target with markerlights.

The Devilfish itself is armed with a burst cannon – an ideal weapon to add suppressive fire in defence of any nearby allies. Two Gun Drones are also standard armament, able to lend the Devilfish their weight of fire, or detach on missions of their own. There are a number of upgrades that can augment the Devilfish, from seeker missiles, for extra power, to embedded MB3 Recon Drones that can analyse firing arcs and transfer targeting coordinates to the Devilfish pilot's holo-array, allowing the craft's weapons to blast foes cowering behind heavy cover with pinpoint accuracy.

SNIPER DRONE TEAMS

Ensconced in cover far from the front lines of battle, a Firesight Marksman scans the battlefield, using advanced optical sights to select prime targets. Above him float the rest of his team – a group of Sniper Drones, adept at picking off enemy leaders. Together they are a deadly addition to any cadre.

MV71 SNIPER DRONES

Sniper Drones are modified from the standard drones, for they carry a longshot pulse rifle and stabilising fins, as well as mini-stealth field generators that partially obscure them from attackers. The longshot pulse rifle is a lethal weapon that can send its plasma pulse over a great distance. A well-placed shot is capable of taking out any target, and there are many accounts of Sniper Drone Teams single-handedly throwing enemy forces into disarray with their ability to rain down sniper fire from long range. When fighting against the humans attempting raids in the Perdus Rift, a lone Sniper Drone Team claimed an entire Terminator squad – each member shot directly through the less-armoured eye lenses of their helmets.

Many Commanders station Sniper Drones behind their own gun-lines, as this affords extra protection for Fire Warrior or XV88 Broadside Teams. Others use Sniper Drones to dominate open territory – deploying them in positions that overlook swathes of the battlefield, often covering the approach towards intervening friendly teams. Thanks to their anti-gravitic jets, the Sniper Drones can move quickly between areas of cover, where the area's natural protection can combine with their stealth fields to make them almost impossible to target with ranged weapons. This particular technique was used to perfection in the battle against Hive Fleet Gorgon on Ke'lshan, with the threat of fire from massed banks of near-invisible Sniper Drones causing even the largest Tyranid monstrosities to cease their headlong charges and instead attempt to move through cover.

FIRESIGHT MARKSMEN

Although Sniper Drones are equipped with impressive artificial intelligence, it is the Firesight Marksman, a shas'la, who is the brains behind the operation. Equipped with a small stealth field generator, a marksman will secret themselves into dense terrain where they will blend in, minimising the threat of return fire and allowing them time to assess the battlefield. From their concealed position, they will use their drone controller to operate their deadly charges, sending them in search of the most vulnerable quarry. A Firesight Marksman is also equipped with a pulse pistol, in case a foe attempts to close with them, and more importantly, a markerlight. This is used to support both the Sniper Drones of their team and their nearby comrades, although some marksmen prefer to keep themselves out of the line of fire, exposing only their drones to incoming shots.

Should a Firesight Marksman be slain – and no other is available to assume control of the fallen warrior's surviving Sniper Drones – his AI team members are able to continue the fight, albeit at suboptimal performance. Earth caste engineers have been amazed to arrive upon a battlefield many hours after the conflict's conclusion to find Sniper Drones still hovering on duty above their fallen controller, their sniper rifles swivelling in search of new targets.

TACTICAL DRONES

T'au make extensive use of machine intelligences called Tactical Drones, and the variant most commonly seen fighting alongside the Fire caste is known as the Gun Drone. Although small and somewhat innocuous, those foes that underestimate Gun Drones often pay for such a costly mistake with their lives. Using anti-gravitic motors and jet-thrusters, Gun Drones hover over the landscape, rotating back and forth as their sensor vane transmits vital information about their surroundings. Should an enemy be encountered, the Gun Drones quickly accelerate – skimming quickly into firing position, their underslung pulse carbines rapidly swivel to unload their firepower upon the acquired target.

The sleek Gun Drone is well armoured and highly mobile, and its programming can cope with any number of battlefield roles. When grouped into a squadron, Gun Drones can produce a withering fusillade of fire – a hailstorm of deadly plasma bursts to support Fire Warriors and bolster defence gun-lines. Because of their speed and mobility, some Commanders choose to send Gun Drone squadrons on seek-and-destroy missions, unleashing the disk-shaped killing machines to advance along a flank, overwhelming enemy scout patrols or even light vehicles. As their jet-thrusters allow them to slow their descent, it is possible to deploy Tactical Drones by Manta or Orca super-heavy dropships. The sudden appearance of a unit of Gun Drones, descending with pulse carbines blazing, can disrupt the best-laid enemy plans and force them to reposition valuable assets.

A remarkable feat of Earth caste engineering, the artificial intelligence of Tactical Drones increases when they are networked together into squadrons, greatly ramping up their processing speed and ability for independent action. Such squadrons have no need for T'au controllers and are capable of impressive feats. It is common to see squadrons of Gun Drones tying up and antagonising enemy infantry with their small arms fire, ready to quickly dart out of harm's way should the foe try to get to grips with them in the press of melee. Other Gun Drone squadrons harry lightly armoured vehicles, using their impressive mobility to keep their targets in range.

Some Tactical Drones are fitted with markerlights or shield generators instead of destructive weaponry. In very rare instances, entire squadrons have been so altered; an MV4 Shield Drone barrier was used with some success in the great tank duels of the Almo'th plains, while Commander Shadowsun's victory over the Orks at Cha'nel colony is widely attributed to the deployment of several MV7 Marker Drone squadrons, whose barrage of markerlights helped wipe out the bulk of the Ork infantry ensconced in ruins.

So deeply do the T'au believe in the Greater Good that even their drones are programmed with saviour protocols – should the life of a warrior of the empire be deemed important to the cause, a drone will position itself with astonishing quickness and at great personal cost to protect them from harm. Despite this, the T'au do not consider drones to be disposable, and the artificial intelligence will analyse every possibility in order to ensure its own survival is not needlessly jeopardised.

The T'au are always intrigued, and more than a little disturbed, to be faced with the Imperium of Man's deep-seated and abiding prejudice against machine intelligences. The Earth caste in particular cannot fully understand the sheer abhorrence that humans reserve for machines that can think for themselves. To the Imperium, the artificially intelligent drones are just another technological tool to use for the advancement of the Greater Good. For the T'au, the drones save time and lives, and to regard machine intelligences with suspicion is yet another example of the backwards, barbaric superstition they must overcome.

TX7 HAMMERHEAD GUNSHIPS

Like a hungry predator on the prowl, the Hammerhead Gunship is a menacing sight. It skims over a planet's surface with its massive turret-mounted gun swivelling back and forth to track potential targets. The Hammerhead Gunship is the main battle tank of the T'au, and all enemies who have encountered it quickly grow to respect, if not outright fear, the might of its main armament – the dreaded railgun.

The railgun is a linear accelerator that uses super-conductive electrodes to project a solid shot at hypersonic speeds. The vast kinetic energy generated by the round on impact has devastating effects, even at long ranges. The Hammerhead can also carry sophisticated submunitions – a shot full of smaller projectiles used for suppressive area fire against soft targets. For close-range protection, the Hammerhead carries a pair of Gun Drones, although at need, these can be switched to full AI mode and detached from the tank to operate independently on the battlefield.

Some Hammerheads do not carry a railgun as their main weapon, but instead use the ion cannon – a unique T'au innovation that shoots an ionic beam that explodes upon contact with its target. Ideal for use against light vehicles and heavily armoured infantry, the ion cannon can also be overcharged; while this risks a dangerous overload, it results in a larger blast capable of destroying even more targets.

It is common to find at least a few Hammerheads deployed in support of Fire Warrior teams. Although well armoured, the Hammerhead is most often kept at a distance to take advantage of the superior range of its weapons. There are many accounts of single Hammerheads demolishing enemy armour with almost contemptuous ease.

During the Damocles Crusade, the Hammerhead gained a particularly fearsome reputation amongst the Astra Militarum. Entire armoured companies were destroyed before they could close with the T'au battle lines, and whole offensives were transformed into fields of wreckage by the formidable Hammerhead Gunship. Not to be denied their advance, the humans massed their remaining armour and sent them all against the T'au lines, seeking to overwhelm them with sheer numbers. But the T'au are veteran Ork-fighters, and they were well accustomed to such tactics; the Imperial tanks were met by expertly placed Armoured Interdiction Cadres – formations of Hammerheads and Sky Rays.

Although outnumbered at least five to one, the superior range and armour penetrating ability of the Hammerhead – along with its ability to quickly reposition into cover or advance into a better firing position – more than made up the difference. By the campaign's end, the Imperial Guard tank regiments were utterly demoralised as they grimly calculated their low odds of survival; they would never leave cover without first thoroughly scanning the horizon for the Hammerhead's distinctive shape.

Although the Hammerhead Gunship performs well in tank duels, the combined arms approach of the T'au requires much more from their main battle tank than just anti-armour capability. It was the legendary Commander Puretide who said that even the most rampant horde attack can be broken through application of firepower, and the submunitions blasts of the railgun can rip enough bloody gaps in charging formations to halt an incoming Waaagh! or smash apart an entire wave of lesser Tyranid creatures. Fire Warrior and Pathfinder Teams often work closely with Hammerheads, mutually supporting each other and frequently using markerlights to guide the gunships' powerful shots towards priority targets.

LONGSTRIKE

HAMMERHEAD PILOT, GUNSHIP ACE, TITAN-SLAYER, TERROR OF T'ROS, HERO OF T'AU

Master gunship pilot Shas'la T'au Sha'ng, now better known as Longstrike, has quickly become the Fire caste's most heralded tank ace. His kill tally far exceeds any other gunship pilot, and the distance between Longstrike and those who would claim his title continues to widen with each fresh engagement. Since his first training session, he exhibited an almost innate ability to handle a Hammerhead. In the wars of the Third Sphere Expansion, his skills were put to the ultimate test in the heat of battle.

It was on T'ros that the young Hammerhead pilot earned the name Longstrike and got his first taste of the repugnant ways in which humans fight their wars. As part of an Armoured Interdiction Cadre, he was assigned to a contingent fighting in the western deserts. There, over the arid flatlands, the Hammerhead Gunships clashed for days against the full might of the Astra Militarum's Leman Russ companies. For all their smoke-spewing and crude design, the human battle tanks were dangerous, even more so as they outnumbered the T'au armour by at least six to one. Early in the engagement, Sha'ng showed poise and a remarkable aim, making every shot count until the horizon was littered with fiery wrecks. Yet the battle was costly for the T'au as well. All of Sha'ng's bond-mates – those who had undergone the version of the ta'lissera unique to gunship pilots – were slain. The human tankers showed no remorse, grinding their heavy tracks over wounded T'au and even their own troops in their eagerness to press the attack.

Sha'ng continued to battle, steadily backing his Hammerhead away to put intervening terrain between himself and incoming fire. With every discharge of his railgun, smoke blossomed from another Leman Russ in the distance. The tank duel went on until a school of Razorshark Strike Fighters flew over to finish off the attackers, and Longstrike's legend was begun. In the ongoing battles that marked the Imperium's retreat from T'ros, Longstrike continued to cull the Imperial armour, including a famous headshot that felled a colossal Warhound Titan.

Due to his unerring aim, Longstrike was chosen to trial the new XV02 pilot battlesuit. With its upgraded interface he could become one with his vehicle, reacting instantaneously alongside various AI functions within the Hammerhead. This would allow Longstrike to provide supporting fire to nearby teams in ways most other vehicles, even those equipped with targeting relays, could not. He would also be able to make better use of incoming markerlight data, enabling him to lock on to targets with even greater accuracy.

The combination of Longstrike's formidable skills and the XV02 battlesuit have made him deadlier than ever. Redeployed for the major battle on Mu'gulath Bay, Longstrike destroyed innumerable gun and bunker emplacements along the Imperial line. As the fighting moved into the narrow hive streets, Longstrike's lightning-fast reactions allowed him to destroy infantry attempting to emerge from cover and attack the surrounding Fire Warriors. Before the last pockets of resistance were wiped out, word of the Hammerhead pilot who could not miss had spread across the Fire caste. By that time, Sha'ng was already on board a transport for the next engagement of the Third Sphere Expansion.

XV02 PILOT BATTLESUITS

One of the most advanced creations of the T'au Sept science divisions, the XV02 pilot battlesuit blends advanced neural interface technology with a network of sub-dermal implants and adrenal stimulators designed to enhance the reaction time of its user. The wearer can visualise and interpret complex streams of markerlight data in an instant, converting these into pinpoint targeting solutions even as they gracefully manoeuvre their vehicle outside of the firing arcs of enemy tanks. The presence of a single pilot wearing an XV02 suit greatly contributes to the already impressive power of an armoured contingent. To the frustration of Earth caste scientists, however, they have thus far been unable to replicate the astonishing success of Shas'la Longstrike. Very few test pilots have proven compatible with the XV02's neural framework, and those who have been able to master the sheer speed of the battlesuit's metasynthetic processing have swiftly succumbed to irreversible encephalic degradation and nerve shock.

TX78 SKY RAY GUNSHIPS

The Sky Ray Missile Defence Gunship is a specialised variant of the Hammerhead that replaces its turret gun with an array of deadly seeker missiles. Although designed to neutralise enemy aircraft, the Sky Ray has also proven itself adept at eliminating assets on the ground.

On the battlefield, a Sky Ray is a grav-tank that glides behind the front lines, using its twin markerlights to sweep the horizon – seeking to find and lock on to either ground or airborne targets. Should enemy targets be acquired, the crew can launch a seeker missile, a deadly rocket that streaks away faster than the eye can follow. If the target is light infantry, not worth one of the limited seeker missiles, the Sky Ray will instead use its pair of markerlights to light up the foe – making them easier prey for the guns of nearby Fire Warriors.

The crew of the Sky Ray rely heavily on their interactions with the forward infantry teams and are in constant contact with them, coordinating fire and determining the viability of targets. Pathfinder Teams range ahead of the T'au advance, utilising markerlight beams to paint enemy vehicles. This vital targeting data is then uploaded into the tactical network, and the Sky Ray Gunship unleashes a pinpoint storm of armour-shredding missiles that devastates the stunned and helpless enemy column.

The Sky Ray was first developed and deployed towards the end of the Damocles Crusade, and served as a counter to the Imperium's air power. Thanks to its velocity tracker, the Sky Ray can lock its missiles onto any target it can see – including the quick-moving flyers of the Imperial Navy. The seeker missiles that they carry are so fast that many enemy pilots are hit and downed before they can even take evasive manoeuvres. During the Taros Campaign, enemy pilots dubbed the vehicle the 'sting ray' or 'stinger' and they came to value confirmed Sky Ray kills above all others. During the Great War of Confederation, so many Ork bombers were lost due to the Sky Ray barriers positioned around T'au cities that even the daredevil Ork pilots soon refused to enter what they termed 'deff alley'. Yet the Sky Ray is not only deadly to flyers, as many enemy tanks have learned. Even enemy commanders have found themselves suddenly lit with markerlights and then targeted by a barrage of seeker missiles. Several notable Space Marine Captains and Lieutenants were thusly obliterated during their recent offensives in the Zeist Sector.

For its secondary weapon system, the Sky Ray is usually equipped with a pair of Gun Drones. Should increased firepower be required, these Gun Drones can be replaced with burst cannons or smart missile systems (SMS). Many Sky Ray crew prefer the SMS as it provides a high degree of close-range protection, and its self-guided missiles allow the Sky Ray to make maximum use of cover, sometimes never exposing itself to return fire.

For all their effectiveness, Sky Rays are rarely encountered in large numbers. Generally, a single vehicle is attached to a Hunter Cadre or deployed near vulnerable locations such as airbases or power generators. With Pathfinders far out front, the Sky Ray is typically positioned behind the main battle line of Fire Warriors. From there it can provide an effective air defence while still being able to aid the infantry against ground targets. It is not unusual to find a Sky Ray as support for an Armoured Interdiction Cadre, although some septs prefer to field impressive Sky Shields – a trio of Sky Rays whose interlocking markerlights and extensive arsenal of missiles provides an umbrella of protection to the ground forces below.

'At Dar'nas, the gue'la generals thought to eliminate our Sky Ray formations in a massed tank assault, believing us vulnerable to attacks from the ground. We repaid their ignorance with a hailstorm of seeker missiles. Our gunship registered no less than seventeen confirmed armour kills in that engagement alone.'

- Shas'vre Yu'tan

XV25 STEALTH BATTLESUITS

Stealth Teams are special operations units that are the 'lone wolves' of the T'au armies, typically operating independently of the cadre. Theirs is a secretive way of war, as they infiltrate enemy lines, seeking vulnerable targets to destroy. In order to pass unseen into enemy territory, Stealth Teams use light-bending disruption technology embedded in their sleek battlesuits to camouflage themselves. Additional cloaking fields deaden sound and shield them from heat-detecting sensors, allowing them to penetrate deep into hostile regions before launching precisely timed ambushes. Suddenly appearing, as if stepping out from nowhere, a Stealth Team unleashes a hail of gunfire to cripple or eliminate their selected targets.

The key to Stealth Teams is the technology behind their XV25 Stealth battlesuits. Only slightly more bulky than the armour worn by Fire Warriors, these 'Stealth suits' have integral stealth field generators that project from nodes situated about the body armour. They surround their bearer with a distortion effect that plays havoc with a full spectrum of light and confounds other detection devices, allowing warriors wearing such armour to move untracked, blending in with their surrounding environment. Because it is hard to focus on their location, a Stealth Team can hide to at least some degree even when standing in open territory. In areas of cover, such as forests or the rubble of an embattled city, they can effectively fade into the background, making themselves extremely difficult targets for enemies to mark out or lock on to effectively.

Built of the same dense nanocrystalline alloy as the larger XV8 Crisis suits, the Stealth suit is equipped with a powerful burst cannon as standard. For added firepower, some teams upgrade specific members to carry a fusion blaster, as these short-ranged weapons are better for engaging heavily armoured targets or vehicles. If a shas'vre is present, he can bring additional equipment, such as a markerlight, drones or even a homing beacon to allow XV8 Crisis Teams to more accurately deploy. Some septs, most notably Tash'var, are known to employ Stealth Teams outfitted with Marker Drones. This is a tactic common against large Ork hordes, as the Stealth Teams use their burst cannons to thin the enemy numbers before painting them with markerlights, allowing the rest of the cadre to wipe them out. Once their ambush is sprung, Stealth Teams use their jet packs to make bounding leaps – moving either to acquire another target or to put obstacles in the way of any return fire.

Due to the nature of their covert role in battle, Stealth Teams enjoy a level of independence that is rare in T'au military operations. Observing comm-silence and unable to receive orders, Stealth Teams are typically left to make their own decisions. Those shas'ui who volunteer for such duty are seen as strange, an unpredictable lot who do not always follow convention – traits generally regarded with much suspicion in the well-regimented and highly structured culture of the T'au. Those who survive long enough to earn the title of shas'vre within the Stealth Teams are, without exception, noted as eccentrics, famous for their tactical innovations and daring raids deep behind enemy lines.

Many a foe of the T'au Empire has learned to be wary of the technologically blurred battlesuits that appear in their midst. During the Taros Campaign, roving Stealth Teams wreaked havoc within Imperial supply lines, sowing panic and confusion and sabotaging their advance before fading back into cover. Entire divisions of Imperial Guard were taken off the front lines in desperate attempts to hunt them down.

XV8 CRISIS BATTLESUITS

No single image represents T'au ingenuity and progress better than XV8 Crisis Battlesuits leaping into battle. Skimming across the battlefield on the jets of their repulsor engines, Crisis Battlesuits close rapidly with their foes. Though twice the size of a Fire Warrior, the speed and resilience of these suits is jaw-dropping; the powered leaps of their skilled pilots evade much of the fire hurled their way, while those shots that do connect simply ricochet from their dense nanocrystalline armour. Yet it is only when the Crisis suits open fire that their lethality is revealed. Multiple hard-points, integrated computational circuitry and recoil absorption buffers allow Crisis Battlesuits to mount diverse weapon and support systems, making them as versatile as they are deadly. Salvoes of missiles and fusion fire bring a swift end to enemy tanks, while with plasma rifles, burst cannons and flamers, the battlesuits exterminate enemy infantry.

The Crisis Battlesuit is far more than a weapon, however. It is a symbol of everything the Fire caste stands for, of wilful and incurable ignorance crushed by the potent combination of technological supremacy and martial skill.

Although the XV8 is by far the most commonly deployed battlesuit in the T'au armoury, only those warriors who have proven their worth are permitted to pilot them. A shas'la must serve four years on the line, fighting as part of a Strike or Breacher Team, before they can even be considered to pilot a battlesuit. Even then, the aspirant must pass their first Trial by Fire in order to earn the honour and secure the rank of shas'ui. Even amongst the Fire caste, known for its tight-knit fellowships, the bond shared by a Crisis Battlesuit Team is remarkably strong. They fight with a cohesion forged by decades of rigorous training and combat.

Crisis Battlesuits provide their pilot with the ultimate balance of firepower, speed and resilience. Able to deploy from the holds of super-heavy Manta dropships lurking in a planet's upper atmosphere, there are few missions at which Crisis Teams do not excel. Whether dropping in to counter an enemy breakthrough, falling upon their foes in the killing blow of a Mont'ka or Kauyon strategy, engaging in opportunist tank-hunting or encircling them in a lethal enfilade, the Crisis Teams are equal to the task.

New technological improvements, such as Iridium armour plating, are made to the Crisis Battlesuit all the time, yet its core aspect remains iconic and unchanged. The XV8 is the armoured embodiment of the T'au'va, its inspirational image blazoned on propaganda holo-vid from Fi'rios to Fal'shia, and even upon the distant worlds of the Farsight Enclaves.

XV88 BROADSIDE BATTLESUITS

Designed to offer long-range support, the XV88 Broadside Teams began as an experiment in blending the manoeuvrability of a ballistic battlesuit with the devastating firepower of a Hammerhead Gunship. After proving their effectiveness in multiples theatres of war, these hulking artillery suits have become mainstays of the Hunter Cadres and tank-killers of legendary proportions.

Powered by a particle accelerator, a Broadside's heavy rail rifle shot can penetrate the thickest plasteel bunkers, often doing so with enough force to punch an exit hole on the other side as well. While the weapon carried by the XV88 Broadside is not as massive as the railgun mounted on the Hammerhead, its range and destructive power are impressive nonetheless. In order to mount the heavy rail rifle on a battlesuit, Earth caste engineers had to modify the XV8 battlesuit. Due to the increased weight of its weapon system, the XV8's jet pack had to be removed, meaning the XV88 Broadside would trade mobility and manoeuvrability in favour of increased weapon power and range. In prototype production, it was quickly noticed that the new battlesuit could not avoid incoming fire, so further protective armour was added. Later modifications added stabilisers and recoil units to the XV88 Broadside suit, and recent Earth caste tinkering has moved the heavy rail rifles from a shoulder mount to a hand-held position.

Like all battlesuits, the XV88 Broadside is worn by a veteran, and can be upgraded with sophisticated support systems such as advanced targeting systems and stimulant injectors. Broadsides are deployed in teams of one to three and, unlike most T'au units, require a static firing position. Commanders have learned to deploy these long-ranged killers with care, for it takes valuable time for them to reposition, and while doing so, their main armament is far less accurate. The secondary weapon – a smart missile system – was chosen to make up for this shortcoming. Deadly in its own right, the smart missile system can fire off a barrage at any target within sensor range, even those in cover or hidden out of sight.

Those races that have faced the T'au in battle have grown to fear these heavily armoured battlesuits. During the Damocles Crusade, the XV88 Broadside was quickly identified by the Imperium as a major threat to armoured vehicles, whose soldiers learned to dread the whip-crack sound made by the hyper-sonic speed of a heavy rail rifle round; the distinct noise could only actually be heard after the shot had already hit home. In open terrain, like on Taros or the ice plains of Issenheim, a few Broadside Teams were sufficient to negate entire tank companies, quickly turning them into smoking wreckage. In the battles against the Tyranid Hive Fleet Gorgon, the XV88 Broadside Teams proved highly adaptive and effective in combating the larger alien creatures, especially after a refitting of their secondary weapons. The mounting of plasma rifles in place of smart missile systems made the battlesuits even more effective when confronting the gargantuan bio-titans of the Tyranids.

Another popular loadout for Broadside pilots is to replace the heavy rail rifle with high-yield missile pods. During the War of Confederation that took place at the time of the Second Sphere Expansion, it was discovered that the sheer density of attacking Ork waves and the light nature of their vehicles meant the heavy rail rifle, although deadly, could not stem the overwhelming tide of attackers. The high-yield missile pod sacrificed some range and hitting strength, but could lay down a greater barrage, and proved more than adequate to destroy the crude scrap-armoured Ork vehicles. Since then, many Commanders have often included this variant in their cadres, either on its own or sometimes in a formation with more traditionally armed Broadsides.

XV95 GHOSTKEEL BATTLESUITS

Huge, deadly and all but impossible to detect until it strikes, the XV95 Ghostkeel is amongst the most effective terror weapons in the galaxy. These mighty battlesuits loom several times the height of a Fire Warrior, and mount a full array of repulsor jets upon their carapace. They are equipped with an arsenal of heavy weaponry, and are supported by a wealth of high-tech hardware and counter-sensory warfare suites. Ghostkeel battlesuits can tear apart entire armoured squadrons and massacre rank upon rank of enemy infantry in sudden ambushes. The firestorm of their onslaught is such that the foe believes a whole army must be attacking them from an unexpected quarter.

Each Ghostkeel is piloted by a single highly trained shas'vre, a former XV25 Stealth Team veteran. This focused warrior is supported by an integrated AI that assists him in operating the Ghostkeel's many complex systems, and monitors his physical and psychological well-being during extended operations. As Ghostkeel pilots spend long periods of time isolated in enemy territory, many form unusually strong bonds with their battlesuit AI. Indeed, in some cases these eccentric warriors become so introverted that they prefer the company of their suit's AI to that of other members of their race.

The tactical applications of the Ghostkeel are many and varied, from unleashing overwhelming strikes behind enemy lines to ambush-hunting alongside Hunter Cadres. However, until recently, the Ghostkeel was restricted to covert missions only. In truth, development of these potent battlesuits was completed around the beginning of the Third Sphere Expansion, but it was decreed that these new weapons should remain hidden until their unveiling held the greatest inspirational value. Pilots were chosen from pre-vetted candidates who were extracted from Stealth Team operations and transported to a secret facility on J'ka'vo Station, on the fringes of the abandoned sept of N'dras. From there, following orders from Aun'Va himself, the first generation of Ghostkeel battlesuits performed a range of deep-cover operations, from the Vadenfall Station sabotage to the assassination of Carnidal Bocsh.

Towards the end of the expansion, the time was judged ripe to reveal the freshly renamed 'Ghosts of N'dras'. Suddenly, the insular band of warriors were thrust into the light, their existence changing from a secret to a propaganda exercise virtually overnight. Recruitment of Ghostkeel pilots across the empire is now well under way, as is production of the battlesuits themselves; the armies of almost every sept now possess Ghostkeel wings of their own.

XV104 RIPTIDE BATTLESUITS

The XV104 Riptide is a wonder of Earth caste engineering, a heavy battlesuit that can blast its way through tanks, formations of infantry and fortified positions while withstanding or evading formidable torrents of return fire. The Riptide stands twice as tall as an XV8 Crisis suit, but its movement is more akin to its smaller cousins than the stiff, servo-motored Imperial walkers that are comparable in size. While the Riptide is huge and bears a number of weapon and support systems, it is still a battlesuit – worn and controlled by a lone warrior, and capable of leaping nimbly out of the path of concentrated enemy fire before unleashing a devastating salvo of its own.

The Riptide's standard armament is the heavy burst cannon, a rapid-firing rotary gun that can chew through dozens of infantry soldiers with each staccato volley. Other Riptides are fitted with an ion accelerator, which fires a wide stream of volatile energy capable of rupturing the thickest armour-plating and tearing great chunks out of reinforced bunkers and fortress walls. A pair of smart missile systems, controlled by sophisticated targeting algorithms, allow the pilot of a Riptide to destroy targets hiding out of sight, though these can be replaced by plasma rifles or fusion blasters should further anti-armour punch be required.

Mobility is the XV104 Riptide's greatest defence, but it also possesses a powerful energy shield that incinerates incoming small-arms fire and turns aside kinetic impacts. During the war for Agrellan – which marked the debut of these advanced battlesuits – there were reports of Riptides being crushed under tonnes of rubble, only to blast their way free of the devastation moments later with their nova shields crackling and cannons blazing.

Production of the Riptide has proven slow; the materials for the dense nanocrystalline alloy armour are difficult to obtain, and the sheer volume required ensures that the XV104 is a rare commodity. As such, the honour of wearing such a powerful battlesuit is only given to the most highly decorated of warriors. To assist its wearer, the Riptide bears a sophisticated AI system – complete with a multi-tracker and numerous comm-links – and the battlesuit is often supported by a pair of MV84 Shielded Missile Drones, each equipped with a missile pod and shield generator.

Powering the Riptide is a nova reactor, an experimental piece of technology that fuses dark matter to produce energy on a scale closer to that of a small star than a conventional engine. Such devices have been utilised by the fleets of the Air caste for some time, but it was only recently that they could be reduced to a size suitable for a battlesuit. Although still in the prototype stage, the nova reactor has proven largely stable, despite some problems in safely releasing the vast energies it produces. The Riptide's higher functions can draw upon this almost unlimited source of power to overcharge its shield, jet-pack thrusters or weapons, but doing so is not without drawback. Pilots who tap these reserves suffer dangerous power vents, capable of crippling the battlesuit or even destroying it entirely, but what they gain in return – increased protection, better mobility or truly frightening destructive potential – could be enough to secure victory.

KV128 STORMSURGES

Towering colossi of destruction, KV128 Stormsurges carry the firepower to annihilate whole columns of tanks, or fell super-heavy walkers with a single earth-shaking volley. Rushed to the front of the escalating war against the Imperium, these mobile bastions have swiftly proved their worth against the numbers and heavy armour of the foe. Though ponderous, a single Stormsurge can alter the course of a battle in seconds. Its armoured resilience and phenomenal firepower make it equally lethal in attack or defence.

weapons so heavy they have previously only seen use on spacecraft.

The Stormsurge is operated by a carefully selected pairing of veteran Hammerhead crewmen, who have graduated through the ballistic suit academies on Bork'an. The prestige of operating a ballistic suit is not equal to that of donning the Hero's Mantle, but the steely eyed graduates of the so-called Ves'oni'vash – or 'giantmaker academy' – are honoured by the Fire Warriors for the countless lives they save.

Working as a seamless team, the crew operate their towering suit, one piloting the Stormsurge while the other monitors, aims, and fires its weapon systems.

In order to keep pace with the fluid strategies of the T'au, Stormsurges are mag-lifted into battle beneath specially modified Manta Missile Destroyers. Once deployed, the ballistic suit stomps into position and unleashes its incredible firepower, annihilating its designated targets before being lifted away once more.

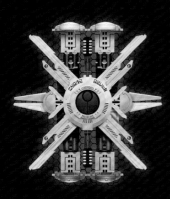

The Stormsurge is the first in a new breed of T'au super-heavy war assets known as ballistic suits. Developed by the noted Earth caste weapons scientist Fio'o Bork'an Ishu'ron, these massive bipedal weapon-platforms are an answer to the super-heavy war engines of their foes. O'Ishu'ron recognised that even heavy battlesuits and aircraft such as the railgun-equipped Tiger Shark AX-1-0 could be outgunned by the Imperium's Titan-class walkers. Furthermore, when the enemy deployed their mightiest war machines en masse – as was the case during the war for Dal'yth and the Great War of Confederation – all the railguns and seeker missiles in the empire could not prevent the Fire caste from sustaining heavy casualties. O'Ishu'ron, however, had a solution: the pinpoint application of overwhelming force.

Each KV128 is essentially an enormous walking gun-tower, whose purpose is to anchor the Fire caste battle line while laying down an insurmountable weight of covering fire. To this end, the ballistic suit is fitted with a secondary generator specifically to power its Titan-killing weaponry, and is regularly used as a platform to field-test experimental

TIDEWALL DEFENCE NETWORKS

In keeping with the tenets contained within the Code of Fire, the T'au make use of highly mobile fortifications known as Tidewalls. Borne aloft and propelled across the battlefield by carefully stabilised grav-repulsor engines, these self-contained redoubts can be used in both attack and defence, and avoid the main weaknesses of traditional strongholds by being in constant motion.

TIDEWALL SHIELDLINES

The most commonly seen fortification utilised by the forces of the T'au Empire is the Tidewall Shieldline, a wall of energy behind which infantry can take cover. As the enemy's fusillades hiss and crack harmlessly from the Shieldline's refractive field, the Fire Warriors it protects unleash a blistering hail of pulse fire in return. Worse still for any aggressor attempting to drive the T'au from cover, this force-wall can redirect kinetic energy, sending las-blasts and armour-piercing shells ricocheting back into the enemy ranks.

Even as a stationary defensive position the Tidewall Shieldline would excel, but it is its manoeuvrability and versatility that makes it so beloved amongst the T'au Empire's soldiery. The Shieldline can be redeployed at will, soaring into the air and carrying its teams of Fire Warriors along with it. This mobility can be used to fall back to another demarcated defensive position should the situation appear dire, but it also means that T'au Commanders can isolate and outflank enemy spearheads – luring them into expending their energy on a frontal assault before simply shifting the lines of battle around them and trapping them in a hellish corridor of enfilading fire.

Commander Shadowsun herself demonstrated the deadly efficacy of such tactics during the Battle for Prefectia, a key conflict of the Third Sphere Expansion. Facing the ferocious and swift assaults of the White Scars Space Marine Chapter, Shadowsun arranged a series of interlocking fire zones. The White Scars were lured in with the illusion of a traditional, static defence. When the Space Marines were entirely committed to their lightning attack, Shadowsun gave the order, and the criss-crossed lines of the T'au Shieldlines rose into the air on waves of anti-grav energy, and then reformed in firing lines on the flanks of the White Scars' force. Suddenly, far from being on the offensive, the Space Marines found themselves subjected to a searing storm of plasma fire. Similar tactics have been used to great effect during the long wars against the Orks, and the purging of Hive Fleet Gorgon.

TIDEWALL DRONEPORTS

Linking and supporting the T'au's fortified lines are Tidewall Droneports, mobile bunkers that carry an arsenal of Tactical Drones. These potent machines begin most battles powered down, passively downloading combat telemetry data from their parent platform while the Droneport's garrisoning Fire Warriors engage the enemy from behind its reinforced walls. However, at the command of the platform's controllers the drones detach, darting out to provide covering fire, marking targets for missile strikes or employing built-in shield generators to provide further protection to those manning the defences. Like the Shieldlines, these support bunkers can be rearranged to suit the ever-changing shape of the battlefield.

TIDEWALL GUNRIGS

With its in-built rail weaponry, the Tidewall Gunrig provides the firepower to deal with heavy enemy assault units or advancing ranks of armour. Manned by hard-eyed Fire Warriors, these mobile turrets mount devastating railguns that are more than capable of ripping apart enemy tanks or monstrous beasts with volleys of hyper-sonic rounds. The combination of manoeuvrability and tremendous firepower possessed by these weapon platforms makes them exceptionally dangerous. Whether hovering inexorably into battle with their guns blazing, backing slowly away from an enemy advance while systematically eliminating their heaviest armour, or rising from concealment to catch the foe in a lethal crossfire, Tidewall Gunrigs provide the T'au's defensive lines with an indispensable anti-armour punch.

When Tidewall Shieldlines, Droneports and Gunrigs are linked together, a truly formidable defence network can be created, against which enemy attacks break like crashing waves on unyielding rock. Safely shielded within their energised redoubts, the T'au's disciplined infantry can unleash the ferocious combined firepower of their pulse weaponry at will, cutting down the helpless foe with cool precision. Should enemy armour threaten to overwhelm their position, Gunrigs unleash a hail of hyper-sonic projectiles that punch

through inch-thick armour to superheat and explode their targets. Meanwhile, Tactical Drones will hover amidst the fray, providing indispensable fire support or shielding the Fire Warriors from incoming rounds. Even in the unlikely event that an enemy assault threatens to break through this fearsome obstacle, the entire array can be rearranged at will, falling back to set out a second killing zone that the enemy must conquer.

When several of these Tidewall defence networks deploy at once, they form a floating fortress, an unbreachable obstacle that dominates the battlefield and obliterates all in its path. At the colony world of Ghynera, T'au from Vior'la Sept held out for three solar spans in such a stronghold, while hordes of slavering Tyranids thrashed and died amidst their unrelenting hails of pulse fire. On Sygna VI, the human warriors of the Mordian 103rd regiment suffered a ninety-six per cent casualty rate when attempting to drive the T'au from their defence networks, despite heavily outnumbering their opponents.

Though the T'au still favour those tactics that involve their teams taking the fight to the enemy on the ground, more and more Commanders are embracing the power of Tidewall fortifications, creating entirely new strategies to take advantage of their unique and dynamic capabilities.

'The ultimate goal of any military technology is to multiply the combat effectiveness of those who utilise it. In this regard, the Tidewall network is perhaps our greatest achievement. A handful of Fire Warriors protected by such a fortification can hold back an enemy force many times their number.'

- Fio'vre Telu of Bork'an Sept

AX3 RAZORSHARK STRIKE FIGHTERS

To the Fire Warriors forming the front ranks of a firing line, there are few sights more gratifying than seeing a Razorshark Strike Fighter swoop out of the cloud cover and streak over enemy formations. Built along a design pattern modified from the Sun Shark Bomber, the Razorshark forgoes the Interceptor Drone in favour of additional manoeuvring thrusters, and it trades the pulse bomb generator for a fearsome quad ion turret. A formidable weapon, the quad ion turret is ideal for turning light vehicles into twisted wrecks. Although it makes the weapon slightly unstable, when fired on its overcharged mode, the quad ion turret can produce an enormous blast radius that consumes entire squads with a single shot.

During the Tyranid invasion on the sept world of Ke'lshan, the aliens quickly grew wary of the dominating T'au air attacks. High in the stratosphere, the super-heavy Manta blasted away the flying terrors, while just above the planet's surface swept the Sun Shark Bombers, their pulse bombs breaking up the swarming Hormagaunt attacks. While the T'au's entire aerial arsenal played a part, it was the Razorshark Strike Fighters that took the highest toll on their foe. Streaking back and forth over the battlefront, the Razorsharks relentlessly targeted the Tyranid Warriors, the beams from their quad ion turrets easily penetrating the Tyranids' thick, chitinous armour. After one of the Razorshark's attack runs, entire squads of the elite alien warriors would be left in ruin, their half-melted bodies continuing to sizzle long after their deaths. A fast-moving craft, the Razorshark was able to seek out and destroy the brains of the invasion – whether they attempted to lurk far behind the front lines, or chose to surround themselves with intervening lesser creatures, the Razorshark was manoeuvrable enough to hunt them down. When infiltrators such as Lictors or Raveners emerged to threaten the Fire Warriors, the Razorsharks could swiftly fly back to target the beasts, minimising both the harm and the distraction of such attacks.

The Razorshark Strike Fighter can engage enemy flyers, but the craft was purpose-built as a ground support attack craft; it is a role in which it excels. Its success is evident from the craft's ever-growing popularity with the Fire Warriors that it flies above. In addition to its main armament, each Razorshark is loaded out with a nose-mounted burst cannon. For further support, it also carries two seeker missiles. These can be auto-fired by the Razorshark's Air caste pilot himself, but are more effective when launched by a ground unit that has painted its target with a markerlight.

AX39 SUN SHARK BOMBERS

Due to their unique fighting tendencies and their highly mobile nature, Hunter Cadres do not use artillery in the conventional sense that most armies do. Instead, in association with the Air caste, they have developed the Sun Shark Bomber – a sleek atmospheric aircraft that is capable of sweeping down from the skies and blasting ground targets with its potent payload. Sun Sharks are apex predators of the skies, and the sight of a formation of these bombers soaring gracefully over the battlefield, rippling explosions trailing beneath them, is enough to strike terror into the enemies of the T'au Empire.

Sun Shark Bombers come equipped with a pulse bomb generator, which produces a ball of deadly plasma beneath the craft. At the pilot's command, the pulsed induction field propels the glaring energy ball towards targets on the battlefield below. Sizzling the air around it, the pulse bomb explodes on the ground with an incandescent fury, spreading destruction over a wide radius. A shoal of Sun Shark Bombers flying in tight formation can blast apart even the most surging of Ork Waaaghs! with a single flyover. An extremely effective weapon, once fired, the pulse bomb generator immediately begins to form another destructive charge.

The Sun Shark has also been equipped with several other weapons, including a pair of seeker missiles. Many a desperate Pathfinder or Fire Warrior Team owe their continued existence to those airborne seeker missiles, which they call in using their markerlights. Their ability to strike enemy vehicles or make short work of armoured infantry with the help of nearby air support greatly increases their chances for survival. The Sun Shark also bears a tail-mounted missile pod, and is often upgraded with a second, as well as a nose-mounted networked markerlight to line up bombing runs.

To ensure the Sun Shark survives long enough to deliver its bombing run, the vehicle is equipped with a pair of wing-mounted Interceptor Drones. Each armed with two powerful ion rifles, Interceptor Drones can either stay attached to the Sun Shark, where they act like turret-mounted weapons, or they can detach from the flyer and serve as an escort. When disembarking from the Sun Shark Bomber, the Interceptor Drones will often position themselves to intervene between the bomber and any oncoming fighters. They also have the ability to boost their jets, providing the Interceptor Drones with a speed unmatched by other drone types and allowing them to better position themselves to lock onto targets, whether in the sky or on the ground.

Few enemies are capable of withstanding the vaporising effects of the ion rifle, and some Interceptor Drones have racked up impressive kill totals; this is a continuing source of bragging rights for the Sun Shark's Air caste pilots, if not for the AI-powered drones themselves.

KROOT

Of all the different species integrated into the T'au Empire, the Kroot are by far the most common auxiliaries serving alongside the Fire caste, with many billions of their kind armed for war and assigned to the Hunter Cadres of nearly every sept. Although their primitive aggression is viewed with distaste by the T'au, such inherent savagery makes them particularly effective shock troops.

KROOT SHAPERS

Kroot mercenary kindreds are led by mysterious figures known as Shapers. It is their duty to negotiate contracts and coordinate strategies with employers, and this position affords them equipment more advanced than that of their brethren; in the case of those Shapers whose kindreds regularly fight alongside the T'au, they will often carry pulse rifles into combat instead of the primitive long-ranged weaponry used by the Carnivores they lead.

As well as leading Kroot warriors in battle, Shapers are believed to be responsible for their race's genetic development. It is said that Kroot can absorb some of the traits of other creatures when they consume their flesh, and as such, the war zones a Shaper chooses to commit his kindreds to, and the foes they face there, will guide their group down a particular evolutionary path.

KROOT CARNIVORES

Given free reign of the battlefield, Kroot Carnivores silently and stealthily creep into flanking positions, burying themselves deep in cover. There, unseen, they carefully level their long rifles, slowly taking aim and waiting for the perfect moment to launch their ambush. When the time is right and a vulnerable target presents itself, they unleash a devastating volley of fire. Only when the foe is whittled down and panicked do the Kroot emerge from their hiding places, closing the distance between themselves and their quarry with a bounding gait. Falling upon their startled prey, the Kroot savagely rip, hack and tear with knives, teeth and the blades strapped to their crude rifles in a display of primal savagery. It is then that they will feast upon the flesh of the fallen, a ritual act that has tremendous spiritual and physical significance to its participants.

KROOT SUBSPECIES

When the Kroot go to war, they often bring with them many of the strange subspecies of Kroot-like beings that are found near any sizable gathering of the aliens. Kroot Hounds, while notoriously bad-tempered, are particularly valued additions. These creatures can track quarry with their keen senses, while in combat they use their beak-like mouths to rip at the vulnerable underbellies of their prey. The Kroot themselves rarely chase a beaten enemy; instead, they release their hounds to run them to ground.

Another beast commonly found alongside Kroot troops is the lumbering Krootox, a hulking creature whose broad back serves as a mobile weapon platform. A heavy cannon-like gun is strapped to the Krootox and a Kroot warrior climbs aboard its mighty haunches to operate the weapon. Although not aggressive as a rule, the Krootox will fight ferociously to defend its comrades, whom the beast sees as herd brothers.

VESPID STINGWINGS

Once heard, the high-pitched hum of Vespid wings is an unforgettable noise, though few hear it and live to tell the tale; the sound is usually picked out just moments before the ominous lightning-crackle report of the neutron blaster releases its deadly charge. Vespids are a flying insectoid race that have joined the T'au Empire; their mobile units – known as Stingwings – fight as auxiliaries alongside the warriors of the Fire caste.

It is a strange to see the Vespids and the T'au allied together, for at first glance, they seem so radically different. The Vespids appear to hover and bob effortlessly in mid-air, their chitinous wings moving so quickly they are seen only as a blur. Although T'au of the Air caste once bore wings, they now rely upon technology to soar. Like the Fire Warriors, the Vespids are covered in segmented plate armour, but their protection is no engineering marvel, but rather a hardened exoskeleton. Where the Fire Warriors use a sophisticated comm-sensor attached to their helmets to supply an array of data, the Vespids rely on natural means – a pair of remarkably sensitive antennae constantly collecting information about their surroundings. Despite their obvious differences, both races are highly deferential to their leaders, obeying even their suggestions as if they were strict orders. While the T'au and Vespid races now share a tight relationship, such was not always the case.

When the Water caste first encountered the Vespids, they had many difficulties – the insectoid mindset seemed too radically different to grasp or reason with. However, at the instruction of the Ethereals, the Earth caste supplied a communication interface device that facilitated a much greater degree of understanding between the two races. More sophisticated versions were soon developed, including the communication-helms worn by the Vespid Strain Leaders, and these cleared the way for integration into the growing T'au Empire. Uniquely, at the time, the Vespids welcomed their new position in the empire and bowed before the pre-eminence of the Ethereals. The Vespids readily agreed to exchange auxiliary troops and regular harvests of the highly coveted crystals of the planet Vespid, for technological support and weapons upgrades. There have been whispers alluding to a hidden connection between the Vespids' calm acceptance of annexation and the interface helms given to their leaders, though no evidence to support such claims has ever been forthcoming.

The Vespid Stingwings are of great use in warfare due to their speed, their ability to navigate over rough terrain and the lethal nature of their weapons. The armament carried by the Stingwings is unique to Vespids. Mounted at the end of each gun's barrel is a highly energetic and unstable crystal harvested from the lowest levels of the Vespids' home world. The T'au have provided the Stingwings with the technology to mount these crystals on advanced neutron containment and projection systems, making them deadly weapons that are able to pass straight through enemy armour to damage flesh or fry inner circuitry. The weapons, however, only function in the hands of a Vespid, for the constant ultrasonic tone emitted by the vibrations of their wings perfectly modulates the energies contained within the crystals.

In battle, the Stingwings are most often integrated into fast-moving mobile cadres. There, the Vespids serve as flying reconnaissance, complementing the ground-based scouts of the Pathfinder Teams.

Some Commanders also use Stingwings to attack alongside their Crisis Teams, for the winged insectoids have the speed and manoeuvrability to keep up with agile T'au jet packs. It is a great compliment that all five castes wholly welcome the Vespid Stingwings, a level of acceptance that has not yet been paid to the more mercenary Kroot of Pech.

ARMIES OF EXPANSION

A T'au Empire force is a dynamic and imposing presence upon the tabletop, filled with sleek war machines and high-tech weaponry. The following pages contain examples of the vibrant colour schemes and armour patterns favoured by the septs.

Commander Shadowsun in her XV22 Stalker battlesuit, with MV52 Shield Drone and MV62 Command-link Drone

Commander Farsight wears an XV8 Crisis battlesuit in his own distinctive colours.

The bloated Death Guard, scions of the Daemon Primarch Mortarion, have trespassed upon a rightful colony of the T'au Empire, and a cadre of Vior'la's finest soldiers has been dispatched to eradicate them. Eager to see these irredeemable foes of the Greater Good scoured from T'au space, the aggressive warriors of Vior'la charge forward into battle, pulse weapons blazing.

A Tidewall Defence Network provides the soldiers of the Fire caste with a vital bastion against the super-swarms of Hive Fleet Leviathan. While the Tyranids crash against a wall of pulse fire, colossal battlesuits including Riptides and Ghostkeels unleash a ceaseless rain of high-explosive death into the chitinous mass of bodies.

MV4 Shield Drone

Vior'la Sept Commander in XV86 Coldstar Battlesuit with high-output burst cannon and missile pod

T'au Sept Crisis Shas'vre with flamer and missile pod

Vior'la Sept XV8 Crisis Shas'vre with burst cannon and target lock

Sa'cea Sept XV8 Crisis Shas'ui with burst cannon and plasma rifle

Farsight Enclaves XV8 Crisis Shas'vre with two fusion blasters

Ethereal Aun'Shi **Ethereal on Hover Drone** **Ethereal Aun'Va** **Ethereal Bodyguard**

XV25 Stealth Battlesuit in default dark colours **T'au Sept XV25 Stealth Battlesuit with burst cannon** **T'au'n Sept XV25 Stealth Battlesuit with burst cannon** **N'dras Sept XV25 Stealth Battlesuit with fusion blaster**

MV31 Pulse Accelerator Drone, which boosts the range of pulse weapons **MB3 Recon Drone, which can be mounted atop a Devilfish transport** **MV33 Grav-inhibitor Drone, which slows oncoming foes**

**T'au Sept
Cadre Fireblade**

**Au'taal Sept
Fire Warrior with
pulse rifle**

**D'yanoi Sept
Fire Warrior with
pulse carbine**

**Bork'an Sept
Fire Warrior with
pulse rifle**

**Ke'lshan Sept
Fire Warrior with
pulse rifle**

**Darkstrider, the
Shadow that Strikes**

**Vash'ya Sept Pathfinder
with Ion Rifle**

**T'au Sept Pathfinder
with pulse carbine**

**Tol'ku Sept Pathfinder
with rail rifle**

**Bork'an Sept Pathfinder
with rail rifle**

**Kroot Shaper with
Kroot rifle**

**Kroot Carnivore with
kroot rifle**

Kroot Hound

Krootox Rider on Krootox

**Vespid Strain Leader with neutron
blaster bearing T'au Sept markings**

**Vespids are equipped with neutron blasters and combat armour, and these bear the
colours and markings of the septs they have joined.**

Vior'la Sept XV95 Ghostkeel Battlesuit with
cyclic ion raker, fusion blasters and MV5 Stealth Drones

T'au Sept AX3 Razorshark Strike Fighter with burst
cannon, quad ion turret and seeker missiles

Amidst the shattered ruins of a Chaos-held world, an Optimised Stealth Cadre hunts for pockets of enemy resistance. Once the foe is
engaged, markerlight beacons are laid down and Sun Shark Bombers are summoned to clear the ground with a deafening, earth-
shaking series of precise bombing runs.

Vior'la Sept KV128 Stormsurge with pulse driver cannon, destroyer missiles, cluster rocket system, smart missile systems and airbursting fragmentation projectors

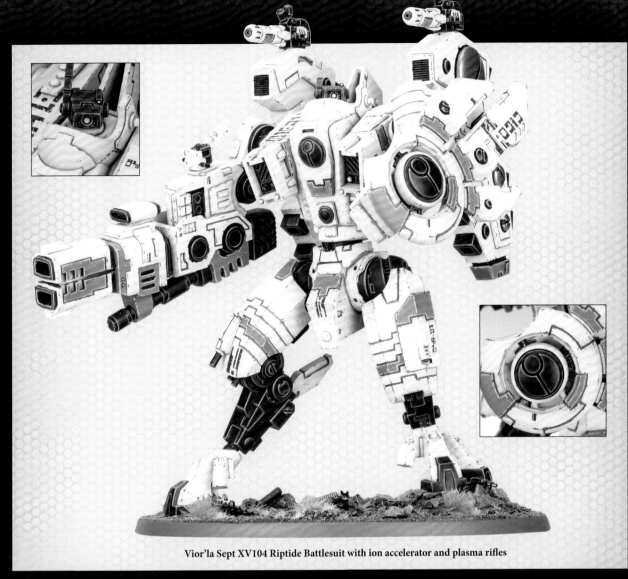

Vior'la Sept XV104 Riptide Battlesuit with ion accelerator and plasma rifles

Having claimed an Imperial hive city in the name of the Greater Good, a Hunter Cadre from Vior'la Sept prepares itself for the inevitable
counter-attack by the forces of Humanity, an enormous KV128 Stormsurge battlesuit the fulcrum of their formidable defensive line.

Longstrike, gunship ace

T'au Sept Hammerhead Gunship with railgun and burst cannons

Longstrike is regarded as the greatest gunship marksman in the T'au Empire. His unerringly accurate salvoes blast ragged holes in the enemy line, opening gaps for his fellow Hammerhead Gunship pilots to exploit.

CHAMPIONS OF UNITY

The T'au military doctrine emphasises speed, adaptability and superior firepower, and these values are exemplified in the starting army below. Though few in number, this strike force boasts formidable offensive capability.

Leading this force is an Ethereal on a hover drone. These serene figures are indispensable – not because of their offensive prowess, but because of their inspiring effect. In the presence of an Ethereal, T'au warriors will fight on through the most grievous wounds, shoot with fearsome accuracy, and show courage in the face of overwhelming odds.

The core of this group is a ten-man Breacher Team, expertly trained Fire Warriors armoured in high-tech composite armour and wielding pulse blasters, perhaps the most powerful standard issue weapons in the galaxy. Keeping the enemy at mid-to-close range, the Breacher Team will unleash blistering fusillades of pulse fire, shredding armour and blasting through thick hide to cut down their foes with ruthless skill.

With the enemy pinned, an XV8 Crisis Battlesuit Team will deliver the killing blow. Equipped with jet-thrusters and a range of heavy weaponry, these ballistic battlesuits leap gracefully into battle with guns blazing, and serve as iconic symbols of the T'au's military might and technological supremacy.

Consisting of one HQ, one Elites and one Troops choice, this collection fulfils the requirements of a Patrol Detachment as detailed in the *Warhammer 40,000* rulebook. As a Battle-forged army, this force gains access to three Command Points to spend on Stratagems.

Ethereal Aun'To and his elite retinue are an excellent starting force for any collection.

FOR THE GREATER GOOD!

Accompanied by his elite retinue, Ethereal Aun'To leads this Spearpoint Assault Cadre to battle, deploying sleek and deadly war machines, devastating ballistic battlesuits and hard-eyed warriors devoted to the T'au'va.

The Spearpoint Assault Cadre is designed to strike hard and fast at the heart of the foe, eliminating command positions and outflanking vulnerable formations. To whit, it is organised around a formidable core of Fire Warriors. Two Breacher Teams epitomise the Vior'la Sept way of war – these aggressive warriors close with the enemy before unleashing close-range volleys from their pulse blasters. A Strike Team provides a stable base of fire, deploying alongside a Sniper Drone Team to pick off targets at range. Should the Fire Warriors need to fall back or defend against a heavy enemy onslaught, they can retreat to the formidable bastion of a Tidewall Gunrig. A TX4 Piranha offers swift reconnaissance and covering fire, and a TY7 Devilfish transport guides infantry teams

safely to their destination while laying down a vicious hail of fire from its prodigious arsenal.

Commander O'Dren studies the flow of battle with the aid of extensive tactical-network feedback built into his Enforcer battlesuit, leading his Crisis Bodyguard Team into the thickest of the fighting. Alongside an XV8 Crisis Team, these warriors are the elite fighters of the Spearpoint Assault Cadre.

Dominating the skies above the battlefield are two AX3 Razorshark Strike Fighters. These swift and sleek hunter-killer aircraft are equally adept at blasting enemy pilots out of the sky and strafing

enemy troops with their rapid-fire burst cannons. Accompanying these fighters is a Sun Shark Bomber, which carries a payload of pulse bombs capable of levelling entire armoured columns.

Speed and manoeuvrability are potent weapons, but the true might of the Spearpoint Assault Cadre lies in its formidable complement of heavy armour. The gigantic form of an XV104 Riptide Battlesuit stalks the front lines, while a Hammerhead Gunship soars gracefully over the battlefield, blasting enemy tanks into piles of melting slag. An XV88 Broadside Battlesuit adds an extra volley of armour-piercing firepower.

This main body of this army fulfils the requirements of a Battalion Detachment, awarding its owner three extra Command Points on top of the three awarded for fielding a Battle-forged force. The three Flyers remaining can be taken as an Air Wing Detachment, adding one more Command Point for an impressive total of seven.

1. **Ethereal Aun'To** on hover drone
2. **XV88 Broadside Battlesuit Shas'ui D'mos**
3. **Strike Team Dawnrunner**
4. **Breacher Team Firetide**
5. **Breacher Team Starlance**
6. **Commander O'Dren**
7. **XV8 Crisis Bodyguards Starseekers**
8. **XV8 Crisis Battlesuits Skybreakers**
9. **XV104 Riptide Shas'vre K'oryn**
10. **MV71 Sniper Drones Vigil**
11. **TX7 Piranha** *Wind Runner*
12. **Hammerhead Gunship** *Flame of Unity*
13. **TY7 Devilfish** *Blue Void*
14. **AX39 Sun Shark Bomber** *Peacemaker*
15. **AX3 Razorshark Strike Fighter** *Blue Flame*
16. **AX3 Razorshark Strike Fighter** *Zephyr*

FORCES OF THE T'AU EMPIRE

This section contains all of the datasheets that you will need to fight battles with your T'au Empire miniatures, and the rules for all of the weapons they can wield in battle. Each datasheet includes the characteristics profiles of the unit it describes, as well as any wargear and special abilities it may have. Any abilities that are common to several units are described below and referenced on the datasheets themselves.

KEYWORDS

Throughout this section you will come across a keyword that is within angular brackets, specifically <Sept>. This is shorthand for a keyword of your own choosing, as described below.

<Septs>

All T'au belong to a sept world, or hail from the breakaway Farsight Enclaves.

Some datasheets specify what sept the unit is drawn from (e.g. Commander Shadowsun has the T'au Sept keyword, so is from the T'au Sept, while Commander Farsight has the Farsight Enclaves keyword, so is from the Farsight Enclaves). If a T'au Empire datasheet does not specify which sept it is drawn from, it will have the <Sept> keyword. When you include such a unit in your army, you must nominate which sept that unit is from (or nominate that unit to be from the Farsight Enclaves). You then simply replace the <Sept> keyword on that unit's datasheet with the name of your chosen sept, or the words 'Farsight Enclaves'. You can use any of the septs that you have read about, or make up your own.

For example, if you were to include a Cadre Fireblade in your army, and you decided they were from the Vior'la Sept, their <Sept> Faction keyword is changed to Vior'la Sept and their 'Volley Fire' ability would then say 'Models in Vior'la Sept units within 6" of any friendly Vior'la Sept Cadre Fireblades may fire an extra shot with pulse pistols, pulse carbines and pulse rifles when shooting at a target within half the weapon's range.'

Note that the T'au of the Enclaves reject the dominion of the Ethereal Caste, and as such Ethereals may not be drawn from the Farsight Enclaves.

ACCOMPANYING DRONES

Many T'au Empire datasheets allow units to be accompanied by Drones. In such instances, unless stated otherwise, all wargear options only apply to the unit that is being accompanied by Drones, and not to the Drones themselves. After deployment, units of accompanying Drones are treated as having the Battlefield Role of the unit they accompany, and are considered to have a Power Rating of 0.

Tactical Drones accompanying units use their own datasheet (pg 109), while profiles, wargear, abilities and keywords for other types of accompanying Drones can be found on their parent unit's datasheet.

'We wield the latest advancements in pulse technology and high-yield munitions. Our tactics are devised and refined by the greatest military minds in the galaxy. And yet, it is our unwavering belief that the galaxy can be saved from itself that is our greatest weapon.'

- Shas'o Vas'kor, Sa'cea Sept

ABILITIES

The following abilities are common to several **T'AU EMPIRE** units:

FOR THE GREATER GOOD

The greatest proof of the superiority of the T'au'va is the sight of a hundred pulse rifles firing in unison.

When an enemy unit declares a charge, a unit with this ability that is within 6" of one of the charging unit's targets may fire Overwatch as if they were also targeted. A unit that does so cannot fire Overwatch again in this turn.

MASTER OF WAR

The academies of the Fire caste produce peerless strategists, true masters of the battlefield.

Once per battle, at the beginning of your turn, a single **COMMANDER** from your army can declare either Kauyon or Mont'ka:

Kauyon: Until the end of the turn, you can re-roll failed hit rolls for friendly <**SEPT**> units within 6" of the **COMMANDER**, but these units cannot move for any reason.

Mont'ka: Friendly <**SEPT**> units within 6" of the **COMMANDER** can both Advance and shoot as if they hadn't moved this turn.

Unless stated otherwise, you can only use the Master of War ability once per battle, irrespective of how many models in your army have this ability.

T'AU EMPIRE WARGEAR LISTS

Many of the units you will find on the following pages reference one or both of the following wargear lists (e.g. Ranged Weapons). When this is the case, the unit may take any item from the appropriate list below. The rules for the items in these lists can be found in the Arsenal of the Empire section (pg 121-123).

RANGED WEAPONS

- Airbursting fragmentation projector
- Burst cannon
- Cyclic ion blaster*
- Flamer
- Fusion blaster
- Missile pod
- Plasma rifle

*Cannot be taken by a Commander in XV86 Coldstar Battlesuit.

SUPPORT SYSTEMS

- Advanced targeting system
- Counterfire defence system
- Drone controller
- Early warning override
- Multi-tracker
- Shield generator
- Target lock
- Velocity tracker

COMMANDER SHADOWSUN

NAME	M	WS	BS	S	T	W	A	Ld	Sv
Commander Shadowsun	8"	3+	2+	4	4	5	4	9	3+
MV52 Shield Drone	8"	5+	5+	3	4	1	1	6	4+
MV62 Command-link Drone	8"	5+	5+	3	4	1	1	6	4+

Commander Shadowsun is a single model equipped with two fusion blasters. She may be accompanied by up to 3 Command Drones (**Power Rating +1**): up to 1 MV62 Command-link Drone and up to 2 MV52 Shield Drones. Only one of this unit can be included in your army.

WEAPON	RANGE	TYPE	S	AP	D	ABILITIES
Fusion blaster	18"	Assault 1	8	-4	D6	If the target is within half range of this weapon, roll two dice when inflicting damage with it and discard the lowest result.

ABILITIES (SHADOWSUN)	For the Greater Good, Master of War (pg 89) **Genius of Kauyon:** Once per battle, Commander Shadowsun can declare Kauyon even if Kauyon or Mont'ka has already been declared. Mont'ka and Kauyon cannot both be declared in the same turn. **XV22 Stalker Battlesuit:** Commander Shadowsun has a 5+ invulnerable save. **Camouflage Fields:** Your opponent must subtract 1 from hit rolls that target Commander Shadowsun or her accompanying Command Drones.	**Defender of the Greater Good:** Roll a D6 each time Shadowsun loses a wound whilst she is within 3" of a friendly unit of XV25 Stealth Battlesuits. On a 2+, a model from that unit can intercept that hit – Shadowsun does not lose a wound but that unit suffers a mortal wound. **Infiltrator:** During deployment, Commander Shadowsun and any accompanying Drones can be set up anywhere on the battlefield that is not within your opponent's deployment zone and is more than 12" away from any enemy unit.
ABILITIES (COMMAND DRONES)	For the Greater Good (pg 89) **MV52 Shield Generator:** MV52 Shield Drones have a 3+ invulnerable save. In addition, roll a D6 each time a **Drone** with this ability loses a wound; on a 5+ that Drone does not lose a wound. **Command-link:** If a friendly Command-link Drone is within 3" of Commander Shadowsun at the start of your Shooting phase, nominate a single friendly **T'au Empire** unit within 12" of the Drone. Re-roll hit rolls of 1 for that unit until the end of the phase.	**Drone Support:** When a unit is set up on the battlefield, any accompanying Drones are set up in unit coherency with it. From that point onwards, the Drones are treated as a separate unit. **Saviour Protocols:** If a <Sept> Infantry or <Sept> Battlesuit unit within 3" of a friendly <Sept> Drones unit is wounded by an enemy attack, roll a D6. On a 2+ you can allocate that wound to the Drones unit instead of the target. If you do, that Drones unit suffers a mortal wound instead of the normal damage.

FACTION KEYWORDS	T'au Empire, T'au Sept
KEYWORDS (SHADOWSUN)	Infantry, Battlesuit, Character, Commander, XV22 Stalker, Jet Pack, Fly, Shadowsun
KEYWORDS (COMMAND DRONES)	Drone, Fly, Command Drones

COMMANDER FARSIGHT

NAME	M	WS	BS	S	T	W	A	Ld	Sv
Commander Farsight	8"	2+	2+	5	5	6	4	9	3+

Commander Farsight is a single model equipped with a high-intensity plasma rifle and the Dawn Blade. Only one of this model can be included in your army.

WEAPON	RANGE	TYPE	S	AP	D	ABILITIES
High-intensity plasma rifle	30"	Rapid Fire 1	6	-4	2	-
Dawn Blade	Melee	Melee	+3	-4	D3	-

ABILITIES	For the Greater Good, Master of War (pg 89)	Manta Strike: During deployment, you can set up Commander Farsight in a Manta hold instead of placing him on the battlefield. At the end of any of your Movement phases he can use a Manta strike to enter the fray – set him up anywhere on the battlefield that is more than 9" from any enemy models.
	Genius of Mont'ka: Once per battle, Commander Farsight can declare Mont'ka even if Kauyon or Mont'ka has already been declared. Mont'ka and Kauyon cannot both be declared in the same turn.	
	Way of the Short Blade: You can re-roll hit rolls of 1 for friendly FARSIGHT ENCLAVES units within 6" of Commander Farsight in the Fight phase (or any phase if the target is an ORK unit).	Shield Generator: Commander Farsight has a 4+ invulnerable save.
FACTION KEYWORDS	T'AU EMPIRE, FARSIGHT ENCLAVES	
KEYWORDS	BATTLESUIT, CHARACTER, COMMANDER, JET PACK, FLY, FARSIGHT	

To some, Commander Farsight is a hero – to others, a pariah. Yet none can deny his strategic and martial brilliance.

COMMANDER
IN XV8 CRISIS BATTLESUIT

NAME	M	WS	BS	S	T	W	A	Ld	Sv
Commander in XV8 Crisis Battlesuit	8"	3+	2+	5	5	5	4	9	3+

A Commander in XV8 Crisis Battlesuit is a single model equipped with a burst cannon and missile pod. It may be accompanied by up to 2 Tactical Drones (pg 109) **(Power Rating +1)**.

WEAPON	RANGE	TYPE	S	AP	D	ABILITIES
Burst cannon	18"	Assault 4	5	0	1	-
Missile pod	36"	Assault 2	7	-1	D3	-

WARGEAR OPTIONS	• This model may replace its burst cannon and missile pod with two items from the *Ranged Weapons* and/or *Support Systems* lists. • This model may take two additional items from the *Ranged Weapons* and/or *Support Systems* lists. • This model may take an XV8-02 Crisis Iridium Battlesuit, increasing its Save characteristic to 2+.
ABILITIES	**For the Greater Good, Master of War** (pg 89) **Manta Strike:** During deployment, you can set up this model and any accompanying Drones in a Manta hold instead of placing them on the battlefield. At the end of any of your Movement phases, they can use a Manta strike to enter the fray – set them up anywhere on the battlefield that is more than 9" from any enemy models.
FACTION KEYWORDS	T'AU EMPIRE, <SEPT>
KEYWORDS	BATTLESUIT, CHARACTER, XV8 CRISIS, JET PACK, FLY, COMMANDER

COMMANDER
IN XV85 ENFORCER BATTLESUIT

NAME	M	WS	BS	S	T	W	A	Ld	Sv
Commander in XV85 Enforcer Battlesuit	8"	3+	2+	5	5	6	4	9	3+

A Commander in XV85 Enforcer Battlesuit is a single model equipped with a burst cannon and missile pod. It may be accompanied by up to 2 Tactical Drones (pg 109) **(Power Rating +1)**.

WEAPON	RANGE	TYPE	S	AP	D	ABILITIES
Burst cannon	18"	Assault 4	5	0	1	-
Missile pod	36"	Assault 2	7	-1	D3	-

WARGEAR OPTIONS	• This model may replace its burst cannon and missile pod with two items from the *Ranged Weapons* and/or *Support Systems* lists. • This model may take two additional items from the *Ranged Weapons* and/or *Support Systems* lists.
ABILITIES	**For the Greater Good, Master of War** (pg 89) **Manta Strike:** During deployment, you can set up this model and any accompanying Drones in a Manta hold instead of placing them on the battlefield. At the end of any of your Movement phases, they can use a Manta strike to enter the fray – set them up anywhere on the battlefield that is more than 9" from any enemy models.
FACTION KEYWORDS	T'AU EMPIRE, <SEPT>
KEYWORDS	BATTLESUIT, CHARACTER, XV85 ENFORCER, JET PACK, FLY, COMMANDER

POWER

COMMANDER
IN XV86 COLDSTAR BATTLESUIT

NAME	M	WS	BS	S	T	W	A	Ld	Sv
Commander in XV86 Coldstar Battlesuit	20"	3+	2+	5	5	6	4	9	3+

A Commander in XV86 Coldstar Battlesuit is a single model equipped with a high-output burst cannon and missile pod. It may be accompanied by up to 2 Tactical Drones (pg 109) **(Power Rating +1)**.

WEAPON	RANGE	TYPE	S	AP	D	ABILITIES
High-output burst cannon	18"	Assault 8	5	0	1	-
Missile pod	36"	Assault 2	7	-1	D3	-

WARGEAR OPTIONS	<ul><li>This model may replace its high-output burst cannon and/or missile pod with two items from the *Ranged Weapons* and/or *Support Systems* lists.</li><li>This model may take two additional items from the *Ranged Weapons* and/or *Support Systems* lists.</li></ul>

ABILITIES	**For the Greater Good, Master of War** (pg 89) **Coldstar:** When this model Advances, add 20" to its Move characteristic for that Movement phase instead of rolling a D6.	**Manta Strike:** During deployment, you can set up this model and any accompanying Drones in a Manta hold instead of placing them on the battlefield. At the end of any of your Movement phases, they can use a Manta strike to enter the fray – set them up anywhere on the battlefield that is more than 9" from any enemy models.

FACTION KEYWORDS	T'AU EMPIRE, <SEPT>

KEYWORDS	BATTLESUIT, CHARACTER, XV86 COLDSTAR, JET PACK, FLY, COMMANDER

Equipped with vectored thrusters and a devastating burst cannon, the Coldstar battlesuit is optimised for high-velocity aerial warfare.

AUN'VA

NAME	M	WS	BS	S	T	W	A	Ld	Sv
Aun'Va	6"	6+	4+	2	3	6	1	9	5+
Ethereal Guard	6"	3+	3+	3	3	2	3	9	5+

This unit contains Aun'Va and two Ethereal Guards. The Ethereal Guards are each armed with an honour blade. Only one of this unit can be included in your army.

WEAPON	RANGE	TYPE	S	AP	D	ABILITIES
Honour blade	Melee	Melee	+2	0	1	-

ABILITIES		
	Failure Is Not An Option: T'AU EMPIRE units within 6" of a friendly ETHEREAL may use the Ethereal's Leadership characteristic instead of their own when taking Morale tests. **Paradox of Duality:** When this unit is attacked during the Shooting phase, it may add, rather than subtract, the AP of the attack to its Save characteristic (e.g. an AP -1 attack would provide a +1 bonus to its saves). **Supreme Loyalty:** Whilst Aun'Va is on the battlefield, you can re-roll Morale tests for all friendly T'AU EMPIRE units.	**Grand Invocation of the Elements:** In your Movement phase, Aun'Va may invoke up to two elemental powers. All friendly T'AU EMPIRE INFANTRY and BATTLESUIT units within 6" of the model invoking an elemental power gain the relevant benefit until the start of your next turn. A unit can only be affected by the same elemental power once per battle round. • **Calm of Tides:** Subtract 1 from any Morale tests made for affected units. • **Storm of Fire:** Re-roll hit rolls of 1 in the Shooting phase for affected units that remain stationary in the Movement phase. • **Sense of Stone:** Whenever a model in an affected unit loses a wound, roll a D6; on a 6, that model does not lose that wound. • **Zephyr's Grace:** You can re-roll the dice for affected units when they Advance.

FACTION KEYWORDS	T'AU EMPIRE, T'AU SEPT
KEYWORDS (AUN'VA)	CHARACTER, INFANTRY, ETHEREAL, AUN'VA
KEYWORDS (ETHEREAL GUARD)	INFANTRY, ETHEREAL GUARD

AUN'SHI

NAME	M	WS	BS	S	T	W	A	Ld	Sv
Aun'Shi	6"	2+	4+	3	3	5	5	9	-

Aun'Shi is a single model armed with an honour blade. Only one of this model can be included in your army.

WEAPON	RANGE	TYPE	S	AP	D	ABILITIES
Honour blade	Melee	Melee	+2	0	1	-

ABILITIES		
	Failure Is Not An Option: T'AU EMPIRE units within 6" of a friendly ETHEREAL may use the Ethereal's Leadership characteristic instead of their own when taking Morale tests. **Shield Generator:** Aun'Shi has a 4+ invulnerable save. **Blademaster:** At the beginning of each Fight phase, choose one of the following effects to last until the end of the phase: • Aun'Shi's close combat attacks have AP -2. • Re-roll failed invulnerable saves for Aun'Shi.	**Invocation of the Elements:** In your Movement phase, Aun'Shi may invoke one of the elemental powers below. All friendly T'AU EMPIRE INFANTRY and BATTLESUIT units within 6" of the model invoking an elemental power gain the relevant benefit until the start of your next turn. A unit can only be affected by the same elemental power once per battle round. • **Calm of Tides:** Subtract 1 from any Morale tests made for affected units. • **Storm of Fire:** Re-roll hit rolls of 1 in the Shooting phase for affected units that remain stationary in the Movement phase. • **Sense of Stone:** Whenever a model in an affected unit loses a wound, roll a D6; on a 6, that model does not lose that wound. • **Zephyr's Grace:** You can re-roll the dice for affected units when they Advance.

FACTION KEYWORDS	T'AU EMPIRE, VIOR'LA SEPT
KEYWORDS	CHARACTER, INFANTRY, ETHEREAL, AUN'SHI

Serene and wise, and unflinching in battle, the T'au Ethereals are the living embodiment of the Greater Good.

ETHEREAL

NAME	M	WS	BS	S	T	W	A	Ld	Sv
Ethereal	6"	3+	4+	3	3	4	3	9	5+

An Ethereal is a single model armed with an honour blade. It may be accompanied by up to 2 Tactical Drones (pg 109) (**Power Rating +1**).

WEAPON	RANGE	TYPE	S	AP	D	ABILITIES
Equalizers	Melee	Melee	User	-1	1	A model armed with equalizers increases its Attacks characteristic by 1.
Honour blade	Melee	Melee	+2	0	1	-

WARGEAR OPTIONS	• This model may replace its honour blade with equalizers. • This model may take a hover drone, increasing its Move characteristic to 8" and giving it the **JET PACK** and **FLY** keywords (**Power Rating +1**).
ABILITIES	**Failure Is Not An Option:** T'AU EMPIRE units within 6" of a friendly ETHEREAL may use the Ethereal's Leadership characteristic instead of their own when taking Morale tests. **Invocation of the Elements:** In your Movement phase, an ETHEREAL may invoke one of the elemental powers below. All friendly T'AU EMPIRE INFANTRY and BATTLESUIT units within 6" of the model invoking an elemental power gain the relevant benefit until the start of your next turn. A unit can only be affected by the same elemental power once per battle round. • **Calm of Tides:** Subtract 1 from any Morale tests made for affected units. • **Storm of Fire:** Re-roll hit rolls of 1 in the Shooting phase for affected units that remain stationary in the Movement phase. • **Sense of Stone:** Whenever a model in an affected unit loses a wound, roll a D6; on a 6, that model does not lose that wound. • **Zephyr's Grace:** You can re-roll the dice for affected units when they Advance.
FACTION KEYWORDS	T'AU EMPIRE, <SEPT>
KEYWORDS	CHARACTER, INFANTRY, ETHEREAL

CADRE FIREBLADE

NAME	M	WS	BS	S	T	W	A	Ld	Sv
Cadre Fireblade	6"	3+	2+	3	3	5	3	8	4+

A Cadre Fireblade is a single model armed with a markerlight, pulse rifle and photon grenades. It may be accompanied by up to 2 Tactical Drones (pg 109) (**Power Rating +1**).

WEAPON	RANGE	TYPE	S	AP	D	ABILITIES
Markerlight	36"	Heavy 1	-	-	-	Markerlights (pg 123)
Pulse rifle	30"	Rapid Fire 1	5	0	1	-
Photon grenade	12"	Grenade D6	-	-	-	This weapon does not inflict any damage. Your opponent must subtract 1 from any hit rolls made for **INFANTRY** units that have suffered any hits from photon grenades until the end of the turn.

ABILITIES	For the Greater Good (pg 89)
	Volley Fire: Models in <SEPT> units within 6" of any friendly <SEPT> Cadre Fireblades may fire an extra shot with pulse pistols, pulse carbines and pulse rifles when shooting at a target within half the weapon's range.

FACTION KEYWORDS	T'AU EMPIRE, <SEPT>

KEYWORDS	CHARACTER, INFANTRY, CADRE FIREBLADE

DARKSTRIDER

NAME	M	WS	BS	S	T	W	A	Ld	Sv
Darkstrider	7"	3+	2+	3	3	5	3	8	5+

Darkstrider is a single model armed with a markerlight, pulse carbine and photon grenades. Only one of this model may be included in your army.

WEAPON	RANGE	TYPE	S	AP	D	ABILITIES
Markerlight	36"	Heavy 1	-	-	-	Markerlights (pg 123)
Pulse carbine	18"	Assault 2	5	0	1	-
Photon grenade	12"	Grenade D6	-	-	-	This weapon does not inflict any damage. Your opponent must subtract 1 from any hit rolls made for **INFANTRY** units that have suffered any hits from photon grenades until the end of the turn.

ABILITIES	For the Greater Good (pg 89)
	Structural Analyser: In your Shooting phase, pick a friendly **T'AU SEPT INFANTRY** unit within 6" of Darkstrider, and pick an enemy unit that is visible to Darkstrider. Until the end of the phase, add 1 to wound rolls made for the friendly **T'AU SEPT INFANTRY** unit's attacks that target the enemy unit you picked.
	Vanguard: At the start of the first battle round but before the first turn begins, you can move Darkstrider up to 7". He cannot end this move within 9" of any enemy models. If both players have units that are able to move at the start of the first battle round but before the first turn begins, the player who is taking the first turn moves their units first.
	Fighting Retreat: Friendly **T'AU SEPT INFANTRY** units within 6" of Darkstrider in the Shooting phase may attack with ranged weapons even if they Fell Back this turn.

FACTION KEYWORDS	T'AU EMPIRE, T'AU SEPT

KEYWORDS	CHARACTER, INFANTRY, DARKSTRIDER

LONGSTRIKE

DAMAGE
Some of this model's characteristics change as it suffers damage, as shown below:

REMAINING W	M	BS	A
7-13+	12"	2+	3
4-6	6"	3+	D3
1-3	3"	4+	1

NAME	M	WS	BS	S	T	W	A	Ld	Sv
Longstrike's Gunship	∗	6+	∗	6	7	13	∗	8	3+
MV1 Gun Drone	8"	5+	5+	3	4	1	1	6	4+

Longstrike's Gunship is a single model equipped with a railgun. It is accompanied by 2 MV1 Gun Drones, each equipped with two pulse carbines. Only one of this unit can be included in your army.

WEAPON	RANGE	TYPE	S	AP	D	ABILITIES
Burst cannon	18"	Assault 4	5	0	1	-
Ion cannon	When attacking with this weapon, choose one of the profiles below.					
- Standard	60"	Heavy 3	7	-2	2	
- Overcharge	60"	Heavy D6	8	-2	3	If you roll one or more hit rolls of 1, the bearer suffers a mortal wound after all of this weapon's shots have been resolved.
Pulse carbine	18"	Assault 2	5	0	1	-
Railgun	When attacking with this weapon, choose one of the profiles below.					
- Solid shot	72"	Heavy 1	10	-4	D6	Each time you make a wound roll of 6+ for this weapon, the target unit suffers D3 mortal wounds in addition to the normal damage.
- Submunitions	72"	Heavy D6	6	-1	1	-
Seeker missile	72"	Heavy 1	8	-2	D6	Each seeker missile can only be used once per battle. This weapon only hits on a roll of 6, regardless of the firing model's Ballistic Skill or any modifiers.
Smart missile system	30"	Heavy 4	5	0	1	This weapon can be fired at units that are not visible to the bearer. Units attacked by this weapon do not gain any bonus to their saving throws for being in cover.

WARGEAR OPTIONS	• Longstrike's Gunship may replace its railgun with an ion cannon. • Longstrike's Gunship may take up to two seeker missiles. • Instead of being accompanied by two MV1 Gun Drones, Longstrike's Gunship may take two burst cannons or two smart missile systems.

ABILITIES (LONGSTRIKE)	**For the Greater Good** (pg 89) **Attached Drones:** When Longstrike's Gunship is set up, any accompanying Gun Drones are attached, and are treated as being embarked. Whilst the Drones remain attached, Longstrike's Gunship is considered to be equipped with their weapons in addition to its own. **Tank Ace:** You can add 1 to wound rolls for Longstrike's Gunship when it shoots at a **VEHICLE** or **MONSTER**. **Hover Tank:** Instead of measuring distances to and from Longstrike's Gunship's base, measure to and from Longstrike's Gunship's hull or base (whichever is closer).	**XV02 Battlesuit:** Longstrike's Gunship treats the number of markerlight counters on an enemy unit affected by the Markerlights ability as being 1 higher. **Explodes:** If Longstrike's Gunship is reduced to 0 wounds, roll a D6 before removing it from the battlefield and before any embarked models disembark. On a 6 it explodes, and each unit within 6" suffers D3 mortal wounds. **Fire Caste Exemplar:** You can add 1 to hit rolls in the Shooting phase for friendly **T'AU SEPT HAMMERHEAD GUNSHIPS** within 6" of Longstrike's Gunship.

ABILITIES (GUN DRONES)	**For the Greater Good** (pg 89) **Saviour Protocols:** If a <SEPT> INFANTRY or <SEPT> BATTLESUIT unit within 3" of a friendly <SEPT> DRONES unit is wounded by an enemy attack, roll a D6. On a 2+ you can allocate that wound to the Drones unit instead of the target. If you do, that Drones unit suffers a mortal wound instead of the normal damage.	**Detach:** Both Gun Drones can detach at the start of your Movement phase by disembarking as if from a transport. From that point onwards, they are treated as a separate unit. They cannot reattach during the battle. **Threat Identification Protocols:** In the Shooting phase, Gun Drones can only target the nearest visible enemy unit. If two units are equally close, you can choose which is targeted.

FACTION KEYWORDS	T'AU EMPIRE, T'AU SEPT
KEYWORDS (LONGSTRIKE)	CHARACTER, VEHICLE, TX7 HAMMERHEAD GUNSHIP, FLY, LONGSTRIKE
KEYWORDS (GUN DRONES)	DRONE, FLY, GUN DRONES

BREACHER TEAM

NAME	M	WS	BS	S	T	W	A	Ld	Sv
Fire Warrior	6"	5+	4+	3	3	1	1	6	4+
Fire Warrior Shas'ui	6"	5+	4+	3	3	1	2	7	4+
DS8 Tactical Support Turret	-	-	4+	3	3	1	0	4	4+
MV36 Guardian Drone	8"	5+	5+	3	4	1	1	6	4+

This unit contains 5 Fire Warriors. It can include up to 5 additional Fire Warriors (**Power Rating +2**). A Fire Warrior Shas'ui can take the place of one Fire Warrior. Each Fire Warrior and Fire Warrior Shas'ui is armed with a pulse blaster and photon grenades. This unit may be accompanied by 2 Tactical Drones (pg 109) or 1 Tactical Drone and 1 MV36 Guardian Drone (**Power Rating +1**).

WEAPON	RANGE	TYPE	S	AP	D	ABILITIES
Markerlight	36"	Heavy 1	-	-	-	Markerlights (pg 123)
Missile pod	36"	Assault 2	7	-1	D3	-
Pulse blaster	When attacking with this weapon, choose one of the profiles below.					
- Close range	5"	Assault 2	6	-2	1	-
- Medium range	10"	Assault 2	5	-1	1	-
- Long range	15"	Assault 2	4	0	1	-
Pulse pistol	12"	Pistol 1	5	0	1	-
Smart missile system	30"	Heavy 4	5	0	1	This weapon can be fired at units that are not visible to the bearer. Units attacked by this weapon do not gain any bonus to their saving throws for being in cover.
Photon grenade	12"	Grenade D6	-	-	-	This weapon does not inflict any damage. Your opponent must subtract 1 from any hit rolls made for **INFANTRY** units that have suffered any hits from photon grenades until the end of the turn.

WARGEAR OPTIONS	
	• The Fire Warrior Shas'ui may take a markerlight.
	• The Fire Warrior Shas'ui may take a pulse pistol or replace their pulse blaster with a pulse pistol.
	• Any Fire Warrior may take a pulse pistol.
	• The unit may take a DS8 Tactical Support Turret equipped with either a missile pod or smart missile system.

ABILITIES (BREACHER TEAM)	
	For the Greater Good (pg 89)
	Bonding Knife Ritual: If you roll a 6 when taking a Morale test for this unit, the test is automatically passed.
	DS8 Tactical Support Turret: Tactical Support Turrets are not set up when their unit is set up. Instead, once per game, at the end of any of your Movement phases, you can set up the Tactical Support Turret within coherency of its unit and more than 2" away from any enemy models.
	The turret cannot move for any reason, and is destroyed if the Breacher Team moves out of unit coherency with it. The destruction of a Tactical Support Turret is ignored for the purposes of Morale tests.

ABILITIES (GUARDIAN DRONE)		
	For the Greater Good (pg 89)	**Drone Support:** When a unit is set up on the battlefield, any accompanying Drones are set up in unit coherency with it. From that point onwards, the Drones are treated as a separate unit.
	Saviour Protocols: If a <SEPT> INFANTRY or <SEPT> BATTLESUIT unit within 3" of a friendly <SEPT> DRONES unit is wounded by an enemy attack, roll a D6. On a 2+ you can allocate that wound to the Drones unit instead of the target. If you do, that Drones unit suffers a mortal wound instead of the normal damage.	**Guardian Field:** Guardian Drones have a 5+ invulnerable save. Breacher Teams within 3" of a friendly Guardian Drone have a 5+ invulnerable save.

FACTION KEYWORDS	T'AU EMPIRE, <SEPT>
KEYWORDS (BREACHER TEAM)	INFANTRY, BREACHER TEAM
KEYWORDS (GUARDIAN DRONE)	DRONE, FLY, GUARDIAN DRONE

98

STRIKE TEAM

NAME	M	WS	BS	S	T	W	A	Ld	Sv
Fire Warrior	6"	5+	4+	3	3	1	1	6	4+
Fire Warrior Shas'ui	6"	5+	4+	3	3	1	2	7	4+
DS8 Tactical Support Turret	-	-	4+	3	3	1	0	4	4+
MV36 Guardian Drone	8"	5+	5+	3	4	1	1	6	4+

This unit contains 5 Fire Warriors. It can include up to 5 additional Fire Warriors (**Power Rating +2**), or up to 7 additional Fire Warriors (**Power Rating +3**). A Fire Warrior Shas'ui can take the place of one Fire Warrior. Each model is armed with a pulse rifle and photon grenades. This unit may be accompanied by 2 Tactical Drones (pg 109) or 1 Tactical Drone and 1 MV36 Guardian Drone (**Power Rating +1**).

WEAPON	RANGE	TYPE	S	AP	D	ABILITIES
Markerlight	36"	Heavy 1	-	-	-	Markerlights (pg 123)
Missile pod	36"	Assault 2	7	-1	D3	-
Pulse carbine	18"	Assault 2	5	0	1	-
Pulse pistol	12"	Pistol 1	5	0	1	-
Pulse rifle	30"	Rapid Fire 1	5	0	1	-
Smart missile system	30"	Heavy 4	5	0	1	This weapon can be fired at units that are not visible to the bearer. Units attacked by this weapon do not gain any bonus to their saving throws for being in cover.
Photon grenade	12"	Grenade D6	-	-	-	This weapon does not inflict any damage. Your opponent must subtract 1 from any hit rolls made for **INFANTRY** units that have suffered any hits from photon grenades until the end of the turn.

WARGEAR OPTIONS	• Any model may replace their pulse rifle with a pulse carbine. • The Fire Warrior Shas'ui may take a markerlight. • The Fire Warrior Shas'ui may take a pulse pistol or replace their pulse rifle with a pulse pistol. • Any Fire Warrior may take a pulse pistol. • The unit may take a DS8 Tactical Support Turret equipped with either a missile pod or smart missile system.

ABILITIES (STRIKE TEAM)	**For the Greater Good** (pg 89) **Bonding Knife Ritual:** If you roll a 6 when taking a Morale test for this unit, the test is automatically passed. **DS8 Tactical Support Turret:** Tactical Support Turrets are not set up when their unit is set up. Instead, once per game, at the end of any of your Movement phases, you can set up the Tactical Support Turret within coherency of its unit and more than 2" away from any enemy models. The turret cannot move for any reason, and is destroyed if the Strike Team moves out of unit coherency with it. The destruction of a Tactical Support Turret is ignored for the purposes of Morale tests.

ABILITIES (GUARDIAN DRONES)	**For the Greater Good** (pg 89) **Saviour Protocols:** If a <SEPT> INFANTRY or <SEPT> BATTLESUIT unit within 3" of a friendly <SEPT> DRONES unit is wounded by an enemy attack, roll a D6. On a 2+ you can allocate that wound to the Drones unit instead of the target. If you do, that Drones unit suffers a mortal wound instead of the normal damage.	**Drone Support:** When a unit is set up on the battlefield, any accompanying Drones are set up in unit coherency with it. From that point onwards, the Drones are treated as a separate unit. **Guardian Field:** Guardian Drones have a 5+ invulnerable save. Strike Teams within 3" of any friendly Guardian Drones have a 6+ invulnerable save.

FACTION KEYWORDS	T'AU EMPIRE, <SEPT>
KEYWORDS (STRIKE TEAM)	INFANTRY, STRIKE TEAM
KEYWORDS (GUARDIAN DRONE)	DRONE, FLY, GUARDIAN DRONE

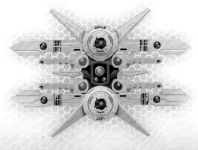

99

KROOT CARNIVORES

NAME	M	WS	BS	S	T	W	A	Ld	Sv
Kroot	7"	3+	4+	3	3	1	1	6	6+

This unit contains 10 Kroot. It can include up to 10 additional Kroot (**Power Rating +2**). Each model is armed with a Kroot rifle.

WEAPON	RANGE	TYPE	S	AP	D	ABILITIES
Kroot rifle (shooting)	24"	Rapid Fire 1	4	0	1	-
Kroot rifle (melee)	Melee	Melee	+1	0	1	-

ABILITIES	**Stealthy Hunters:** At the start of the first battle round but before the first turn begins, you can move this unit up to 7". It cannot end this move within 9" of any enemy models. If both players have units that are able to move at the start of the first battle round but before the first turn begins, the player who is taking the first turn moves their units first.
FACTION KEYWORDS	T'AU EMPIRE, KROOT
KEYWORDS	INFANTRY, KROOT CARNIVORES

As savage as they are cunning, Kroot Carnivores are expert trackers and ambush specialists who range ahead of the T'au armies.

KROOT SHAPER

NAME	M	WS	BS	S	T	W	A	Ld	Sv
Kroot Shaper	7"	3+	4+	3	3	5	3	7	6+

A Kroot Shaper is a single model armed with a Kroot rifle and a ritual blade.

WEAPON	RANGE	TYPE	S	AP	D	ABILITIES
Kroot rifle (shooting)	24"	Rapid Fire 1	4	0	1	-
Pulse rifle	30"	Rapid Fire 1	5	0	1	-
Kroot rifle (melee)	Melee	Melee	+1	0	1	-
Ritual blade	Melee	Melee	User	0	1	If any models are destroyed by this weapon, friendly **Kroot** units within 6" of the bearer do not have to take Morale tests in the Morale phase of that turn.

WARGEAR OPTIONS	• This model may replace its Kroot rifle with a pulse rifle.	
ABILITIES	**Wisest of Their Kind: Kroot** units within 6" of a friendly Kroot Shaper may use the Shaper's Leadership characteristic instead of their own when taking Morale tests.	**The Shaper Commands:** Re-roll wound rolls of 1 for friendly **Kroot** units within 6" of this model.
FACTION KEYWORDS	T'au Empire, Kroot	
KEYWORDS	Character, Infantry, Kroot Shaper	

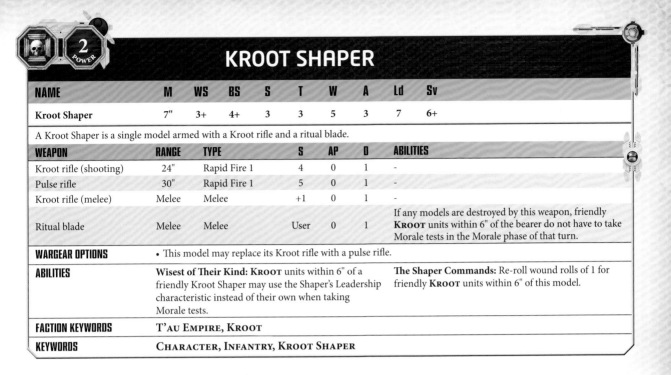

'The be'gel had us surrounded, and the last of our ammunition reserves had run dry. We resolved to meet our deaths with honour. Then we heard the shrill baying of hounds, and the crack of hard-round rifles. The Kroot emerged from the forest with howls that chilled the blood, and fell upon the be'gel. It was over in minutes. Our auxiliaries saved many lives that day, and I will not forget their bravery. Nor will I forget the awful sounds of tearing flesh and snapping bone that followed, as they butchered and devoured the bodies of their foes.'

- Shas'ui Dau, Vior'la Sept

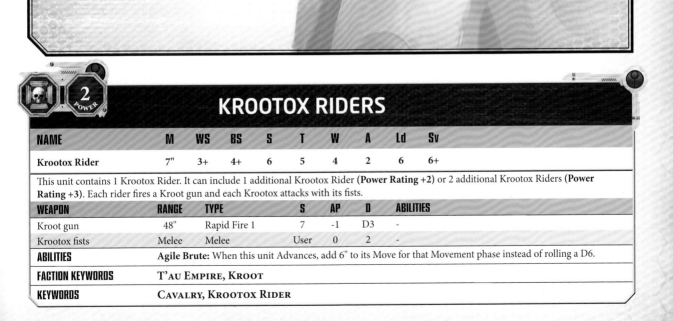

KROOTOX RIDERS

NAME	M	WS	BS	S	T	W	A	Ld	Sv
Krootox Rider	7"	3+	4+	6	5	4	2	6	6+

This unit contains 1 Krootox Rider. It can include 1 additional Krootox Rider (**Power Rating +2**) or 2 additional Krootox Riders (**Power Rating +3**). Each rider fires a Kroot gun and each Krootox attacks with its fists.

WEAPON	RANGE	TYPE	S	AP	D	ABILITIES
Kroot gun	48"	Rapid Fire 1	7	-1	D3	-
Krootox fists	Melee	Melee	User	0	2	-

ABILITIES	**Agile Brute:** When this unit Advances, add 6" to its Move for that Movement phase instead of rolling a D6.
FACTION KEYWORDS	T'au Empire, Kroot
KEYWORDS	Cavalry, Krootox Rider

XV25 STEALTH BATTLESUITS

NAME	M	WS	BS	S	T	W	A	Ld	Sv
Stealth Shas'ui	8"	5+	4+	4	4	2	2	7	3+
Stealth Shas'vre	8"	5+	4+	4	4	2	3	8	3+

This unit contains 3 Stealth Shas'ui. It can include up to 3 additional Stealth Shas'ui (**Power Rating +6**). A Stealth Shas'vre can take the place of one Stealth Shas'ui. Each model is equipped with a burst cannon. This unit may be accompanied by up to 2 Tactical Drones (pg 109) (**Power Rating +1**).

WEAPON	RANGE	TYPE	S	AP	D	ABILITIES
Burst cannon	18"	Assault 4	5	0	1	-
Fusion blaster	18"	Assault 1	8	-4	D6	If the target is within half range of this weapon, roll two dice when inflicting damage with it and discard the lowest result.
Markerlight	36"	Heavy 1	-	-	-	Markerlights (pg 123)

WARGEAR OPTIONS	
	• Any model may take a single item from the *Support Systems* list. • One model may replace its burst cannon with a fusion blaster. If the unit numbers six models, one additional model may do this. • The Shas'vre may take a markerlight and target lock. • The unit may take a homing beacon.

ABILITIES	
	For the Greater Good (pg 89) **Camouflage Fields:** Your opponent must subtract 1 from all hit rolls for attacks that target this unit. **Homing Beacon:** A homing beacon may be used at the start of your Movement phase by placing it within 1" of its unit. If there are any friendly homing beacons on the battlefield at the end of your Movement phase, one of your <Sept> units that has been set up in a Manta hold can perform a low-altitude drop instead of a Manta strike. Set up the unit wholly within 6" of the homing beacon. The homing beacon then shorts out and is removed from the battlefield. Homing beacons are deactivated and removed from the battlefield if an enemy model ends a move within 9" of it.	**Bonding Knife Ritual:** If you roll a 6 when taking a Morale test for this unit, the test is automatically passed. **Infiltrators:** During deployment, this unit and any accompanying Drones can be set up anywhere on the battlefield that is not within your opponent's deployment zone and is more than 12" from any enemy unit. **Target Lock:** A model with a target lock does not suffer the penalty to their hit rolls for moving and firing Heavy weapons, or for Advancing and firing Assault weapons. This model can also Advance and fire Rapid Fire weapons, but you must subtract 1 from its hit rolls when it does so.

FACTION KEYWORDS	T'au Empire, <Sept>
KEYWORDS	Battlesuit, Infantry, Jet Pack, Fly, XV25 Stealth Battlesuits

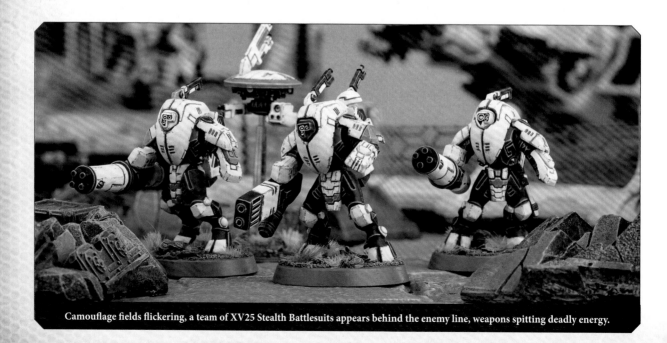

Camouflage fields flickering, a team of XV25 Stealth Battlesuits appears behind the enemy line, weapons spitting deadly energy.

Crisis Battlesuits are an iconic symbol of T'au technological might, sleek and lethal killing machines piloted by elite Fire Caste warriors.

XV8 CRISIS BATTLESUITS

POWER 12

NAME	M	WS	BS	S	T	W	A	Ld	Sv
Crisis Shas'ui	8"	5+	4+	5	5	3	2	7	3+
Crisis Shas'vre	8"	5+	4+	5	5	3	3	8	3+

This unit contains 3 Crisis Shas'ui. It can include up to 3 additional Crisis Shas'ui (**Power Rating +12**) or up to 6 additional Crisis Shas'ui (**Power Rating +24**). A Crisis Shas'vre can take the place of one Crisis Shas'ui. Each model is equipped with a burst cannon, and may be accompanied by up to 2 Tactical Drones (pg 109) (**Power Rating +1 for each model accompanied by any Drones**).

WEAPON	RANGE	TYPE	S	AP	D	ABILITIES
Burst cannon	18"	Assault 4	5	0	1	-

WARGEAR OPTIONS	• Any model may replace its burst cannon with up to three items from the *Ranged Weapons* and/or *Support Systems* list. • For every three models in the unit, one model may take an XV8-02 Crisis Iridium Battlesuit, increasing that model's Save characteristic to 2+.

ABILITIES	**For the Greater Good** (pg 89) **Bonding Knife Ritual:** If you roll a 6 when taking a Morale test for this unit, the test is automatically passed.	**Manta Strike:** During deployment, you can set up this unit and any accompanying Drones in a Manta hold instead of placing them on the battlefield. At the end of any of your Movement phases they can use a Manta strike to enter the fray – set them up anywhere on the battlefield that is more than 9" from any enemy models.

FACTION KEYWORDS	T'AU EMPIRE, <SEPT>
KEYWORDS	BATTLESUIT, JET PACK, FLY, XV8 CRISIS BATTLESUITS

XV8 CRISIS BODYGUARDS

NAME	M	WS	BS	S	T	W	A	Ld	Sv
Crisis Bodyguard	8"	5+	4+	5	5	3	3	8	3+

This unit contains 3 Crisis Bodyguards. It can include up to 3 additional Crisis Bodyguards (**Power Rating +12**) or up to 6 additional Crisis Bodyguards (**Power Rating +24**). Each model is equipped with a burst cannon, and may be accompanied by up to 2 Tactical Drones (pg 109) (**Power Rating +1 for each model accompanied by any Drones**).

WEAPON	RANGE	TYPE		S	AP	D	ABILITIES
Burst cannon	18"	Assault 4		5	0	1	-

WARGEAR OPTIONS	
	• Any model may replace their burst cannon with up to three items from the *Ranged Weapons* and/or *Support Systems* list.
	• For every three models in the unit, one model may take an XV8-02 Crisis Iridium Battlesuit, increasing that model's Save characteristic to 2+.

ABILITIES	
	For the Greater Good (pg 89) **Manta Strike:** During deployment, you can set up this unit and any accompanying Drones in a Manta hold instead of placing them on the battlefield. At the end of any of your Movement phases they can use a Manta strike to enter the fray – set them up anywhere on the battlefield that is more than 9" from any enemy models.	**Sworn Protectors:** Roll a D6 each time a friendly <Sept> Character loses a wound whilst they are within 3" of this unit. On a 2+, a model from this unit can intercept that hit – the **Character** does not lose a wound but this unit suffers a mortal wound. **Bonding Knife Ritual:** If you roll a 6 when taking a Morale test for this unit, the test is automatically passed.

FACTION KEYWORDS	T'au Empire, <Sept>

KEYWORDS	Battlesuit, Jet Pack, Fly, XV8 Crisis Bodyguards

'I take no pleasure in the death we must deliver, but by the same token I will shed no tears for those too blind to accept the deliverance of the T'au'va. Let them burn. All of them. From their ashes shall arise a better world.'

- Crisis Shas'ui Nu'ma, D'yanoi Sept

FIRESIGHT MARKSMAN

NAME	M	WS	BS	S	T	W	A	Ld	Sv
Firesight Marksman	5"	5+	3+	3	3	3	2	7	4+

A Firesight Marksman is a single model armed with a markerlight and pulse pistol.

WEAPON	RANGE	TYPE		S	AP	D	ABILITIES
Markerlight	36"	Heavy 1		-	-	-	Markerlights (pg 123)
Pulse pistol	12"	Pistol 1		5	0	1	-

ABILITIES	
	For the Greater Good (pg 89) **Marksman Stealth Field:** This model adds 2 rather than 1 to its saving throws when benefiting from cover.	**Drone Uplink:** You can add 1 to hit rolls for <Sept> MV71 Sniper Drones in the Shooting phase when they attack a unit visible to a friendly <Sept> Firesight Marksman.

FACTION KEYWORDS	T'au Empire, <Sept>

KEYWORDS	Character, Infantry, Firesight Marksman

XV95 GHOSTKEEL BATTLESUIT

DAMAGE			
Some of this model's characteristics change as it suffers damage, as shown below:			
REMAINING W	M	BS	A
6-10+	12"	4+	3
3-5	8"	5+	2
1-2	4"	5+	1

NAME	M	WS	BS	S	T	W	A	Ld	Sv
Ghostkeel Shas'vre	✱	5+	✱	6	6	10	✱	8	3+
MV5 Stealth Drones	12"	5+	5+	4	4	1	1	6	4+

A Ghostkeel Shas'vre is a single model equipped with a fusion collider and two flamers. It is accompanied by 2 MV5 Stealth Drones.

WEAPON	RANGE	TYPE	S	AP	D	ABILITIES
Burst cannon	18"	Assault 4	5	0	1	-
Cyclic ion raker	When attacking with this weapon, choose one of the profiles below.					
- Standard	24"	Heavy 6	7	-1	1	
- Overcharge	24"	Heavy 6	8	-1	D3	If you roll one or more hit rolls of 1, the bearer suffers a mortal wound after all of this weapon's shots have been resolved.
Flamer	8"	Assault D6	4	0	1	This weapon automatically hits its target.
Fusion blaster	18"	Assault 1	8	-4	D6	If the target is within half range of this weapon, roll two dice when inflicting damage with it and discard the lowest result.
Fusion collider	18"	Heavy D3	8	-4	D6	If the target is within half range of this weapon, roll two dice when inflicting damage with it and discard the lowest result.

WARGEAR OPTIONS	• This model may replace its fusion collider with a cyclic ion raker. • This model may replace both its flamers with two burst cannons or two fusion blasters. • This model may take up to two items from the *Support Systems* list.

ABILITIES (GHOSTKEEL)	**For the Greater Good** (pg 89) **Ghostkeel Electrowarfare Suite:** Your opponent must subtract 1 from hit rolls for models attacking this model from more than 6" away.	**Infiltrator:** During deployment, this model and any accompanying Drones may be set up anywhere on the battlefield that is not within your opponent's deployment zone and is more than 12" from any enemy unit.

ABILITIES (STEALTH DRONES)	**For the Greater Good** (pg 89) **Saviour Protocols:** If a <Sept> Infantry or <Sept> Battlesuit unit within 3" of a friendly <Sept> Drones unit is wounded by an enemy attack, roll a D6. On a 2+ you can allocate that wound to the Drones unit instead of the target. If you do, that Drones unit suffers a mortal wound instead of the normal damage.	**Drone Support:** When a unit is set up on the battlefield, any accompanying Drones are set up in unit coherency with it. From that point onwards, the Drones are treated as a separate unit. **Stealth Field:** Models shooting at a Stealth Drone or an **XV95 Ghostkeel Battlesuit** within 3" of any friendly Stealth Drones subtract 1 from their hit rolls. (This is cumulative with the Ghostkeel Electrowarfare Suite ability.)

FACTION KEYWORDS	T'au Empire, <Sept>
KEYWORDS (GHOSTKEEL)	Battlesuit, Monster, Jet Pack, Fly, XV95 Ghostkeel Battlesuit
KEYWORDS (STEALTH DRONES)	Drone, Fly, MV5 Stealth Drones

14 POWER

XV104 RIPTIDE BATTLESUIT

DAMAGE
Some of this model's characteristics change as it suffers damage, as shown below:

REMAINING W	M	BS	A
7-14+	12"	4+	4
4-6	8"	5+	3
1-3	4"	5+	2

NAME	M	WS	BS	S	T	W	A	Ld	Sv
Riptide Shas'vre	*	5+	*	6	7	14	*	8	2+
MV84 Shielded Missile Drone	12"	5+	5+	4	4	1	1	6	4+

A Riptide Shas'vre is a single model equipped with a heavy burst cannon and two smart missile systems. It may be accompanied by up to 2 MV84 Shielded Missile Drones (**Power Rating +2**), each equipped with a missile pod.

WEAPON	RANGE	TYPE	S	AP	D	ABILITIES
Fusion blaster	18"	Assault 1	8	-4	D6	If the target is within half range of this weapon, roll two dice when inflicting damage with it and discard the lowest result.
Heavy burst cannon	36"	Heavy 12	6	-1	2	-
Ion accelerator	When attacking with this weapon, choose one of the profiles below.					
- Standard	72"	Heavy D6	8	-3	D3	-
- Overcharge	72"	Heavy D6	9	-3	3	If you roll one or more hit rolls of 1, the bearer suffers a mortal wound after all of this weapon's shots have been resolved.
Missile pod	36"	Assault 2	7	-1	D3	-
Plasma rifle	24"	Rapid Fire 1	6	-3	1	-
Smart missile system	30"	Heavy 4	5	0	1	This weapon can be fired at units that are not visible to the bearer. Units attacked by this weapon do not gain any bonus to their saving throws for being in cover.

WARGEAR OPTIONS	• This model may replace both its smart missile systems with two plasma rifles or two fusion blasters. • This model may replace its heavy burst cannon with an ion accelerator. • This model may take up to two items from the *Support Systems* list.

ABILITIES (RIPTIDE)	**For the Greater Good** (pg 89) **Riptide Shield Generator:** This model has a 5+ invulnerable save. **Nova Reactor:** In your Movement phase you can choose to use this model's Nova Reactor. If you do, the model suffers a mortal wound. Choose one of the following effects to last until the beginning of your next turn: • **Nova Shield:** This model has a 3+ invulnerable save. • **Boost:** This model can move 2D6" in your charge phase (even if it doesn't declare a charge). • **Nova-charge:** Choose for either this model's heavy burst cannon Type to change to Heavy 18, or its ion accelerator Type (both standard and overcharge) to change to Heavy 6.

ABILITIES (SHIELDED MISSILE DRONES)	**For the Greater Good** (pg 89) **Saviour Protocols:** If a \<Sept\> Infantry or \<Sept\> Battlesuit unit within 3" of a friendly \<Sept\> Drones unit is wounded by an enemy attack, roll a D6. On a 2+ you can allocate that wound to the Drones unit instead of the target. If you do, that Drones unit suffers a mortal wound instead of the normal damage.	**Drone Support:** When a unit is set up on the battlefield, any accompanying Drones are set up in unit coherency with it. From that point onwards, the Drones are treated as a separate unit. **Shield Generator:** Shielded Missile Drones have a 4+ invulnerable save. In addition, roll a D6 each time a **Drone** with this ability loses a wound; on a 5+ that Drone does not lose a wound.

FACTION KEYWORDS	T'au Empire, \<Sept\>
KEYWORDS (RIPTIDE)	Battlesuit, Monster, Jet Pack, Fly, XV104 Riptide Battlesuit
KEYWORDS (SHIELDED MISSILE DRONES)	Drone, Fly, MV84 Shielded Missile Drones

'Launch an ambush not to slay, but rather to seize the initiative and thereby win the war.'

- Commander Puretide

PATHFINDER TEAM

NAME	M	WS	BS	S	T	W	A	Ld	Sv
Pathfinder	7"	5+	4+	3	3	1	1	6	5+
Pathfinder Shas'ui	7"	5+	4+	3	3	1	2	7	5+
MV31 Pulse Accelerator Drone	8"	5+	5+	3	4	1	1	6	4+
MV33 Grav-inhibitor Drone	8"	5+	5+	3	4	1	1	6	4+
MB3 Recon Drone	8"	5+	5+	4	4	2	1	6	4+

This unit contains 5 Pathfinders. It can include up to 5 additional Pathfinders (**Power Rating +2**). A Pathfinder Shas'ui can take the place of one Pathfinder. Each model is armed with a markerlight, pulse carbine and photon grenades. This unit may be accompanied by up to 2 Tactical Drones (pg 109) (**Power Rating +1**) and/or an MB3 Recon Drone (**Power Rating +1**) equipped with a burst cannon and up to 2 Support Drones: 1 MV31 Pulse Accelerator Drone and/or 1 MV33 Grav-inhibitor Drone (**Power Rating +1**).

WEAPON	RANGE	TYPE	S	AP	D	ABILITIES
Ion rifle	When attacking with this weapon, choose one of the profiles below.					
- Standard	30"	Rapid Fire 1	7	-1	1	
- Overcharge	30"	Heavy D3	8	-1	2	If you roll one or more hit rolls of 1, the bearer suffers a mortal wound after all of this weapon's shots have been resolved.
Markerlight	36"	Heavy 1	-	-	-	Markerlights (pg 123)
Pulse carbine	18"	Assault 2	5	0	1	-
Pulse pistol	12"	Pistol 1	5	0	1	-
Rail rifle	30"	Rapid Fire 1	6	-4	D3	For each wound roll of 6+ made for this weapon, the target unit suffers a mortal wound in addition to the normal damage.
Photon grenade	12"	Grenade D6	-	-	-	This weapon does not inflict any damage. Your opponent must subtract 1 from any hit rolls made for INFANTRY units that have suffered any hits from photon grenades until the end of the turn.

WARGEAR OPTIONS	• Up to three Pathfinders may replace their markerlight and pulse carbine with an ion rifle or a rail rifle. • The Pathfinder Shas'ui may take a pulse pistol.

ABILITIES (PATHFINDERS)

For the Greater Good (pg 89)

Vanguard: At the start of the first battle round but before the first turn begins, you can move this unit and any accompanying Drones up to 7". They cannot end this move within 9" of any enemy models. If both players have units that are able to move at the start of the first battle round but before the first turn begins, the player who is taking the first turn moves their units first.

Recon Suite: Units making saves against attacks made by a Pathfinder Team that is within 3" of a friendly Recon Drone do not gain any bonus to their saving throws for being in cover.

Bonding Knife Ritual: If you roll a 6 when taking a Morale test for this unit, the test is automatically passed.

ABILITIES (DRONES)

For the Greater Good (pg 89)

Drone Support: When a unit is set up on the battlefield, any accompanying Drones are set up in unit coherency with it. From that point onwards, the Drones are treated as a separate unit.

Pulse Accelerator: Whilst a T'AU EMPIRE INFANTRY unit is within 3" of any friendly Pulse Accelerator Drones, increase the Range characteristic of that unit's pulse pistols, pulse carbines and pulse rifles by 6".

Saviour Protocols: If a <SEPT> INFANTRY or <SEPT> BATTLESUIT unit within 3" of a friendly <SEPT> DRONES unit is wounded by an enemy attack, roll a D6. On a 2+ you can allocate that wound to the Drones unit instead of the target. If you do, that Drones unit suffers a mortal wound instead of the normal damage.

Gravity Wave Projector: Enemy units beginning a charge move within 12" of any Grav-inhibitor Drones reduce their charge distance by D3".

FACTION KEYWORDS	T'AU EMPIRE, <SEPT>
KEYWORDS (PATHFINDERS)	INFANTRY, PATHFINDER TEAM
KEYWORDS (SUPPORT DRONES)	DRONE, FLY, SUPPORT DRONES
KEYWORDS (RECON DRONE)	DRONE, FLY, RECON DRONE

TX4 PIRANHAS

NAME	M	WS	BS	S	T	W	A	Ld	Sv
TX4 Piranha	16"	6+	4+	4	5	6	2	6	4+
MV1 Gun Drone	8"	5+	5+	3	4	1	1	6	4+

This unit contains 1 TX4 Piranha accompanied by 2 MV1 Gun Drones. It can include up to 4 additional TX4 Piranhas, each of which is accompanied by 2 MV1 Gun Drones (**Power Rating +4 per TX4 Piranha**). Each TX4 Piranha is equipped with a burst cannon, and each MV1 Gun Drone is equipped with two pulse carbines.

WEAPON	RANGE	TYPE	S	AP	D	ABILITIES
Burst cannon	18"	Assault 4	5	0	1	-
Fusion blaster	18"	Assault 1	8	-4	D6	If the target is within half range of this weapon, roll two dice when inflicting damage with it and discard the lowest result.
Pulse carbine	18"	Assault 2	5	0	1	-
Seeker missile	72"	Heavy 1	8	-2	D6	Each seeker missile can only be used once per battle. This weapon only hits on a roll of 6, regardless of the firing model's Ballistic Skill or any modifiers.

WARGEAR OPTIONS	• Any model may replace its burst cannon with a fusion blaster and may take up to two seeker missiles.

ABILITIES (PIRANHAS)	**Attached Drones:** When a Piranha is set up, its accompanying Gun Drones are attached, and are treated as being embarked. Whilst the Drones remain attached, the Piranha is considered to be equipped with their weapons in addition to its own.	**Explodes:** If a Piranha is reduced to 0 wounds, roll a D6 before removing it from the battlefield and before any embarked models disembark. On a 6 it explodes, and each unit within 3" suffers a mortal wound.

ABILITIES (GUN DRONES)	**For the Greater Good** (pg 89) **Saviour Protocols:** If a <Sept> Infantry or <Sept> Battlesuit unit within 3" of a friendly <Sept> Drones unit is wounded by an enemy attack, roll a D6. On a 2+ you can allocate that wound to the Drones unit instead of the target. If you do, that Drones unit suffers a mortal wound instead of the normal damage.	**Detach:** Both Gun Drones can detach at the start of your Movement phase by disembarking as if from a transport. From that point onwards, they are treated as a separate unit. They cannot reattach during the battle. **Threat Identification Protocols:** In the Shooting phase, Gun Drones can only target the nearest visible enemy unit. If two units are equally close, you can choose which is targeted.

FACTION KEYWORDS	T'au Empire, <Sept>
KEYWORDS (PIRANHA)	Vehicle, Fly, TX4 Piranhas
KEYWORDS (GUN DRONES)	Drone, Fly, Gun Drones

A TX4 Piranha darts nimbly between arcs of enemy fire, spitting death from its fore-mounted fusion blaster.

Tactical Drones provide warriors of the Fire caste with strategic versatility and prodigious firepower.

TACTICAL DRONES

NAME	M	WS	BS	S	T	W	A	Ld	Sv
MV1 Gun Drone	8"	5+	5+	3	4	1	1	6	4+
MV4 Shield Drone	8"	5+	5+	3	4	1	1	6	4+
MV7 Marker Drone	8"	5+	5+	3	4	1	1	6	4+

This unit contains 4 Tactical Drones. It can include up to 4 additional Tactical Drones (**Power Rating +2**), or up to 8 additional Tactical Drones (**Power Rating +4**). Each Drone in the unit must be either an MV1 Gun Drone armed with two pulse carbines, an MV4 Shield Drone or an MV7 Marker Drone armed with a markerlight. Note that this datasheet is also used for Tactical Drones that accompany many T'au Empire units (see Drone Support, below).

WEAPON	RANGE	TYPE	S	AP	D	ABILITIES
Markerlight	36"	Heavy 1	-	-	-	Markerlights (pg 123)
Pulse carbine	18"	Assault 2	5	0	1	-

ABILITIES	
	For the Greater Good (pg 89)

Manta Strike: During deployment, you can set up this unit in a Manta hold instead of placing them on the battlefield. At the end of any of your Movement phases, they can use a Manta strike to enter the fray – set them up anywhere on the battlefield that is more than 9" from any enemy models.

Saviour Protocols: If a **\<Sept\> Infantry** or **\<Sept\> Battlesuit** unit within 3" of a friendly **\<Sept\> Drones** unit is wounded by an enemy attack, roll a D6. On a 2+ you can allocate that wound to the Drones unit instead of the target. If you do, that Drones unit suffers a mortal wound instead of the normal damage.

Stable Platform: Marker Drones do not suffer the penalty for moving and firing Heavy weapons.

Shield Generator: Shield Drones have a 4+ invulnerable save. In addition, roll a D6 each time a **Drone** with this ability loses a wound; on a 5+ that Drone does not lose a wound. | **Drone Support:** Tactical Drones often accompany other T'au Empire units. In such instances, a unit's datasheet will instruct you if, and how many, Tactical Drones may accompany it. Tactical Drones included in your army in this way have the Battlefield Role of the unit they accompany.

When a unit is set up on the battlefield, any accompanying Drones must be placed in unit coherency with it. From that point onwards, the accompanying Drones are treated as a separate unit.

Threat Identification Protocols: In the Shooting phase, Gun Drones can only target the nearest visible enemy unit. If two units are equally close, you can choose which is targeted. |

FACTION KEYWORDS	T'au Empire, \<Sept\>
KEYWORDS	Drone, Fly, Tactical Drones

Vespid Stingwings are swift and deadly assault troops, armed with radiation-emitting neutron blasters.

VESPID STINGWINGS

3 POWER

NAME	M	WS	BS	S	T	W	A	Ld	Sv
Vespid Stingwing	14"	4+	4+	3	4	1	1	5	4+
Vespid Strain Leader	14"	4+	4+	3	4	1	2	8	4+

This unit contains 4 Vespid Stingwings. It can include up to 4 additional Vespid Stingwings (**Power Rating +3**), or up to 8 additional Vespid Stingwings (**Power Rating +5**). A Vespid Strain Leader can take the place of one Vespid Stingwing. Each model is equipped with a neutron blaster.

WEAPON	RANGE	TYPE	S	AP	D	ABILITIES
Neutron blaster	18"	Assault 2	5	-2	1	-

ABILITIES	**Plunge from the Sky:** During deployment, you can set up this unit high in the sky, instead of placing it on the battlefield. If you do so, it can plunge from the sky at the end of any of your Movement phases – set it up anywhere that is more than 9" from any enemy models.
FACTION KEYWORDS	T'AU EMPIRE, VESPID
KEYWORDS	INFANTRY, FLY, VESPID STINGWINGS

KROOT HOUNDS

1 POWER

NAME	M	WS	BS	S	T	W	A	Ld	Sv
Kroot Hound	12"	3+	-	3	3	1	2	5	6+

This unit contains 4 Kroot Hounds. It can include up to 4 additional Kroot Hounds (**Power Rating +1**) or up to 8 additional Kroot Hounds (**Power Rating +2**). Each model attacks with its ripping fangs.

WEAPON	RANGE	TYPE	S	AP	D	ABILITIES
Ripping fangs	Melee	Melee	User	-1	1	-

ABILITIES	**Voracious Predators:** You can re-roll failed charge rolls for this unit when targeting a unit that has suffered any unsaved wounds this turn.
FACTION KEYWORDS	T'AU EMPIRE, KROOT
KEYWORDS	BEASTS, KROOT HOUNDS

XV88 BROADSIDE BATTLESUITS

NAME	M	WS	BS	S	T	W	A	Ld	Sv
Broadside Shas'ui	5"	5+	4+	5	5	6	2	7	2+
Broadside Shas'vre	5"	5+	4+	5	5	6	3	8	2+
MV8 Missile Drone	8"	5+	5+	3	4	1	1	6	4+

This unit contains 1 Broadside Shas'ui. It can include 1 additional Broadside Shas'ui (**Power Rating +7**) or 2 additional Broadside Shas'ui (**Power Rating +14**). A Broadside Shas'vre can take the place of one Broadside Shas'ui. Each model is equipped with a heavy rail rifle and two smart missile systems, and may either be accompanied by up to 2 MV8 Missile Drones, each equipped with a missile pod (**Power Rating +2 for each model accompanied by any Drones**), or up to 2 Tactical Drones (pg 109) (**Power Rating +1 for each model accompanied by any Drones**).

WEAPON	RANGE	TYPE	S	AP	D	ABILITIES
Heavy rail rifle	60"	Heavy 2	8	-4	D6	Each time you make a wound roll of 6+ for this weapon, the target unit suffers a mortal wound in addition to the normal damage.
High-yield missile pod	36"	Heavy 4	7	-1	D3	-
Missile pod	36"	Assault 2	7	-1	D3	-
Plasma rifle	24"	Rapid Fire 1	6	-3	1	-
Seeker missile	72"	Heavy 1	8	-2	D6	Each seeker missile can only be used once per battle. This weapon only hits on a roll of 6, regardless of the firing model's Ballistic Skill or any modifiers.
Smart missile system	30"	Heavy 4	5	0	1	This weapon can be fired at units that are not visible to the bearer. Units attacked by this weapon do not gain any bonus to their saving throws for being in cover.

WARGEAR OPTIONS	• Any model may replace its heavy rail rifle with two high-yield missile pods. • Any model may replace both its smart missile systems with two plasma rifles. • Any model may take a seeker missile. • Any model may take one item from the *Support Systems* list.
ABILITIES (BROADSIDES)	**For the Greater Good** (pg 89) **Bonding Knife Ritual:** If you roll a 6 when taking a Morale test for this unit, the test is automatically passed.
ABILITIES (MISSILE DRONES)	**For the Greater Good** (pg 89) **Drone Support:** When a unit is set up on the battlefield, any accompanying Drones are set up in unit coherency with it. From that point onwards, the Drones are treated as a separate unit.	**Saviour Protocols:** If a <Sept> Infantry or <Sept> Battlesuit unit within 3" of a friendly <Sept> Drones unit is wounded by an enemy attack, roll a D6. On a 2+ you can allocate that wound to the Drones unit instead of the target. If you do, that Drones unit suffers a mortal wound instead of the normal damage.
FACTION KEYWORDS	T'au Empire, <Sept>
KEYWORDS (BROADSIDES)	Battlesuit, XV88 Broadside Battlesuits
KEYWORDS (MISSILE DRONES)	Drone, Fly, MV8 Missile Drones

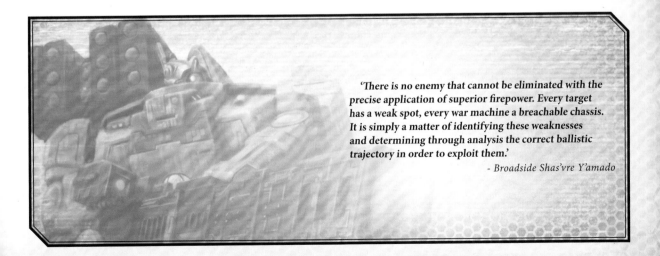

'There is no enemy that cannot be eliminated with the precise application of superior firepower. Every target has a weak spot, every war machine a breachable chassis. It is simply a matter of identifying these weaknesses and determining through analysis the correct ballistic trajectory in order to exploit them.'

- Broadside Shas'vre Y'amado

TX7 HAMMERHEAD GUNSHIP

NAME	M	WS	BS	S	T	W	A	Ld	Sv
TX7 Hammerhead Gunship	*	6+	*	6	7	13	*	8	3+
MV1 Gun Drone	8"	5+	5+	3	4	1	1	6	4+

DAMAGE
Some of this model's characteristics change as it suffers damage, as shown below:

REMAINING W	M	BS	A
7-13+	12"	3+	3
4-6	6"	4+	D3
1-3	3"	5+	1

A TX7 Hammerhead Gunship is a single model equipped with a railgun. It is accompanied by 2 MV1 Gun Drones, each equipped with two pulse carbines.

WEAPON	RANGE	TYPE	S	AP	D	ABILITIES
Burst cannon	18"	Assault 4	5	0	1	-
Ion cannon	When attacking with this weapon, choose one of the profiles below.					
- Standard	60"	Heavy 3	7	-2	2	-
- Overcharge	60"	Heavy D6	8	-2	3	If you roll one or more hit rolls of 1, the bearer suffers a mortal wound after all of this weapon's shots have been resolved.
Pulse carbine	18"	Assault 2	5	0	1	-
Railgun	When attacking with this weapon, choose one of the profiles below.					
- Solid shot	72"	Heavy 1	10	-4	D6	Each time you make a wound roll of 6+ for this weapon, the target unit suffers D3 mortal wounds in addition to the normal damage.
- Submunitions	72"	Heavy D6	6	-1	1	-
Seeker missile	72"	Heavy 1	8	-2	D6	Each seeker missile can only be used once per battle. This weapon only hits on a roll of 6, regardless of the firing model's Ballistic Skill or any modifiers.
Smart missile system	30"	Heavy 4	5	0	1	This weapon can be fired at units that are not visible to the bearer. Units attacked by this weapon do not gain any bonus to their saving throws for being in cover.

WARGEAR OPTIONS
- This model may replace its railgun with an ion cannon.
- This model may take up to two seeker missiles.
- Instead of being accompanied by two MV1 Gun Drones, this model may take two burst cannons or two smart missile systems.

ABILITIES (HAMMERHEAD)

Attached Drones: When this model is set up, any accompanying Gun Drones are attached, and are treated as being embarked. Whilst the Drones remain attached, this model is considered to be equipped with their weapons in addition to its own.

Hover Tank: Instead of measuring distances to and from this model's base, measure to and from this model's hull or base (whichever is closer).

Explodes: If this model is reduced to 0 wounds, roll a D6 before removing it from the battlefield and before any embarked models disembark. On a 6 it explodes, and each unit within 6" suffers D3 mortal wounds.

ABILITIES (GUN DRONES)

For the Greater Good (pg 89)

Saviour Protocols: If a <Sept> Infantry or <Sept> Battlesuit unit within 3" of a friendly <Sept> Drones unit is wounded by an enemy attack, roll a D6. On a 2+ you can allocate that wound to the Drones unit instead of the target. If you do, that Drones unit suffers a mortal wound instead of the normal damage.

Detach: Both Gun Drones can detach at the start of your Movement phase by disembarking as if from a transport. From that point onwards, they are treated as a separate unit. They cannot reattach during the battle.

Threat Identification Protocols: In the Shooting phase, Gun Drones can only target the nearest visible enemy unit. If two units are equally close, you can choose which is targeted.

FACTION KEYWORDS
T'au Empire, <Sept>

KEYWORDS (HAMMERHEAD)
Vehicle, Fly, Hammerhead, TX7 Hammerhead Gunship

KEYWORDS (GUN DRONES)
Drone, Fly, Gun Drones

TX78 SKY RAY GUNSHIP

DAMAGE
Some of this model's characteristics change as it suffers damage, as shown below:

REMAINING W	M	BS	A
7-13+	12"	3+	3
4-6	6"	4+	D3
1-3	3"	5+	1

NAME	M	WS	BS	S	T	W	A	Ld	Sv
TX78 Sky Ray Gunship	*	6+	*	6	7	13	*	8	3+
MV1 Gun Drone	8"	5+	5+	3	4	1	1	6	4+

A TX78 Sky Ray Gunship is a single model equipped with two markerlights and six seeker missiles.
It is accompanied by 2 MV1 Gun Drones, each equipped with two pulse carbines.

WEAPON	RANGE	TYPE	S	AP	D	ABILITIES
Burst cannon	18"	Assault 4	5	0	1	-
Markerlight	36"	Heavy 1	-	-	-	Markerlights (pg 123)
Pulse carbine	18"	Assault 2	5	0	1	-
Seeker missile	72"	Heavy 1	8	-2	D6	Each seeker missile can only be used once per battle. This weapon only hits on a roll of 6, regardless of the firing model's Ballistic Skill or any modifiers.
Smart missile system	30"	Heavy 4	5	0	1	This weapon can be fired at units that are not visible to the bearer. Units attacked by this weapon do not gain any bonus to their saving throws for being in cover.

WARGEAR OPTIONS	• Instead of being accompanied by two MV1 Gun Drones, this model may take two burst cannons or two smart missile systems.
ABILITIES (SKY RAY)	**Attached Drones:** When this model is set up, any accompanying Gun Drones are attached, and are treated as being embarked. Whilst the Drones remain attached, this model is considered to be equipped with their weapons in addition to its own. **Velocity Tracker:** Add 1 to hit rolls for this model when it shoots at a unit that can **FLY**.	**Explodes:** If this model is reduced to 0 wounds, roll a D6 before removing it from the battlefield and before any embarked models disembark. On a 6 it explodes, and each unit within 6" suffers D3 mortal wounds. **Hover Tank:** Instead of measuring distances to and from this model's base, measure to and from this model's hull or base (whichever is closer).
ABILITIES (GUN DRONES)	**For the Greater Good** (pg 89) **Saviour Protocols:** If a <SEPT> INFANTRY or <SEPT> BATTLESUIT unit within 3" of a friendly <SEPT> DRONES unit is wounded by an enemy attack, roll a D6. On a 2+ you can allocate that wound to the Drones unit instead of the target. If you do, that Drones unit suffers a mortal wound instead of the normal damage.	**Detach:** Both Gun Drones can detach at the start of your Movement phase by disembarking as if from a transport. From that point onwards, the Drones are treated as a separate unit. They cannot reattach during the battle. **Threat Identification Protocols:** In the Shooting phase, Gun Drones can only target the nearest visible enemy unit. If two units are equally close, you can choose which is targeted.
FACTION KEYWORDS	T'AU EMPIRE, <SEPT>
KEYWORDS (SKY RAY)	VEHICLE, FLY, TX78 SKY RAY GUNSHIP
KEYWORDS (GUN DRONES)	DRONE, FLY, GUN DRONES

MV71 SNIPER DRONES

NAME	M	WS	BS	S	T	W	A	Ld	Sv
MV71 Sniper Drone	8"	5+	5+	3	4	1	1	6	4+

This unit contains 3 MV71 Sniper Drones. It can include up to 3 additional MV71 Sniper Drones (**Power Rating +3**), or up to 6 additional MV71 Sniper Drones (**Power Rating +5**). Each MV71 Sniper Drone is equipped with a longshot pulse rifle.

WEAPON	RANGE	TYPE	S	AP	D	ABILITIES
Longshot pulse rifle	48"	Rapid Fire 1	5	0	1	This weapon may target a **CHARACTER** even if it is not the closest enemy unit. If you make a wound roll of 6+ for this weapon, it inflicts a mortal wound on the target in addition to its normal damage.

ABILITIES	**For the Greater Good** (pg 89), **Saviour Protocols** (see above) **Sniper Drone Stealth Field:** Subtract 1 from hit rolls in the Shooting phase for attacks made against this unit unless it is within 12" of the firing model.
FACTION KEYWORDS	T'AU EMPIRE, <SEPT>
KEYWORDS	DRONE, FLY, MV71 SNIPER DRONES

TY7 DEVILFISH

NAME	M	WS	BS	S	T	W	A	Ld	Sv
TY7 Devilfish	*	6+	*	6	7	12	*	8	3+
MV1 Gun Drone	8"	5+	5+	3	4	1	1	6	4+

DAMAGE
Some of this model's characteristics change as it suffers damage, as shown below:

REMAINING W	M	BS	A
7-12+	12"	4+	3
4-6	6"	5+	D3
1-3	3"	6+	1

A TY7 Devilfish is a single model equipped with a burst cannon. It is accompanied by 2 MV1 Gun Drones, each equipped with two pulse carbines.

WEAPON	RANGE	TYPE	S	AP	D	ABILITIES
Burst cannon	18"	Assault 4	5	0	1	-
Pulse carbine	18"	Assault 2	5	0	1	-
Seeker missile	72"	Heavy 1	8	-2	D6	Each seeker missile can only be used once per battle. This weapon only hits on a roll of 6, regardless of the firing model's Ballistic Skill or any modifiers.
Smart missile system	30"	Heavy 4	5	0	1	This weapon can be fired at units that are not visible to the bearer. Units attacked by this weapon do not gain any bonus to their saving throws for being in cover.

WARGEAR OPTIONS	• Instead of being accompanied by two MV1 Gun Drones, this model may take two smart missile systems. • This model may take up to two seeker missiles.
ABILITIES (DEVILFISH)	**Attached Drones:** When this model is set up, any accompanying Gun Drones are attached, and are treated as being embarked (though they do not count towards the total number of models embarked). Whilst the Drones remain attached, this model is considered to be equipped with their weapons in addition to its own. **Hover Tank:** Instead of measuring distances to and from this model's base, measure to and from this model's hull or base (whichever is closer).	**Turret Mounting:** Units attacked by a Devilfish with an MB3 Recon Drone embarked within it do not gain any bonus to their saving throws for being in cover. **Explodes:** If this model is reduced to 0 wounds, roll a D6 before removing it from the battlefield and before any embarked models disembark. On a 6 it explodes, and each unit within 6" suffers D3 mortal wounds.
ABILITIES (GUN DRONES)	**For the Greater Good** (pg 89) **Saviour Protocols:** If a <Sept> Infantry or <Sept> Battlesuit unit within 3" of a friendly <Sept> Drones unit is wounded by an enemy attack, roll a D6. On a 2+ you can allocate that wound to the Drones unit instead of the target. If you do, that Drones unit suffers a mortal wound instead of the normal damage.	**Detach:** Both Gun Drones can detach at the start of your Movement phase by disembarking as if from a transport. From that point onwards, they are treated as a separate unit. They cannot reattach during the battle. **Threat Identification Protocols:** In the Shooting phase, Gun Drones can only target the nearest visible enemy unit. If two units are equally close, you can choose which is targeted.
TRANSPORT	A Devilfish can transport up to 12 <Sept> Infantry or Drone models. It cannot transport Battlesuits. It can transport only a single MB3 Recon Drone, but it does not count towards the total number of models embarked on the Devilfish.
FACTION KEYWORDS	T'au Empire, <Sept>
KEYWORDS (DEVILFISH)	Vehicle, Transport, Fly, TY7 Devilfish
KEYWORDS (GUN DRONES)	Drone, Fly, Gun Drones

AX3 RAZORSHARK STRIKE FIGHTER

NAME	M	WS	BS	S	T	W	A	Ld	Sv
AX3 Razorshark Strike Fighter	*	6+	*	6	6	12	*	6	4+

DAMAGE
Some of this model's characteristics change as it suffers damage, as shown below:

REMAINING W	M	BS	A
7-12+	20"-50"	4+	3
4-6	20"-30"	5+	D3
1-3	20"-25"	5+	1

An AX3 Razorshark Strike Fighter is a single model equipped with a burst cannon, a quad ion turret and two seeker missiles.

WEAPON	RANGE	TYPE	S	AP	D	ABILITIES
Burst cannon	18"	Assault 4	5	0	1	-
Missile pod	36"	Assault 2	7	-1	D3	-
Quad ion turret		When attacking with this weapon, choose one of the profiles below. Add 1 to hit rolls for this weapon against targets that can't **FLY**.				
- Standard	30"	Assault 4	7	-1	1	-
- Overcharge	30"	Assault 4	8	-1	D3	If you roll one or more hit rolls of 1, the bearer suffers a mortal wound after all of this weapon's shots have been resolved.
Seeker missile	72"	Heavy 1	8	-2	D6	Each seeker missile can only be used once per battle. This weapon only hits on a roll of 6, regardless of the firing model's Ballistic Skill or any modifiers.

WARGEAR OPTIONS	• This model may replace its burst cannon with a missile pod.

ABILITIES	**Airborne:** This model cannot charge, can only be charged by units that can **FLY**, and can only attack or be attacked in the Fight phase by units that can **FLY**. **Supersonic:** Each time this model moves, first pivot it on the spot up to 90° (this does not contribute to how far the model moves), and then move the model straight forwards. Note that it cannot pivot again after the initial pivot. When this model Advances, increase its Move characteristic by 20" until the end of the phase – do not roll a dice.	**Hard to Hit:** Your opponent must subtract 1 from hit rolls for attacks that target this model in the Shooting phase. **Crash and Burn:** If this model is reduced to 0 wounds, roll a D6 before removing it from the battlefield. On a 6 it explodes, and each unit within 6" suffers D3 mortal wounds.

FACTION KEYWORDS	T'AU EMPIRE, <SEPT>
KEYWORDS	VEHICLE, FLY, AX3 RAZORSHARK STRIKE FIGHTER

Air caste assets sweep over the battlefield, devastasting enemy formations with vicious strafing fire and pulse bombs.

AX39 SUN SHARK BOMBER

DAMAGE
Some of this model's characteristics change as it suffers damage, as shown below:

NAME	M	WS	BS	S	T	W	A	Ld	Sv
AX39 Sun Shark Bomber	✱	6+	✱	6	6	12	✱	6	4+
MV17 Interceptor Drone	20"	5+	5+	3	4	1	1	6	4+

REMAINING W	M	BS	A
7-12+	20"-50"	4+	3
4-6	20"-30"	5+	D3
1-3	20"-25"	5+	1

An AX39 Sun Shark Bomber is a single model equipped with a markerlight, a missile pod and two seeker missiles. It is accompanied by 2 MV17 Interceptor Drones, each equipped with two ion rifles.

WEAPON	RANGE	TYPE	S	AP	D	ABILITIES
Ion rifle	When attacking with this weapon, choose one of the profiles below.					
- Standard	30"	Rapid Fire 1	7	-1	1	
- Overcharge	30"	Heavy D3	8	-1	2	If you roll one or more hit rolls of 1, the bearer suffers a mortal wound after all of this weapon's shots have been resolved.
Markerlight	36"	Heavy 1	-	-	-	Markerlights (pg 123)
Missile pod	36"	Assault 2	7	-1	D3	-
Seeker missile	72"	Heavy 1	8	-2	D6	Each seeker missile can only be used once per battle. This weapon only hits on a roll of 6, regardless of the firing model's Ballistic Skill or any modifiers.

WARGEAR OPTIONS	• This model may take a second missile pod.

ABILITIES (SUN SHARK BOMBER)	**Pulse Bombs:** This model may drop a pulse bomb as it flies over enemy units in its Movement phase. To do so, after this model has moved, pick one enemy unit that it moved across. Then, roll a D6 for each model in that unit (up to a maximum of 10), adding 1 to the result if the enemy unit is **INFANTRY**. For each roll of 5+, the target unit suffers 1 mortal wound. **Airborne:** This model cannot charge, can only be charged by units that can **FLY**, and can only attack or be attacked in the Fight phase by units that can **FLY**. **Supersonic:** Each time this model moves, first pivot it on the spot up to 90° (this does not contribute to how far the model moves), and then move the model straight forwards. Note that it cannot pivot again after the initial pivot. When this model Advances, increase its Move characteristic by 20" until the end of the phase – do not roll a dice.	**Attached Drones:** When this model is set up, its accompanying Interceptor Drones are attached, and are treated as being embarked. Whilst the Drones remain attached, this model is considered to be equipped with their weapons in addition to its own. However, a hit roll of 1 when firing the ion rifle on overcharge setting results in one of the Drones being slain rather than this model suffering a mortal wound. **Hard to Hit:** Your opponent must subtract 1 from hit rolls for attacks that target this model in the Shooting phase. **Crash and Burn:** If this model is reduced to 0 wounds, roll a D6 before removing it from the battlefield and before any embarked models disembark. On a 6 it explodes, and each unit within 6" suffers D3 mortal wounds.

ABILITIES (INTERCEPTOR DRONES)	**For the Greater Good** (pg 89) **Detach:** Both Interceptor Drones can detach at the start of your Movement phase by disembarking as if from a transport. From that point onwards, they are treated as a separate unit. They cannot reattach during the battle.	**Saviour Protocols:** If a \<SEPT\> **INFANTRY** or \<SEPT\> **BATTLESUIT** unit within 3" of a friendly \<SEPT\> **DRONES** unit is wounded by an enemy attack, roll a D6. On a 2+ you can allocate that wound to the Drones unit instead of the target. If you do, that Drones unit suffers a mortal wound instead of the normal damage.

FACTION KEYWORDS	T'AU EMPIRE, \<SEPT\>

KEYWORDS (SUN SHARK BOMBER)	VEHICLE, FLY, AX39 SUN SHARK BOMBER

KEYWORDS (INTERCEPTOR DRONES)	DRONE, FLY, INTERCEPTOR DRONES

TIDEWALL SHIELDLINE

NAME	M	WS	BS	S	T	W	A	Ld	Sv
Tidewall Shieldline	6"	-	-	-	6	10	-	-	4+
Tidewall Defence Platform	6"	-	-	-	7	10	-	-	4+

A Tidewall Shieldline is a single model. It can also include a Tidewall Defence Platform (**Power Rating +3**).

ABILITIES	**Fortification:** Tidewall Shieldlines and Tidewall Defences Platforms cannot move independently (see below), nor can they fight in the Fight phase. Enemy models automatically hit these model in the Fight phase – do not make hit rolls. However, friendly units can still target enemy units that are within 1" of these models. **Tidewall Network:** When a Tidewall Shieldline that includes a Tidewall Defence Platform is set up on the battlefield, both models are placed within 1" of each other. From that point onwards, both are treated as separate units. **Mobile Defence Platform:** If a friendly T'au Empire Infantry unit is embarked on a Tidewall Shieldline or a Tidewall Defence Platform at the beginning of your Movement phase, you can move that Tidewall Shieldline or Tidewall Defence Platform in the Movement phase. Neither a Tidewall Shieldline or a Tidewall Defence Platform can Advance or charge.	**Open-topped:** Models embarked on a Tidewall Shieldline or Defence Platform can attack in their Shooting phase. Measure the range and draw line of sight from any point on the model they are embarked on. When they do so, any restrictions or modifiers that apply to this model also apply to its passengers; for example, the passengers cannot shoot if this model has Fallen Back in the same turn, the passengers cannot shoot (except with Pistols) if this model is within 1" of an enemy unit, and so on. **Tidewall Field:** A Tidewall Shieldline can reflect shots back at the enemy. For each unmodified save roll of 6 you make in the Shooting phase for a Tidewall Shieldline, the attacking unit suffers one mortal wound after they have finished shooting. **Explodes:** If a Tidewall Defence Platform is reduced to 0 wounds, roll a dice before removing the model from the battlefield and before any embarked models disembark; on a 6 it explodes, and each unit within 6" suffers D3 mortal wounds.
BUILDING	A Tidewall Shieldline and Tidewall Defence Platform can each transport any number of T'au Empire Infantry Characters and one other T'au Empire Infantry unit, but each can transport no more than 10 models in total.	
FACTION KEYWORDS	T'au Empire, <Sept>	
KEYWORDS	Building, Vehicle, Transport, Tidewall Shieldline	

A Tidewall Shieldline slams to earth ahead of the enemy advance, its defenders unleashing a deadly fusillade of pulse energy.

Fire Warriors man a Tidewall Droneport, directing its suite of Tactical Drones while using their pulse rifles to pick off enemies.

TIDEWALL DRONEPORT

5 POWER

NAME	M	WS	BS	S	T	W	A	Ld	Sv
Tidewall Droneport	6"	-	-	-	7	10	-	-	4+

A Tidewall Droneport is a single model. It is fitted with up to 4 Tactical Drones (see below).

ABILITIES	

Fortification: A Tidewall Droneport cannot move independently (see below), nor can it fight in the Fight phase. Enemy models automatically hit this model in the Fight phase – do not make hit rolls. However, friendly units can still target enemy units that are within 1" of this model.

Mobile Defence Platform: If a friendly T'AU EMPIRE INFANTRY unit is embarked on a Tidewall Droneport at the beginning of your Movement phase, you can move that Tidewall Droneport in the Movement phase. A Tidewall Droneport cannot Advance or charge.

Open-topped: Models embarked on this model can attack in their Shooting phase. Measure the range and draw line of sight from any point on this model. When they do so, any restrictions or modifiers that apply to this model also apply to its passengers; for example, the passengers cannot shoot if this model has Fallen Back in the same turn, the passengers cannot shoot (except with Pistols) if this model is within 1" of an enemy unit, and so on.

Drone Control Systems: When you set up a Tidewall Droneport, you can also set up a unit of up to 4 Tactical Drones in the slots in the Droneport. These Drones begin the battle fully automated – if able to, they must shoot in your Shooting phase at the nearest enemy unit to the Droneport that is visible to it. If there is a friendly T'AU EMPIRE INFANTRY unit embarked on the Droneport at the beginning of your Movement phase, you can take control of the Drones, which then detach from the Droneport and act as a separate unit. In addition, while a friendly T'AU EMPIRE INFANTRY unit is embarked on the Droneport, the Tactical Drones activated in this way can use that unit's Ballistic Skill instead of their own when making shooting attacks. If the Droneport is destroyed before the Drones are activated, they are destroyed as well.

Explodes: If this model is reduced to 0 wounds, roll a dice before removing it from the battlefield and before any embarked models disembark; on a 6 it explodes, and each unit within 6" suffers D3 mortal wounds.

BUILDING	This model can transport any number of T'AU EMPIRE INFANTRY CHARACTERS and one other T'AU EMPIRE INFANTRY unit, but no more than 10 models in total.
FACTION KEYWORDS	T'AU EMPIRE, <SEPT>
KEYWORDS	BUILDING, VEHICLE, TRANSPORT, TIDEWALL DRONEPORT

TIDEWALL GUNRIG

NAME	M	WS	BS	S	T	W	A	Ld	Sv
Tidewall Gunrig	6"	-	5+	-	7	10	-	-	4+

A Tidewall Gunrig is a single model equipped with a supremacy railgun.

WEAPON	RANGE	TYPE	S	AP	D	ABILITIES
Supremacy railgun	72"	Heavy 2	10	-4	D6	Each time you make a wound roll of 6+ for this weapon, the target unit suffers D3 mortal wounds in addition to the normal damage.

ABILITIES	
	Fortification: This model cannot move independently (see below), nor can it fight in the Fight phase. Enemy models automatically hit this model in the Fight phase – do not make hit rolls. However, this model can still shoot if there are enemy models within 1" of it, and friendly units can still target enemy units that are within 1" of this model. **Open-topped:** Models embarked on this model can attack in their Shooting phase. Measure the range and draw line of sight from any point on this model. When they do so, any restrictions or modifiers that apply to this model also apply to its passengers; for example, the passengers cannot shoot if this model has Fallen Back in the same turn and so on. Note that the passengers cannot shoot (except with Pistols) if this model is within 1" of an enemy unit, even though this model itself can.	**Mobile Defence Platform:** If a friendly T'au Empire Infantry unit is embarked on this model at the beginning of your Movement phase, you may move this model in the Movement phase. This model cannot Advance or charge. **Automated Weapon:** Unless a friendly T'au Empire Infantry unit is embarked on this model, its supremacy railgun can only target the nearest visible enemy. If two units are equally close, you may choose which is targeted. **Explodes:** If this model is reduced to 0 wounds, roll a dice before removing it from the battlefield and before any embarked models disembark; on a 6 it explodes, and each unit within 6" suffers D3 mortal wounds.

BUILDING	This model can transport any number of T'au Empire Infantry Characters and one other T'au Empire Infantry unit, but no more than 10 models in total.
FACTION KEYWORDS	T'au Empire, <Sept>
KEYWORDS	Building, Vehicle, Transport, Tidewall Gunrig

A Tidewall Gunrig provides brutal anti-armour firepower, crippling enemy tanks with every shot of its supremacy railgun.

KV128 STORMSURGE

DAMAGE
Some of this model's characteristics change as it suffers damage, as shown below:

REMAINING W	BS	S	A
11-20+	4+	8	3
6-10	5+	7	D3
1-5	6+	6	1

NAME	M	WS	BS	S	T	W	A	Ld	Sv
KV128 Stormsurge	6"	5+	*	*	7	20	*	8	3+

A KV128 Stormsurge is a single model equipped with a cluster rocket system, four destroyer missiles, two flamers, a pulse blastcannon and two smart missile systems.

WEAPON	RANGE	TYPE	S	AP	D	ABILITIES
Airbursting fragmentation projector	18"	Assault D6	4	0	1	This weapon can be fired at units that are not visible to the bearer.
Burst cannon	18"	Assault 4	5	0	1	-
Cluster rocket system	48"	Heavy 4D6	5	0	1	-
Destroyer missile	60"	Heavy 1	-	-	-	A unit hit by this weapon suffers D3 mortal wounds. Each destroyer missile can only be used once per battle. This weapon only hits on a roll of 6, regardless of the firing model's Ballistic Skill or any modifiers.
Flamer	8"	Assault D6	4	0	1	This weapon automatically hits its target.
Pulse blastcannon	When attacking with this weapon, choose one of the profiles below.					
- Close range	10"	Heavy 2	14	-4	6	-
- Medium range	20"	Heavy 4	12	-2	4	-
- Long range	30"	Heavy 6	10	0	2	-
Pulse driver cannon	72"	Heavy D6	10	-3	D6	-
Smart missile system	30"	Heavy 4	5	0	1	This weapon can be fired at units that are not visible to the bearer. Units attacked by this weapon do not gain any bonus to their saving throws for being in cover.

WARGEAR OPTIONS	
	• This model may replace both its flamers with two burst cannons or two airbursting fragmentation projectors.
	• This model may replace its pulse blastcannon with a pulse driver cannon.
	• This model may be equipped with up to three items from the *Support Systems* list.

ABILITIES	
	Explodes: If this model is reduced to 0 wounds, roll a D6 before removing it from the battlefield. On a 6 it explodes, and each unit within 6" suffers D6 mortal wounds. **Stabilising Anchors:** A Stormsurge may deploy its anchors at the end of your Shooting phase. While its anchors are deployed it may not move for any reason and it cannot pile in and attack in the Fight phase, but you can add 1 to its hit rolls. The Stormsurge can retract its anchors at the beginning of any of your Movement phases, and can then move, shoot and fight normally.	**Walking Battleship:** This model can Fall Back in the Movement phase and still shoot and/or charge in the same turn. When this model Falls Back, it can move over enemy **INFANTRY** models, though it must end its move more than 1" from any enemy units. In addition, this model can move and fire Heavy weapons without suffering a penalty to its hit rolls. Finally, this model only gains a bonus to its save for being on or within cover if at least half of the model is obscured from the firer.

FACTION KEYWORDS	T'AU EMPIRE, <SEPT>
KEYWORDS	VEHICLE, TITANIC, KV128 STORMSURGE

ARSENAL OF THE EMPIRE

The forces of the T'au Empire employ a wide arsenal of devastating weaponry, from the compact but powerful pulse pistols and carbines to the tank killing power of the immense pulse driver cannons. The profiles for all of their wargear are detailed below.

RANGED WEAPONS

WEAPON	RANGE	TYPE	S	AP	D	ABILITIES
Airbursting fragmentation projector	18"	Assault D6	4	0	1	This weapon can target units that are not visible to the bearer.
Burst cannon	18"	Assault 4	5	0	1	-
Cluster rocket system	48"	Heavy 4D6	5	0	1	-
Cyclic ion blaster	When attacking with this weapon, choose one of the profiles below.					
- Standard	18"	Assault 3	7	-1	1	-
- Overcharge	18"	Assault 3	8	-1	D3	If you roll one or more hit rolls of 1, the bearer suffers a mortal wound after all of this weapon's shots have been resolved.
Cyclic ion raker	When attacking with this weapon, choose one of the profiles below.					
- Standard	24"	Heavy 6	7	-1	1	-
- Overcharge	24"	Heavy 6	8	-1	D3	If you roll one or more hit rolls of 1, the bearer suffers a mortal wound after all of this weapon's shots have been resolved.
Destroyer missile	60"	Heavy 1	-	-	-	A unit hit by this weapon suffers D3 mortal wounds. Each destroyer missile can only be used once per battle. This weapon only hits on a roll of 6, regardless of the firing model's Ballistic Skill or any modifiers.
Flamer	8"	Assault D6	4	0	1	This weapon automatically hits its target.
Fusion blaster	18"	Assault 1	8	-4	D6	If the target is within half range of this weapon, roll two dice when inflicting damage with it and discard the lowest result.
Fusion collider	18"	Heavy D3	8	-4	D6	If the target is within half range of this weapon, roll two dice when inflicting damage with it and discard the lowest result.
Heavy burst cannon	36"	Heavy 12	6	-1	2	-
Heavy rail rifle	60"	Heavy 2	8	-4	D6	For each wound roll of 6+, the target unit suffers a mortal wound in addition to the normal damage.
High-intensity plasma rifle	30"	Rapid Fire 1	6	-4	2	-
High-output burst cannon	18"	Assault 8	5	0	1	-
High-yield missile pod	36"	Heavy 4	7	-1	D3	-
Ion accelerator	When attacking with this weapon, choose one of the profiles below.					
- Standard	72"	Heavy D6	8	-3	D3	-
- Overcharge	72"	Heavy D6	9	-3	3	If you roll one or more hit rolls of 1, the bearer suffers a mortal wound after all of this weapon's shots have been resolved.
Ion cannon	When attacking with this weapon, choose one of the profiles below.					
- Standard	60"	Heavy 3	7	-2	2	-
- Overcharge	60"	Heavy D6	8	-2	3	If you roll one or more hit rolls of 1, the bearer suffers a mortal wound after all of this weapon's shots have been resolved.
Ion rifle	When attacking with this weapon, choose one of the profiles below.					
- Standard	30"	Rapid Fire 1	7	-1	1	-
- Overcharge	30"	Heavy D3	8	-1	2	If you roll one or more hit rolls of 1, the bearer suffers a mortal wound after all of this weapon's shots have been resolved.
Kroot gun	48"	Rapid Fire 1	7	-1	D3	-
Kroot rifle (shooting)	24"	Rapid Fire 1	4	0	1	-
Longshot pulse rifle	48"	Rapid Fire 1	5	0	1	This weapon may target a **CHARACTER** even if they are not the closest enemy unit. If you make a wound roll of 6+ for this weapon, it inflicts a mortal wound on the target in addition to its normal damage.
Markerlight	36"	Heavy 1	-	-	-	Markerlights (pg 123)
Missile pod	36"	Assault 2	7	-1	D3	-
Neutron blaster	18"	Assault 2	5	-2	1	-
Photon grenade	12"	Grenade D6	-	-	-	This weapon does not inflict any damage. Your opponent must subtract 1 from any hit rolls made for **INFANTRY** units that have suffered any hits from photon grenades until the end of the turn.
Plasma rifle	24"	Rapid Fire 1	6	-3	1	-

WEAPON	RANGE	TYPE	S	AP	D	ABILITIES
Pulse blastcannon	When attacking with this weapon, choose one of the profiles below.					
- Close range	10"	Heavy 2	14	-4	6	-
- Medium range	20"	Heavy 4	12	-2	4	-
- Long range	30"	Heavy 6	10	0	2	-
Pulse blaster	When attacking with this weapon, choose one of the profiles below.					
- Close range	5"	Assault 2	6	-2	1	-
- Medium range	10"	Assault 2	5	-1	1	-
- Long range	15"	Assault 2	4	0	1	-
Pulse bomb						Pulse Bombs (pg 116)
Pulse carbine	18"	Assault 2	5	0	1	-
Pulse driver cannon	72"	Heavy D6	10	-3	D6	-
Pulse pistol	12"	Pistol 1	5	0	1	-
Pulse rifle	30"	Rapid Fire 1	5	0	1	-
Quad ion turret	When attacking with this weapon, choose one of the profiles below. Add 1 to hit rolls for this weapon against targets that can't **FLY**.					
- Standard	30"	Assault 4	7	-1	1	-
- Overcharge	30"	Assault 4	8	-1	D3	If you roll one or more hit rolls of 1, the bearer suffers a mortal wound after all of this weapon's shots have been resolved.
Rail rifle	30"	Rapid Fire 1	6	-4	D3	For each wound roll of 6+ made for this weapon, the target unit suffers a mortal wound in addition to the normal damage.
Railgun	When attacking with this weapon, choose one of the profiles below.					
- Solid shot	72"	Heavy 1	10	-4	D6	Each time you make a wound roll of 6+ for this weapon, the target unit suffers D3 mortal wounds in addition to the normal damage.
- Submunitions	72"	Heavy D6	6	-1	1	-
Seeker missile	72"	Heavy 1	8	-2	D6	Each seeker missile can only be used once per battle. This weapon only hits on a roll of 6, regardless of the firing model's Ballistic Skill or any modifiers.
Smart missile system	30"	Heavy 4	5	0	1	This weapon can be fired at units that are not visible to the bearer. Units attacked by this weapon do not gain any bonus to their saving throws for being in cover.
Supremacy railgun	72"	Heavy 2	10	-4	D6	Each time you make a wound roll of 6+ for this weapon, the target unit suffers D3 mortal wounds in addition to the normal damage.

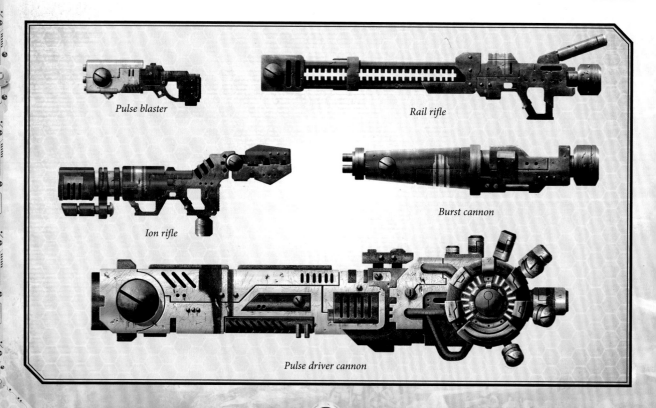

Pulse blaster

Rail rifle

Ion rifle

Burst cannon

Pulse driver cannon

MELEE WEAPONS

WEAPON	RANGE	TYPE	S	AP	D	ABILITIES
Dawn Blade	Melee	Melee	+3	-4	D3	-
Equalizers	Melee	Melee	User	-1	1	A model armed with equalizers increases its Attacks characteristic by 1.
Honour blade	Melee	Melee	+2	0	1	-
Kroot rifle (melee)	Melee	Melee	+1	0	1	-
Krootox fists	Melee	Melee	User	0	2	-
Ripping fangs	Melee	Melee	User	-1	1	-
Ritual blade	Melee	Melee	User	0	1	If any enemy models are destroyed by this weapon, friendly **KROOT** units within 6" of the bearer do not have to take Morale tests in the Morale phase of that turn.

SUPPORT SYSTEMS

A model cannot have more than one of the same Support System.

SYSTEM	EFFECT
Advanced targeting system	A model equipped with an advanced targeting system increases the AP characteristic of all of its weapons by 1 (e.g. an AP of 0 becomes -1, an AP of -1 becomes -2).
Counterfire defence system	A model equipped with a counterfire defence system re-rolls failed hit rolls when firing Overwatch.
XV8-02 Crisis Iridium battlesuit	A model equipped with an XV8-02 Crisis Iridium battlesuit increases its Save characteristic to 2+.
Drone controller	**\<SEPT\> DRONE** units within 6" of any friendly models equipped with a drone controller add one to their hit rolls.
Early warning override	If any enemy units are set up within 12" of a model from your army equipped with an early warning override as the result of an ability that allows them to arrive mid-battle (i.e. teleporting to the battlefield), then at the end of that phase the model may immediately shoot at one of those units as if it were your Shooting phase, but you must subtract 1 from hit rolls when resolving these shots.
Multi-tracker	Re-roll hit rolls of 1 in the Shooting phase for a model equipped with a multi-tracker if it fires all of its weapons at the same target and that target contains 5 or more models.
Shield generator	A model with a shield generator has a 4+ invulnerable save. You cannot take this support system on a Riptide battlesuit.
Target lock	A model with a target lock does not suffer the penalty for moving and firing Heavy weapons, or for Advancing and firing Assault weapons. The model can also Advance and fire Rapid Fire weapons, but must subtract 1 from its hit rolls when doing so.
Velocity tracker	Add 1 to hit rolls for a model with a velocity tracker when it shoots at a unit that can **FLY**.

MARKERLIGHTS

A projected holo-beam illuminates the target, rendering it vulnerable to pinpoint fusillades from supporting units.

If a model (other than a **VEHICLE**) fires a markerlight, it cannot fire any other weapons in that phase. When a unit is hit by a markerlight, place a counter next to it for the remainder of the phase. The table below describes the benefits **T'AU EMPIRE** models receive when shooting at a unit that has markerlight counters. All benefits are cumulative.

MARKERLIGHT TABLE

MARKERLIGHTS	BENEFIT
1	You can re-roll hit rolls of 1 for **T'AU EMPIRE** models attacking this unit.
2	Destroyer and seeker missiles fired at this unit use the firing model's Ballistic Skill (and any modifiers) rather than only hitting on a 6.
3	The target unit does not gain any bonus to its saving throws for being in cover.
4	**T'AU EMPIRE** models attacking this unit do not suffer the penalty for moving and firing Heavy weapons or Advancing and firing Assault weapons.
5 or more	Add 1 to hit rolls for **T'AU EMPIRE** models attacking this unit.

The T'au war machine encircles a last redoubt of the Astra Militarum. Outmanoeuvred and outgunned, the warriors of Humanity are overwhelmed with pinpoint barrages of pulse fire and swarms of micro-missiles, their lumbering war machines brought low with blistering beams of hyper-volatile energy.

SUPREMACY THROUGH UNITY

In this section you'll find rules for Battle-forged armies that include T'AU EMPIRE Detachments – that is, any Detachment which includes only T'AU EMPIRE units. These rules include the abilities below and a series of Stratagems that can only be used by the T'au. This section also includes the T'au Empire's unique Warlord Traits, Signature Systems and Tactical Objectives. Together, these rules reflect the character and fighting style of the T'au Empire in your games of Warhammer 40,000.

WARRIORS OF THE GREATER GOOD

Every Fire Warrior is a zealous believer in the T'au's utilitarian philosophy, and will lay down their life without a second thought to advance the empire's cause.

If your army is Battle-forged, all Troops (except **DRONES**) units in **T'AU EMPIRE** Detachments gain this ability. Such a unit that is within range of an objective marker (as specified in the mission) controls that objective marker even if there are more enemy models within range of that objective marker. If an enemy unit within range of the same objective marker has a similar ability, then the objective marker is controlled by the player who has the most models within range of it as normal.

> ### MATCHED PLAY RULE: COMMANDERS
>
> If you are playing a matched play game, then in a Battle-forged army, you can include no more than one **COMMANDER** in each Detachment.

SEPT TENETS

The septs have developed their own unique ways of war, contributing reams of combat-tested doctrine and tactical data to the academies of the Fire caste.

If your army is Battle-forged, all <**SEPT**> units in **T'AU EMPIRE** Detachments gain a Sept Tenet, so long as every unit in that Detachment is from the same sept. The Sept Tenet gained depends upon the sept they are drawn from, as shown on the table on the right. For example, all units in a **VIOR'LA** Detachment gain the Strike Fast Sept Tenet.

If you have chosen a sept that does not have an associated Sept Tenet, you can choose the tenet that best suits the fighting style and strategies of the warriors that hail from it.

Alien Auxiliaries

The inclusion of **KROOT** and/or **VESPID** units in a **T'AU EMPIRE** Detachment does not prevent other units in that Detachment from gaining a Sept Tenet. Note, however, that **KROOT** and **VESPID** units can never themselves benefit from a Sept Tenet.

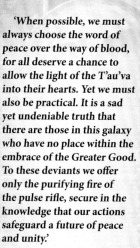

'When possible, we must always choose the word of peace over the way of blood, for all deserve a chance to allow the light of the T'au'va into their hearts. Yet we must also be practical. It is a sad yet undeniable truth that there are those in this galaxy who have no place within the embrace of the Greater Good. To these deviants we offer only the purifying fire of the pulse rifle, secure in the knowledge that our actions safeguard a future of peace and unity.'

- Aun'Tol, Flame of Bork'an

SEPT TENETS

T'AU SEPT: COORDINATED FIRE ARCS

The rigorously drilled Fire Warriors of T'au Sept utilise overlapping fields of fire to envelop charging enemies in a kill-storm of searing pulse energy.

When a unit with this tenet uses their For the Greater Good ability, or when they fire Overwatch whilst they are within 6" of a friendly **T'au Sept** unit, a 5 or 6 is required for a successful hit roll, irrespective of the firing model's Ballistic Skill or any modifiers.

VIOR'LA SEPT: STRIKE FAST

The Commanders of Vior'la harness their warriors' fiery temperament by embracing a highly mobile and aggressive form of warfare, taking the fight to the heart of the enemy.

If a unit with this tenet Advances, it treats all Rapid Fire weapons it is armed with as Assault weapons until the end of the turn (e.g. a Rapid Fire 1 weapon is treated as an Assault 1 weapon). In addition, models with this tenet do not suffer the penalty to their hit rolls for Advancing and firing Assault weapons.

DAL'YTH SEPT: ADAPTIVE CAMOUFLAGE

The T'au of Dal'yth prize victory at any cost, and have mastered the art of sudden ambushes and elaborate traps. They utilise adaptive camouflage fields to elude and disorient their foes.

A unit with this tenet that does not Manta Strike, move, Fall Back, charge, pile in or consolidate in its turn may claim the benefit of cover in the opponent's subsequent turn, even while in the open.

SA'CEA SEPT: CALM DISCIPLINE

The Fire Warriors of the densely populated Sa'cea Sept train extensively for the close-range hell of city combat, learning the vital importance of fire discipline and combined arms.

Add 1 to the Leadership characteristic of models with this tenet. In addition, in the Shooting phase you can re-roll a single failed hit roll when a unit with this tenet shoots.

BORK'AN SEPT: SUPERIOR CRAFTSMANSHIP

From Bork'an Sept's renowned applied science divisions come the most advanced and ingenious weapon prototypes, field tested by elite contingents of Fire caste soldiers.

Models with this tenet may add 6" to the maximum Range of any Rapid Fire and Heavy weapons they are armed with.

FARSIGHT ENCLAVES: DEVASTATING COUNTER-STRIKE

Commander O'Shovah's mastery of Mont'ka has bled into the martial culture of the Farsight Enclaves. Its warriors are experts in the deadly art of engaging the enemy in close confines.

Re-roll wound rolls of 1 for models with this tenet for shooting attacks against enemy units that are within 6" of the firing model.

'Those with superior reach can dictate the terms of battle and impose their will upon their foe. Remember, the first step on the path to victory is often the most important.'

- Commander Puretide

STRATAGEMS

If your army is Battle-forged and includes any T'AU EMPIRE Detachments (excluding Auxiliary Support Detachments), you have access to the Stratagems shown below, meaning you can spend Command Points to activate them. These help to reflect the unique tactics and strategies used by the forces of the T'au Empire on the battlefield.

MULTI-SPECTRUM SENSOR SUITE
1CP

T'au Empire Stratagem

The battlesuit's integrated sensor suite scans multiple ranges on the electromagnetic spectrum, analysing telemetric data and feeding optimised firing solutions to the pilot.

Use this Stratagem before a **BATTLESUIT** unit from your army shoots. Enemy units cannot claim the benefit of cover against shots made by this unit this phase.

FAIL-SAFE DETONATOR
1CP

T'au Empire Stratagem

The battlesuits of high-value T'au operatives are equipped with a fail-safe self-destruct algorithm, ensuring that the pilot cannot be taken alive for interrogation.

Use this Stratagem when a **BATTLESUIT** unit from your army is destroyed in the Fight phase, before removing the last model. Roll a dice for each unit (friend or foe) within 3" of that model. On a 4+ that unit suffers one mortal wound.

AUTOMATED REPAIR SYSTEM
2CP

T'au Empire Stratagem

Nanite repair drones swarm over the damaged battlesuit or vehicle, knitting together ruptured composite plating and repairing vital life-support systems.

Use this Stratagem at the start of any turn. Pick a **VEHICLE** or **BATTLESUIT** model from your army. That model regains D3 lost wounds.

NEUROWEB SYSTEM JAMMER
2CP

T'au Empire Stratagem

This device emits an intense electrostatic jamming field, causing the enemy's weapons to malfunction.

Use this Stratagem at the start of the enemy Shooting phase. Pick an enemy unit within 18" of a **BATTLESUIT COMMANDER** from your army. Your opponent must subtract 1 from hit rolls made for that unit this phase.

REPULSOR IMPACT FIELD
1CP

T'au Empire Stratagem

Detecting an incoming enemy assault, the pilot's battlesuit unleashes a hammer-pulse of kinetic energy strong enough to shatter bone.

Use this Stratagem after an enemy unit successfully charges a **BATTLESUIT** unit from your army. Roll a dice for each model in the enemy unit within 3" of your unit. On a 6 that model suffers a mortal wound.

COMMAND-AND-CONTROL NODE
1CP

T'au Empire Stratagem

The Commander's AI-networked transition system generates firing arcs and enhanced strike-patterns, feeding this raw data to nearby battlesuit teams.

Use this Stratagem at the start of your Shooting phase. Pick a **<SEPT> COMMANDER** from your army. That Commander may not shoot this phase, but one **<SEPT> BATTLESUIT** unit from your army that is within 6" of that Commander may re-roll failed wound rolls this phase.

EMP GRENADE
1CP

T'au Empire Stratagem

This device emits an intense electrostatic field capable of overloading vital computer systems.

Use this Stratagem when a **T'AU EMPIRE** model from your army is chosen to throw a photon grenade at an enemy **VEHICLE** unit. Only make a single hit roll with the weapon this phase; if it hits, the target suffers D3 mortal wounds.

HUNTING HOUNDS
1CP

T'au Empire Stratagem

The Kroot unleash their razor-beaked hounds, and a tide of mottled green flesh tears into the enemy ranks.

Use this Stratagem when a Kroot Hound unit from your army completes a charge against an enemy unit. Until the end of the phase, you can re-roll failed charge rolls for other friendly **KROOT** units that are within 12" of that Kroot Hound unit after it completes its charge move.

UPLINKED MARKERLIGHT
T'au Empire Stratagem

Some markerlights are uplinked directly into the T'au command network, enabling a much faster and more accurate tactical targeting support.

Use this Stratagem after an enemy unit has been hit by a markerlight fired by a model from your army. Place D3+1 markerlight counters next to that unit instead of only 1.

BRANCHED NOVA CHARGE
T'au Empire Stratagem

This prototype power router floods the intense energy generated by a nova reactor to multiple engine systems.

Use this Stratagem when you choose to use a **XV104 RIPTIDE BATTLESUIT**'s Nova Reactor. You may choose two effects from those listed rather than one.

SUPPORT TURRET REPLACEMENT
T'au Empire Stratagem

Field-logistics drones swoop down from above, bearing a replacement support turret in an underslung grav-harness.

Use this Stratagem at the end of your Movement phase. Pick a friendly **STRIKE TEAM** or **BREACHER TEAM** whose DS8 Tactical Support Turret has been destroyed. You may immediately set up a new DS8 Tactical Support Turret in unit coherency with the unit as described in their DS8 Tactical Support Turret ability.

POINT-DEFENCE TARGETING RELAY
T'au Empire Stratagem

Automated subroutines direct this vehicle's secondary weapon systems towards encroaching enemies.

Use this Stratagem when an enemy unit declares a charge against a **VEHICLE** unit from your army. When your unit fires Overwatch this phase, a 5 or 6 is required for a successful hit roll, instead of only 6.

EMERGENCY DISPENSATION
T'au Empire Stratagem

Multiple advanced prototypes and ultra-rare technologies have been provided for the war effort by Ethereal decree.

Use this Stratagem before the battle. Your army can have one extra Signature System for 1 CP, or two extra Signature Systems for 3 CPs. All of the Signature Systems that you include must be different and be given to different **T'AU EMPIRE CHARACTERS**. You can only use this Stratagem once per battle.

ORBITAL ION BEAM
3CP
T'au Empire Stratagem

A kor'vattra cruiser in high orbit unleashes a pulse from an immense ion cannon, engulfing the target in white-hot energy.

Use this Stratagem in your Shooting phase if a **T'AU EMPIRE COMMANDER** from your army did not move or use their Manta Strike ability in the preceding Movement phase. Pick two points on the battlefield 2D6" apart. Draw an imaginary straight line 1mm wide between these two points and roll a dice for each unit (friend or foe) that has models under this line. Subtract 1 from the result if the unit being rolled for is a **CHARACTER**. On a 4+ the unit being rolled for suffers D3 mortal wounds. This Stratagem can only be used once per battle.

BREACH AND CLEAR!
1CP
T'au Empire Stratagem

Breacher Teams excel at clearing enemy-held structures with blinding photon grenades and disciplined bursts of pulse fire.

Use this Stratagem in your Shooting phase, before a **BREACHER TEAM** from your army shoots at an enemy unit that is receiving the benefit of cover. The Breacher Team re-rolls failed wound rolls against the enemy unit until the end of this phase.

RECON SWEEP
1CP
T'au Empire Stratagem

Pathfinders are the eyes and ears of the T'au war machine, always operating ten steps ahead of the foe.

Use this Stratagem at the start of your Shooting phase. Select a **PATHFINDER TEAM** from your army. That unit can immediately move 2D6" but cannot shoot or charge this turn.

WALL OF MIRRORS
1CP
T'au Empire Stratagem

The T'au Stealth Cadres utilise interwoven obfuscation fields and wide-band refraction beams to mask their deadly advance. This process is known as mesme'j'kaara – the wall of mirrors.

Use this Stratagem at the start of your Movement phase. Pick a <SEPT> **XV25 STEALTH BATTLESUITS** unit from your army that is within 6" of a <SEPT> **XV95 GHOSTKEEL BATTLESUIT** from your army. You may immediately remove the Stealth Battlesuits unit from the battlefield and set it up again, anywhere within 12" of that Ghostkeel Battlesuit and more than 9" from any enemy models. Note that this does not count as Falling Back if the Stealth Battlesuits unit was within 1" of an enemy unit when it was removed.

STIMULANT INJECTOR
T'au Empire Stratagem
Many battlesuits contain an emergency revivication system to bring their injured pilot back from the brink of death.

Use this Stratagem at the start of any turn. Choose a **Battlesuit** model from your army with a Wounds characteristic of 10 or more. Until the end of this turn, use the top row of the model's damage table, regardless of how many wounds it has left. This ends immediately if the model is reduced to 0 wounds.

1CP

POSITIONAL RELAY
T'au Empire Stratagem
Zeroing in on the pulse flares of a Recon Drone, T'au reinforcements strike their target drop zone with unerring accuracy.

Use this Stratagem at the start of your Movement phase. Pick a <Sept> MB3 Recon Drone from your army. One of your <Sept> units that has been set up in a Manta hold can perform a low-altitude drop instead of a Manta strike. Set up the unit wholly within 6" of the MB3 Recon Drone.

2CP

FOCUSED FIRE
T'au Sept Stratagem
T'au Sept doctrine heavily emphasises the massed concentration of fire upon a single target at a time, obliterating each component of the enemy force in succession with a series of unrelenting barrages.

Use this Stratagem after a **T'au Sept** unit from your army inflicts an unsaved wound on an enemy unit in the Shooting phase. You can add 1 to wound rolls for any other **T'au Sept** units from your army that target the same enemy unit this phase.

3CP

HOT-BLOODED
Vior'la Stratagem
The daredevil Fire Warriors of Vior'la stray dangerously close to enemy formations in order to maximise the killing power of their pulse volleys.

Use this Stratagem at the start of your shooting phase. Pick a **Vior'la Sept Infantry** unit from your army. That unit may be chosen to shoot twice this phase, but all models in the unit must target the closest enemy unit each time they do so.

2CP

STRIKE AND FADE
Dal'yth Stratagem
Dal'yth T'au are experts at harrying and outmanoeuvring their foes, bleeding them with accurate bursts of fire before fading away into the shadows.

Use this Stratagem at the start of your Shooting phase. Pick a **Dal'yth Sept** unit from your army. That unit may shoot and then immediately move up to 6" as if it were the Movement phase. They cannot Advance as part of this move.

1CP

ORBITAL MARKER DISTRIBUTION UPLINK
Sa'cea Stratagem
Sa'cea Sept has innovated the use of markerlight scatter-flares, dropped from the upper atmosphere by networked Recon Drones to illuminate the greatest concentrations of enemy troops.

Use this Stratagem at the start of your Shooting phase. Pick an enemy unit visible to a **Sa'cea Sept Character** from your army. That unit and all other enemy units within 6" of it gain a markerlight counter.

2CP

EXPERIMENTAL WEAPONRY
Bork'an Stratagem
Bork'an scientists have distributed the latest prototype weapons amongst their Sept's Fire caste contingents, optimised to increase range and accuracy.

Use this Stratagem when a **Bork'an Sept** unit from your army fires a ranged weapon that makes a random number of attacks (e.g. Heavy D6, Heavy 2D6 etc.). You can re-roll one of the dice used to determine the number of attacks made.

1CP

DROP ZONE CLEAR
Farsight Enclaves Stratagem
O'Shovah's warriors have mastered the art of the drop-zone assault. There are few more imposing sights than a cadre of battlesuits raining from low orbit, jump-jets blazing and cannons spitting death at the helpless foe.

Use this Stratagem at the start of your Shooting phase. Choose a **Farsight Enclaves Battlesuit** unit from your army that was set up on the battlefield using its Manta Strike ability this turn. Add 1 to hit rolls for that unit this phase.

2CP

WARLORD TRAITS

The Commanders of the T'au strive from birth to master the theory and practice of warfare. Each specialises in a distinct arena of battle, from the precise lethality of stealth combat to the aggressive ebb and surge of close-quarters engagements.

If a T'au Empire Character is your Warlord, they can generate a Warlord Trait from the following table instead of the one in the *Warhammer 40,000* rulebook. You can either roll on the table below to randomly generate a Warlord Trait, or you can select the one that best suits their temperament and preferred style of waging war.

D6	RESULT
1	**Precision of the Hunter:** *The Warlord stalks the deadliest enemy war machines.* Re-roll wound rolls of 1 made for your Warlord against enemy Vehicles or Monsters.
2	**Through Unity, Devastation:** *The Warlord is an expert in the application of concentrated fire.* In each of your Shooting phases, you can pick an enemy unit that is visible to your Warlord. Until the end of the phase, each time you make a wound roll of 6+ against that unit for an attack made by a friendly <Sept> unit within 6" of your Warlord, the Armour Penetration characteristic of that attack is improved by 1 (e.g. AP0 becomes AP-1).
3	**A Ghost Walks Among Us:** *The Warlord walks unseen until the moment is right to strike.* When your Warlord Advances, add 6" to their Move characteristic for that Movement phase instead of rolling a dice.
4	**Through Boldness, Victory:** *The Warlord favours bold and aggressive action.* If your Warlord is within 12" of an enemy unit at the start of your Shooting phase, you can re-roll failed hit rolls made for your Warlord until the end of the phase.
5	**Exemplar of the Kauyon:** *The Warlord has mastered the art of Kauyon, the Patient Hunter.* You can re-roll failed hit rolls for your Warlord as long as they have not moved this turn. If they have moved for any reason, they lose this trait until the start of the next turn.
6	**Exemplar of the Mont'ka:** *The Warlord has mastered the art of Mont'ka, the Killing Blow.* Your Warlord can Advance and still shoot as if they hadn't Advanced this turn.

NAMED CHARACTERS AND WARLORD TRAITS

If one of the following named characters is your Warlord, they must be given the associated Warlord Trait shown below.

NAMED CHARACTER	WARLORD TRAIT
Commander Shadowsun	Exemplar of the Kauyon
Commander Farsight	Hero of the Enclaves
Longstrike	Strength of Belief
Aun'Va	Through Unity, Devastation
Aun'Shi	Academy Luminary
Darkstrider	A Ghost Walks Among Us

SEPT WARLORD TRAITS

If you wish, you can pick a Sept Warlord Trait from the list below instead of the T'au Empire Warlord Traits to the left, but only if your Warlord is from the relevant sept.

SEPT	TRAIT
T'au	**Strength of Belief:** *The Warlord's unwavering belief in the Greater Good grants them formidable resolve.* Roll a D6 for each mortal wound inflicted on your Warlord; on a 5+, that mortal wound is ignored and has no effect.
Vior'la	**Academy Luminary:** *This Warlord was marked for greatness by the exacting Fire caste tutors of Vior'la.* If your Warlord has the Master of War, Volley Fire or Failure is Not an Option ability, the range of that ability is increased to 9". In addition, if your army is Battle-forged, you receive an additional 1 Command Point.
Dal'yth	**Gunship Diplomat:** *This Warlord is held in the highest favour by the T'au's alien auxiliaries.* Whilst within 12" of your Warlord, friendly Kroot and Vespid units gain the For the Greater Good ability.
Sa'cea	**Beacon of Honour:** *This Warlord is a noble and honourable leader, beloved of their troops.* Friendly Sa'cea units within 6" of this model reduce the number of models that flee as a result of a failed Morale test by 1.
Bork'an	**Seeker of Perfection:** *The Warlord seeks mastery in all aspects of warfare.* For each hit roll of 6+ made for your Warlord, add 1 to the wound roll for that attack.
Farsight Enclaves	**Hero of the Enclaves:** *The Warlord's very name inspires devotion and awe amongst his warriors.* Your Warlord can perform a Heroic Intervention if they are within 6" of any enemy units after the enemy has completed all their charge moves. Your Warlord can move up to 6" when performing a Heroic Intervention, so long as they end the move closer to the nearest enemy model. In addition, if your Warlord charged, was charged or performed a Heroic Intervention, then until the end of the turn you can re-roll failed hit rolls made for them.

SIGNATURE SYSTEMS

The greatest inventions of the Earth caste's science divisions are bestowed to the T'au Empire's war leaders to use as they see fit. These ingenious examples of bleeding-edge technology range from solar-charged doomsday weapons to neural personality matrices and devious holo-illusion projectors.

If your army is led by a T'AU EMPIRE Warlord, then before the battle you may give one of the following Signature Systems to a T'AU EMPIRE CHARACTER. Named characters such as Commander Shadowsun already have one or more specialised systems and cannot be given any of the following systems. KROOT CHARACTERS may not be given any Signature Systems.

Note that some weapons replace one of the character's existing weapons. Where this is the case, if you are playing a matched play game or are otherwise using points values, you must still pay the cost of the weapon that is being replaced. Write down any Signature Systems your characters have on your army roster.

PURETIDE ENGRAM NEUROCHIP

Commander Puretide was undoubtedly the most gifted T'au war leader of all time. The T'au were unwilling to lose his tactical and strategic brilliance, and upon his death, his mind was scanned and his accumulated memories committed to a massive hologram on his birth world of Dal'yth. A sliver of that genius has been crafted into a bio-chip. When surgically implanted into the brain of a Fire caste commander, the bearer can access much of the wisdom of Puretide himself, drawing upon a great reservoir of tactical acumen.

Once per battle, you can re-roll a single hit roll, wound roll or damage roll made for the bearer, or a friendly <SEPT> unit within 6" of the bearer. In addition, if your army is Battle-forged and the bearer is on the battlefield, roll a D6 each time you or your opponent use a Stratagem; on a 6 you gain a command point.

ONAGER GAUNTLET

Onager gauntlets were developed during the Damocles Crusade to counter the massed heavy armour spearheads of the Imperium. Armed with such a weapon, a warrior could punch straight through the thick armour of a tank. Though the technology proved successful, the casualty rate amongst bearers was extremely high, and of the original twelve prototypes, only one remains.

BATTLESUIT COMMANDER only.

WEAPON	RANGE	TYPE	S	AP	D
Onager Gauntlet	Melee	Melee	10	-4	D6
Abilities: Each time the bearer fights, it can make one (and only one) attack with this weapon.					

MULTI-SENSORY DISCOURAGEMENT ARRAY

The Multi-Sensory Discouragement Array was first designed as a non-lethal response to quell rioting civilians. The device resembles a pulsing sensor beacon, and emits both sub-sonic frequencies and scatter-bursts of ultraviolet colour, stunning and nauseating targets and rendering them compliant.

Enemy units within 6" of the bearer subtract 1 from their Leadership characteristics.

SOLID-IMAGE PROJECTION UNIT

The tragic demise of Supreme Ethereal Aun'Va led the Ethereal High Council to assign several science divisions to the development of portable defensive technologies. A recent innovation is the solid-image projection unit. This miniaturised holowave-emitter drone projects beams of so-called 'heavy light', forming an utterly convincing illusory image that is solid to the touch, while simultaneously masking the true target with an advanced refraction field.

Ethereal with hover drone only. Once per phase, when an enemy unit declares the bearer as the target of a charge, you may move the bearer up to 3" before the charge roll is made.

SEISMIC DESTABILISER

Designed to undermine fortified positions and drive enemy soldiers from cover, the Seismic Destabiliser emits an ultra-low resonating frequency that causes localised earth tremors. The targeted structure is riven by a spider's web of fractures, and any garrisoned troops must evacuate or risk being buried under tonnes of rubble.

At the start of each Shooting phase, you may either pick an enemy INFANTRY unit claiming the benefit of cover, or a BUILDING, within 12" of the bearer. If you picked a BUILDING, it suffers D3 mortal wounds. If you picked an INFANTRY unit, roll a dice for each model in the unit. For each roll of 6, that unit suffers a mortal wound.

SUPERNOVA LAUNCHER

The Supernova Launcher was developed during the bloody fighting against Hive Fleet Gorgon. Unable to get close enough to effectively deploy anti-armour ordnance against the Tyranids' deadliest bio-organisms, Earth caste scientists adapted several fragmentation launchers to hurl experimental plasma grenades. Launched high into the air, these projectiles drop amongst the enemy and explode in a coruscating fireball that evaporates metal and flesh alike.

Model with airbursting fragmentation projector only. The Supernova Launcher replaces one of the model's airbursting fragmentation projectors and has the following profile:

WEAPON	RANGE	TYPE	S	AP	D
Supernova Launcher	18"	Assault D6	6	-2	2
Abilities: This weapon can target units that are not visible to the bearer.					

VECTORED MANOEUVRING THRUSTERS

This enhanced movement system can be adapted for both battlesuits and vehicles. It consists of multiple high-output thruster nozzles, each hardwired into the pilot's neural interface, allowing them to react with startling speed to any changes in the strategic situation.

T'au Sept Battlesuit only. This model may immediately move up to 6" after attacking in the Shooting phase.

THERMONEUTRONIC PROJECTOR

Vior'la weapons developers have focused their efforts heavily on flamer technology, responding to their Commanders' desire for maximum-impact close-range ordnance. The Thermoneutronic Projector uses volatile gases siphoned from the corona of a neutron star to expel a flame capable of searing through the armour plating of a battle tank.

Vior'la Sept model with flamer only. The Thermoneutronic Projector replaces one of the model's flamers and has the following profile:

WEAPON	RANGE	TYPE	S	AP	D
Thermoneutronic Projector	8"	Assault D6	6	-1	2

Abilities: This weapon automatically hits its target.

DYNAMIC MIRROR FIELD

Commanders hailing from Dal'yth prefer stealth and subterfuge to overt aggression, and their demands for improved camouflage technology have led to the development of the Dynamic Mirror Field. This advanced prototype is based upon the refraction technology utilised to such tremendous effect by Ghostkeel battlesuits, adapted for alternative armour chassis. Armour nodes project multiple light-distortion fields, creating false images of the bearer to draw enemy fire.

Dal'yth Sept model only. Your opponent must subtract 1 from hit rolls that target the bearer.

GRAV-INHIBITOR FIELD

It was Commander O'Jir of Sa'cea who first utilised the Grav-Inhibitor Field during the defence of Laguna Shard against Ork raiders. The gravitic-field generator mounted upon the Commander's battlesuit unleashed waves of battering kinetic force, disrupting each and every attempt by the be'gel to overwhelm his position.

Sa'cea Sept model only. Enemy units that choose the bearer's unit as the target of a charge must subtract 2" from their charge distance.

PLASMA ACCELERATOR RIFLE

The Plasma Accelerator Rifle is one of the deadliest inventions from Bork'an's renowned science divisions, blending pulse-induction technology with a high-yield plasma generator. The result is a long-range armour-piercing weapon that is highly effective against both infantry and light vehicles.

Bork'an Sept model with plasma rifle only. The Plasma Accelerator Rifle replaces one of the model's plasma rifles and has the following profile:

WEAPON	RANGE	TYPE	S	AP	D
Plasma Accelerator Rifle	30"	Rapid Fire 1	7	-3	2

FUSION BLADES

This deadly innovation was first created by the third Commander Brightsword, and refined over the following decades by the Earth caste division of the Farsight Enclaves. Fusion blades resemble modified versions of the familiar T'au fusion blaster. However, when the firing impulse is activated, each weapon unleashes a continuous beam of volatile energy that extends from the muzzle of the weapon like a shining sword of pure light. Fusion blades are intensely powerful but drain a battlesuit's energy reserves at a prodigious pace, and so must be utilised sparingly.

Farsight Enclaves model with at least two fusion blasters only. The Fusion Blades replace two of the model's fusion blasters and have the following profile:

WEAPON	RANGE	TYPE	S	AP	D
Fusion Blades (Ranged)	18"	Assault 2	8	-4	D6
Fusion Blades (Melee)	Melee	Melee	8	-4	D6

Abilities (Ranged): If the target is within half the weapon's range, roll two dice when inflicting damage and discard the lowest result.

Abilities (Melee): Each time the bearer fights, it can make two (and only two) attacks with this weapon.

POINTS VALUES

If you are playing a matched play game, or a game that uses a points limit, you can use the following lists to determine the total points cost of your army. Simply add together the points costs of all your models and the wargear they are equipped with to determine your army's total points value.

HQ

UNIT	MODELS PER UNIT	POINTS PER MODEL (Does not include wargear or Drones)
Cadre Fireblade	1	39
Commander in XV8 Crisis Battlesuit	1	72
Commander in XV85 Enforcer Battlesuit	1	76
Commander in XV86 Coldstar Battlesuit	1	90
Ethereal	1	45
Ethereal with Hover Drone	1	50
Longstrike	1	137

TROOPS

UNIT	MODELS PER UNIT	POINTS PER MODEL (Does not include wargear or Drones)
Breacher Team	5-10	7
- DS8 Tactical Support Turret	0-1	0
Kroot Carnivores	10-20	5
Strike Team	5-12	7
- DS8 Tactical Support Turret	0-1	0

DEDICATED TRANSPORTS

UNIT	MODELS PER UNIT	POINTS PER MODEL (Does not include wargear or Drones)
TY7 Devilfish	1	80

ELITES

UNIT	MODELS PER UNIT	POINTS PER MODEL (Does not include wargear or Drones)
XV8 Crisis Battlesuits	3-9	42
XV8 Crisis Bodyguards	3-9	45
Firesight Marksman	1	21
XV95 Ghostkeel Battlesuit	1	82
Krootox Riders	1-3	34
Kroot Shaper	1	31
XV104 Riptide Battlesuit	1	185
XV25 Stealth Battlesuit	3-6	20

FAST ATTACK

UNIT	MODELS PER UNIT	POINTS PER MODEL (Does not include wargear or Drones)
Kroot Hounds	4-12	4
Pathfinder Team	5-10	5
TX4 Piranhas	1-5	38
Tactical Drones	4-12	See Drones, below
Vespid Stingwings	4-12	14

DRONES

UNIT	MODELS PER UNIT	POINTS PER MODEL (Includes wargear)
MV62 Command-link Drone	N/A	6
MV33 Grav-inhibitor Drone	N/A	8
MV36 Guardian Drone	N/A	8
MV1 Gun Drone	N/A	12
MV17 Interceptor Drone	N/A	15
MV7 Marker Drone	N/A	10
MV8 Missile Drone	N/A	20
MV31 Pulse Accelerator Drone	N/A	8
MB3 Recon Drone	N/A	12
MV4 Shield Drone	N/A	10
MV52 Shield Drone	N/A	11
MV84 Shielded Missile Drone	N/A	25
MV71 Sniper Drone	N/A	18
MV5 Stealth Drones	N/A	10

HEAVY SUPPORT

UNIT	MODELS PER UNIT	POINTS PER MODEL (Does not include wargear or Drones)
XV88 Broadside Battlesuit	1-3	60
TX7 Hammerhead Gunship	1	100
TX78 Sky Ray Gunship	1	100

FLYERS

UNIT	MODELS PER UNIT	POINTS PER MODEL (Does not include wargear or Drones)
AX3 Razorshark Strike Fighter	1	72
AX39 Sun Shark Bomber	1	90

FORTIFICATIONS

UNIT	MODELS PER UNIT	POINTS PER MODEL (Does not include wargear or Drones)
Tidewall Droneport	1	70
Tidewall Gunrig	1	70
Tidewall Shieldline	1	70
-Tidewall Defence Platform	0-1	70

LORDS OF WAR

UNIT	MODELS PER UNIT	POINTS PER MODEL (Does not include wargear)
KV128 Stormsurge	1	180

NAMED CHARACTERS

UNIT	MODELS PER UNIT	POINTS PER MODEL (Includes wargear but not Drones)
Aun'Shi	1	60
Aun'Va	1	85
- Ethereal Guard	2	5
Commander Farsight	1	151
Commander Shadowsun	1	167
Darkstrider	1	45

SUPPORT SYSTEMS

SUPPORT SYSTEM	POINTS PER SYSTEM
Advanced targeting system (Ghostkeel, Riptide and Stormsurge)	18
Advanced targeting system (all other models)	12
Counterfire defence system	10
XV8-02 Crisis Iridium battlesuit	15
Drone controller	5
Early warning override (Ghostkeel, Riptide and Stormsurge)	10
Early warning override (all other models)	5
Homing beacon	20
Multi-tracker	10
Shield generator (Stormsurge)	40
Shield generator (all other models)	8
Target lock (Ghostkeel, Riptide and Stormsurge)	12
Target lock (all other models)	6
Velocity tracker (Ghostkeel, Riptide and Stormsurge)	10
Velocity tracker (all other models)	2

RANGED WEAPONS

WEAPON	POINTS PER WEAPON
Airbursting fragmentation projector	8
Burst cannon	8
Cluster rocket system	25
Cyclic ion blaster	18
Cyclic ion raker	39
Destroyer missile	10
Flamer	9
Fusion blaster	21
Fusion collider	35
Heavy burst cannon	35
Heavy rail rifle	35
High-output burst cannon	20
High-yield missile pod	25
Ion accelerator	65
Ion cannon	35
Ion rifle	7
Kroot gun	0
Kroot rifle	0
Longshot pulse rifle	0
Markerlight	3
Missile pod	24
Neutron blaster	0
Photon grenades	0
Plasma rifle	11
Pulse blastcannon	43
Pulse blaster	0
Pulse bomb	0
Pulse carbine	0
Pulse driver cannon	97
Pulse pistol	1
Pulse rifle	0
Quad ion turret	45
Rail rifle	17
Railgun	38
Seeker missile	5
Smart missile system	15
Supremacy railgun	50

MELEE WEAPONS

WEAPON	POINTS PER WEAPON
Equalizers	1
Honour blade	0
Kroot rifle	0
Krootox fists	0
Ripping fangs	0
Ritual blade	0

TACTICAL OBJECTIVES

The forces of the T'au use a variety of complex strategies on the battlefield to confound and destroy their enemies in the pursuit of conquest and expansion, as well as to defend the holdings of their empire. Each unit acts in perfect synchronicity with those around them, proving the maxim that cooperation brings victory.

If your army is led by a **T'au Empire** Warlord, these Tactical Objectives replace the Capture and Control Tactical Objectives (numbers 11-16) in the *Warhammer 40,000* rulebook. If a mission uses Tactical Objectives, players use the normal rules for using Tactical Objectives with the following exception: when a T'au Empire player generates a Capture and Control objective (numbers 11-16), they instead generate the corresponding T'au Empire Tactical Objective, as shown below. Other Tactical Objectives (numbers 21-66) are generated normally.

D66	TACTICAL OBJECTIVE
11	The Lure
12	Patient Hunter
13	Ambush
14	Multiple Distractions
15	Tactical Withdrawal
16	The Greater Good

11 — THE LURE — *T'au Empire*

Use the enemy's small-minded aggression against them. Provide a tempting target, and they will stray within the range of our rifles. That will be their final mistake.

Score 1 victory point if at least one enemy unit that made a successful charge in your opponent's last turn was destroyed. Score D3 victory points instead if three or more enemy units that made a successful charge in your opponent's last turn were destroyed.

12 — PATIENT HUNTER — *T'au Empire*

Using skill and foresight, the patient hunter will deploy in the perfect position to destroy the foe.

Score 1 victory point if one or more enemy units were slain by a unit from your army that is in your deployment zone this turn.

13 — AMBUSH — *T'au Empire*

Draw the enemy into the jaws of the trap. Then strike hard and true, routing their warriors and eliminating with the utmost prejudice any that persist in their ignorance.

Score 1 victory point if an enemy unit was destroyed and/or failed a Morale test during this turn. If at least three enemy units were destroyed and/or failed Morale tests during this turn, score D3 victory points instead.

14 — MULTIPLE DISTRACTIONS — *T'au Empire*

A divided opponent is a weakened opponent. Harry the flanks of the enemy formation, drawing their battle lines apart before unleashing the killing thrust.

Score 1 victory point if there is at least one enemy unit wholly within 12" of a battlefield edge, and at least one enemy unit wholly within 12" of the opposite battlefield edge, at the end of this turn.

15 — TACTICAL WITHDRAWAL — *T'au Empire*

The T'au do not sacrifice lives in vain. If our forces are overmatched we shall withdraw, preserving lives for the ongoing war.

Score 1 victory point if at least one enemy unit is destroyed in the Shooting phase that was within 1" of any of your units at the start of this turn.

16 — THE GREATER GOOD — *T'au Empire*

Our desire to claim the galaxy in the name of the T'au'va is not born from greed or arrogant pride, but from our sense of moral duty.

Score D3 victory points if you control an objective marker that was controlled by your opponent at the start of this turn. If you control three or more objective markers that were controlled by your opponent at the start of this turn, score D3+3 victory points instead.

'THE QUESTION OF THE TIMING OF THE COMMENCEMENT OF HOSTILITIES IS ONE UPON WHICH YOU MUST MEDITATE MOST DEEPLY. ONCE YOUR DECISION IS ARRIVED AT, IT MUST BE PURSUED WITH THE UTMOST ENERGY.'

- *Commander Puretide, The 37th Meditation on the Way of the Warrior*